UP THE YEARS
FROM BLOOMSBURY

GEORGE ARLISS

From the painting by George Sneed Williams

GEORGE ARLISS

UP THE YEARS
FROM BLOOMSBURY

An Autobiography

WITH ILLUSTRATIONS

LITTLE, BROWN, AND COMPANY

BOSTON · 1927

TO
THE GIRL
With the Nice Arms

❧

CONTENTS

ILLUSTRATIONS

UP THE YEARS
FROM BLOOMSBURY

I

STARTING A "CAREER"

If any one can tell me of a more highly respectable neighborhood than Bloomsbury, London, W. C., England, about 1880, I should like to hear of it. Not that I have any use for it; I am not seeking such a spot in which to pass my declining years; but I do not believe it exists, and I will go so far as to defy any one to produce it. But if Bloomsbury, W. C., was respectable, what about Museum Street, Bloomsbury, W. C., with Mudie's Library at one end and the British Museum at the other! Could any street have its morals more securely guarded?

Of course there were some shops in Museum Street, but what respectable shops! The stationer's opposite (Mr. Hickman's), filled with all the things that industrious people need — ruled paper and steel pens, some photographs of Greek statues (the originals of which are to be seen in the British Museum), Guides to London, nice red blotting-paper — all looking so restful and good. And farther along, Mr. Stubbs', the bookseller's, kept by old Mr. Stubbs and young Mr. Stubbs. When you entered Mr. Stubbs' shop you knew at once you were in the Holy of Holies: in the half light you saw nothing distinctly, but by degrees you became conscious of the presence of Old Mr. Stubbs and Young Mr. Stubbs in soundless shoes, approaching you over a soundless floor. Old Mr. Stubbs

3

with white whiskers, Young Mr. Stubbs with black. I am sure that if any one asked for any literature lighter than Homer's "Iliad" or Gibbon's "Decline and Fall" he was coldly and firmly bowed out by the two Mr. Stubbs.

Then there was Mr. Parr at the corner shop. Mr. Parr had a long white beard, and at once suggested the twelve apostles. He sold cough drops — good old established cough drops that had the unmistakable odor and flavor of doing you good about them. I am sure they helped to give a smell of venerable respectability to the British Museum.

And then there was Miss Ryan's — nice, plump, pleasant, kindly Miss Ryan, who sold cakes — but wait, not the ordinary vulgar-looking cakes that you might see in any shop window. Miss Ryan's cakes were such as you would buy coming from Mudie's Library on your way to the British Museum, or, having left the British Museum, you might get them to stay your stomach while you called at Mudie's Library. They were the kind of cakes that fall comfortably into a highly respectable paper bag, such as no College Professor need be ashamed to be seen carrying. Miss Ryan's door had a little old-fashioned bell on it that had the ingenuity to waggle backwards and forwards all by itself, as soon as you opened the door, thus acquainting Miss Ryan, who was frequently taking a cup of tea with her mother in the back parlor, with your presence.

But if this is Museum Street on a week day, what is it on a Sunday? It is the aisle of a cathedral. Its

4

respectability acts upon you like a narcotic. It is as ostentatiously respectable as a shiny Bible in the center of a round table. Nothing stirs till the bells of St. George's Church ring out; then if you peep from behind the drawing-room curtains you may see Mr. Parr walking steadfastly along the pavement, prayer book in hand, answering the call. No cough drops are sold on Sunday. It must be confessed that as an apostle he is rather spoilt by his top hat and his gloves; his gloves are too dark, and his boots are too shiny, for an apostle. But he typifies Museum Street on Sunday. Other worshippers follow in the wake of Mr. Parr.

All the men's boots look too obvious on Sunday, for some reason or other; and you distinctly hear them squeak through the closed windows. When the last trump is sounded, I am sure the day will be spoilt for Museum Street if its boots are forbidden to squeak and it is denied its top hat and gloves.

And then nothing happens until they bring their prayer books and their hats and their boots back from church, all to be put away until next Sunday. From now on, apparently nobody moves all day; although there is a feeling of eyes behind curtains. No sign of life is visible within any of the houses opposite, except when Mr. Hickman feeds his goldfish. Outside, the street is deserted except, of course, for Mr. Pavey. Mr. Pavey is a builder's laborer; he lives in Gilbert Street, a narrow and surprisingly poor street running off Museum Street just opposite. On week days he may be seen going or returning from work in shabby corduroys, a nondescript hat, a dirty clay pipe in his

5

mouth, and a grimy growth of beard. On Sundays he is dressed in a suit of unrelieved black: too large, but otherwise immaculate; on his head is an irreproachable bowler and in his mouth a cigar — carefully conserved, for he will not look upon its like again until next Sunday. He is shaven. He has no gloves on, it is true, but you might almost be deceived about this, because his hands are not aggressively white. He appears at the corner of Museum Street and Gilbert Street every Sunday about three. You never see him come and you never see him go. When you look he is either there or he has gone. He remains at the corner till about five. During this time he makes no movement except to afford his left foot some relief by shifting the burden of weight to his right and vice versa; and having gazed fixedly with a sad eye towards one end of the street, to turn his head and gaze fixedly with unchanged expression towards the other. What pleasure he found in this weekly vigil, why ever he did it, was always a mystery to me and to all Museum Street. I never saw a soul speak to him, and never saw him open his mouth. He might have been something out of the British Museum — except that there could be no possible reason why he should ever have been taken in there.

During the afternoon the dead silence is broken by the Muffin Man. He carries a large tray upon his head filled with muffins and covered with a green baize, and as he calls "Muffins", he rings a bell. During the walnut season, another man with a basket on his head cries "Walnuts — ten a penny — Walnuts." Their

6

voices sound like the cry of an imprisoned soul in an otherwise deserted cave. I suppose the vendors of these succulent commodities took on this mournful tone that they might blend in with the awesomeness of their surroundings. They must have found their customers in less holy places, but I never saw any one in Museum Street so far forget himself as to buy a muffin or a walnut.

I have dwelt upon the majesty of Museum Street on a Sunday, not in order to create an atmosphere through which to introduce the moment of my birth (I was born on a Good Friday, April 10, 1868), but rather to conjure up in my own mind what the effect could have been on the owners of those eyes blinking behind the curtains opposite on a certain Sunday afternoon, when they saw a small boy of five or six or perhaps seven dash out in the full and gorgeous costume of a circus clown, rush round the block of houses round to the right into Little Russell Street, to the right again into Duke Street (where I was born, by the way), to the right again into Great Russell Street, along by the British Museum, and once more into Museum Street and a quick dive for home, panting and victorious. How many deaths there were behind the closed curtains — what happened to Mr. Pavey — what my father and mother had to endure from the neighbors afterward I shall never know. For my parents had a way, when we did anything very terrible that brought distressing results, of saying nothing to us about it. They allowed a clear field for conscience. I don't know how this silent reproach would succeed with

7

other children, but it was most effective with me. It made me feel awful! To learn from the chance words of others how surprised and hurt my mother and father had been at my conduct — and yet no word from them, just a coolness and an unresponsive eye — dreadful!

Of course this particular, horrible thing would never have happened if I hadn't had brothers. I was perhaps seven; that would make my brother Fred nine, and Charley eleven. We were good boys, really; not at all the "boys will be boys" type. We could generally be trusted to behave. But we had been doing "daggs." Referring to the Oxford Dictionary I do not find the word "daggs" recorded. Perhaps it belonged to our family (there are family words), or perhaps it was schoolboy slang that is no longer in vogue; I certainly do not ever remember seeing it written or printed before. But to do daggs is not only to dare, but to do the thing first yourself and then dare the others to do it. We had done every kind of daggs (there is no singular to daggs) that we could think of: stood on our heads on the end of the sofa, walked once across the room on our hands, crawled head downwards over the banisters — we were all just about the age that has tired of the more conventional methods of locomotion. If, after my long experience on the stage, I might give advice to boys of six or seven, I should say do not spend too long in attempting to walk easily and nonchalantly upon the palms of your hands. I devoted very many hours to it between the age of six and eight, and although I became fairly proficient, I have never found it of any real use to me

in the legitimate drama, and I have not observed that
it is of value in other walks of public life.

Well, daggs were beginning to pall upon us, when,
during a lull in our activities, the clown's dress that
my sister had made for me suddenly sprang into my
mind. I had been recently taken to the children's pantomime at Drury Lane Theatre. At that time the
pantomime always closed with a Harlequinade in
which figured the Clown and Pantaloon, and the Har-
lequin and Columbine. I have heard with regret that
this part of the pantomime has been discontinued of
recent years. The Clown was always the children's
hero: he played every imaginable prank on the Pantaloon and the Policeman and the Fishmonger — and
every boy in the theatre wanted to be a clown. I
always had the childish taste for "dressing up"
strongly developed, and so my tender-hearted elder
sister had spent many hours duplicating the striking
costume of my hero of Drury Lane.

It might have been a budding sense of the drama
that led me to realize the violent contrast between
this gorgeous apparel and the deadly dull street without; anyhow, I slipped away and reappeared in a few
minutes in full costume, including some kind of comic
headpiece. I announced to my astonished brothers that
I proposed running clear round the houses — round
the entire block — just as I stood. They yelped with
scornful incredulity, knowing full well that such a
thing could never happen in Museum Street, and they
felt safe in daring me and daring me — until of course
I had to do it.

9

This was my first appearance in public. It is, I think, my earliest recollection of anything that appertains to my subsequent stage career. There comes to my mind another character effort at about this time, when I was dressed up as a Holy Friar and sang "The Friar of Orders Grey." For this Charley made the wig out of a shiny pink material (much used at that time for putting underneath a lace covering on the dressing table in the spare bedroom) and some tow; Daisy (my tender-hearted elder sister) made the gray frock with rope around the waist, and my mother taught me the song. I must have been quite small, because I remember I was lifted up and stood on a chair to sing. That may have antedated my other more spectacular appearance — I am not sure. But the clown episode was my first hit. In a certain sense it was unfortunate, because I reached the very pinnacle of fame at one bound; I can never hope to make such a sensation again. For some year or more after this I held steadfastly to my determination to be a Clown when I grew up. Later, I decided the life of an omnibus conductor would be perhaps more to my taste. Still later, I decided that I would be a schoolmaster and at the age of twelve I finally concluded that I would be a clergyman. At this time I was writing a severe commentary on the Bible; that was perhaps why I decided to go into the Church.

Looking back on this selection of vocations, which I made before the age of twelve, I perceive that they all gave the opportunity for what is known to-day as "Self Expression." It was undoubtedly this attribute that so strongly suggested to me the appeal of the life of an omnibus conductor. The 'bus conductor and the driver were at that time London's chief public humorists — the recognized jesters of the streets. They knew it and they strained every nerve to hold their reputation; they played into each other's hands for the benefit of passengers on top; and they brought off some kind of *bon mot* at almost every stopping place. It is true that the public was easily amused by the 'busmen's repartee, and would laugh uproariously at very mild humor; but there is no doubt that the 'busmen did develop an unusual readiness of reply and a certain gutter humor that was most entertaining and frequently clever.

This class gradually but surely passed out as the motor bus came in. They were able however to have a fairly long fling at the approaching competitor, that was destined at last to drive them out of business. Motor vehicles of all kinds were tried in the London streets for years before they became a possible reliable means of locomotion. They were continually breaking down and having to be hauled away, as the horse-bus drove blithely past. How often have I sat on the box seat with the driver as we have passed one of those derelicts and heard him murmur in my ear, "They won't never be no good, sir."

Just about the time that I had decided to become a clergyman and to revolutionize the Church with my commentaries on the Bible, something happened which firmly and irrevocably drew me to the stage. It was Christmastime and we were to have a children's party. All the nice children that we knew were to be asked and all the others were to be discreetly overlooked. Of course, cousins had to be included, whether we liked them or not. My cousin "Fatty" who lived at Clapham Common we liked particularly; my mother liked him too. So when he wrote accepting the invitation and saying that he would not only come himself but that he would bring two friends with him, and that the trio would play a one-act farce for us during the evening, no objection was raised by my parents. And of course we were excited beyond words. Charlie at once commenced to erect a stage with curtains, at one end of the drawing-room. Charlie was always ready to make things. I remember how thrilled I was when I saw the curtains draw backwards and forwards; that seemed to me to give an unmistakably professional air to the entire thing — curtains to draw backwards and forwards. There was some discussion as to footlights, Charlie contending that it would be quite easy for him to lay them on. But my father decided against this, much to my disappointment. Is there anything to-day as exciting as a children's party was then? I doubt it. I do not suggest that human nature has changed, but it seems as though much more is done nowadays to give pleasure and amusement to the young, and children quickly become blasé. I doubt whether they get the pleasure that we experienced at our annual Christmas Party. The keen enjoyment of each arrival. The surprise at seeing our grubby little friends all dressed up and with smooth hair. And the little girls

be-ribboned out of all knowledge, and looking absolutely pretty, some of them. Extraordinary! And so
amazingly well-behaved. And the Ohs! And the
Oohs! at the sight of the stage. And the scent of the
Christmas tree and the unmistakable smell of new
clothes. Oh, it was wonderful!

And nurses and sisters and mothers brought children, hundreds of children it seemed to me, although
there were probably not more than thirty — all with
glittering eyes and burning cheeks and hearts thump-
ing with pleasurable anticipation.

And in the midst of this bubble of excitement there
appeared the thing that was to definitely decide my
"career." Two boys, rather tall for their age, dressed
in immaculate "Etons" with very low-cut waistcoats
and the whitest of white Camellias in their coats —
Master Henry Soutar, and Master Joseph Soutar (these
were Fatty's friends) arrived alone, with the terrible
news that Fatty had been taken ill and could not
come. I regret to say that my first thought was not
one of sympathy for Fatty — as to whether he was
very ill, or even likely to get better — but of what
was to happen to the stage, and the curtain that drew
backwards and forwards: was there to be no farce
after all; no entertainment at all?

I asked them about this, breathlessly, and found
that the situation was hopeless. "Mrs. Bottlewasher's
Apartment" was a farce for three people, the whole
story pivoted round Fatty's part, and could not be
played any other way. It was entirely unlike many
of Shakespeare's plays, or even some of Sheridan's,

in which certain scenes may be cut without great detriment to the story. "Mrs. Bottlewasher's Apartment" was not that kind of play: it had been written by Master Joseph Soutar and could not be condensed.

It was a desperate situation. The news must be kept from the "party" for the time; this terrible wet blanket must not be allowed to descend upon them so early in the evening. Could nothing be done? My brothers and sister joined us and we held a council of war. Could "Mrs. Jarley's Waxworks" be revived at a moment's notice? My mother did Mrs. Jarley the year before last with great success.

We approached her, but she not only could not remember the part, but pointed out that it was necessary to have costumes that could not be got at a moment's notice. Of course, there were always charades to fall back upon, but all children's parties had charades, and we had hoped for something so different. As we paused, seeking for inspiration, I became conscious that the eyes of Joseph were fixed upon me in an unnatural gaze. He looked me up and down appraisingly, as other gifted authors have done since, and then suddenly said, "Why shouldn't you play the part?" My heart stood still with astonishment and excitement. All the others said, "Why of course," "That's it," "Why not?" with that unanimity that so frequently ensues when a way out is discovered which does not involve ourselves.

"But I don't know the part," I said.

"That's all right," said Joseph, "I'll tell you about it and you can 'gag' it."

We were hustled into a small adjoining room where we remained closeted for about half an hour. The author described in great detail the kind of young man I was supposed to be — a very nervous young man, etc. "And then I say to you" and then "You say to me" — perhaps the most intensive study I have ever had.

Well, to bring a thrilling and palpitating adventure down to plain unvarnished facts, "Mrs. Bottlewasher's Apartment" was played that night, with enormous and overwhelming success. Little girls screamed with laughter, boys howled, and aunts and uncles applauded vigorously. It is true that the curtain which had drawn backwards to perfection at the opening of the play was seized with violent hysterics at the end and had to be pushed and shoved, and jerked by a million unseen hands, supported by obvious feet, before it would consent to close the entertainment. But this, so far from being a tragedy, seemed to add to the merriment and success.

The important result to me was that I had made a hit with Joseph and his brother, and there sprang up a friendship between Joseph and me — a close friendship which has lasted to the present day. But for this chance adventure I might never have gone on the stage.

I don't think the success of "Mrs. Bottlewasher's Apartment" led me to believe that I had any special ability as an actor. I think I knew enough even then to realize that no entertainment given at a children's party by children has ever been anything but a huge success. But I knew that I liked it, and that that was the kind of thing I wanted to do, and from that moment I never changed my mind.

Joseph and Henry gave me a pressing invitation to visit them, and held out the prospect of unlimited acting in the cellar of their house. I will describe some of those stirring entertainments later.

The children's party was the turning point which led me to the stage. How I was going to get there I had no idea, but I hadn't any doubt that I should arrive there sooner or later. My first step towards the goal was to join an Elocution Class. And since I may be expected perhaps to give some advice to aspirants to the stage, I am tempted to say, "Never join an Elocution Class." This may be unfair of me, because perhaps there are other kinds of elocution classes nowadays, and on second thoughts there may be some value in the association, if you keep a tight hold on yourself. But our master of elocution taught us to speak so beautifully, so much better and more correctly than anybody else in the world, that no theatre audience could have tolerated us. The desire to throw something would have been so strong that I doubt if they could have resisted. There in the charmed circle of our elocution class we all elocuted at one another till our mouths took on strange shapes and our faces cracked. Everything that could be done to ruin the student for a stage career was done in that class.

The only value in allying oneself to such a group is that it gives the student an opportunity of speaking before an audience; from my association with the other students I got invitations to recite at all sorts of charity concerts, penny readings, church socials. I went everywhere I was asked and was soon inflicting myself in various suburbs of London upon two or three audiences a week.

I believe I was saved from speaking beautifully by my association with my friends Joseph and Henry. But for them I should probably have had the delivery which marks one at once as a Shakespearian actor. But it happened that Joseph and Henry were the sons of an actress and of an actor. Their mother was Nellie Farren, so long associated with the Old Gaiety Theatre, under John Hollingshead, and later under George Edwardes; she was the darling of the London public. I don't recall any actress of my time who had such a strong hold on the affections of all classes in London, from the Prince of Wales (the late King Edward) to the poorest gallery boy. Their father, Robert Soutar, was a stage manager, who will be remembered by many of the older theatregoers of London.

Through them I occasionally met actors and actresses of the London stage, and I found that they spoke and behaved in a manner quite different from the members of my elocution class; in fact they seemed just like human beings. Previous to this time I had never met an actor. I saw one once. I believe he came to see my father in connection with publishing some reminiscences (they did it even then, occasionally). I remember he was a red-faced man in a tall hat and shepherd's plaid trousers and his name was Stevenson. I know I followed him all down Museum Street and registered his every movement; I thought that perhaps I might never see an actor again off the stage and I must make the most of my opportunity.

The next actor I remember seeing off the stage was a dark dashing fellow in a cape-coat, or a cloak, who swung into my father's office one day to see about the printing of a play. He seemed to me a striking figure. That was Maurice Barrymore, the father of the present Barrymore family. He was probably looking up some data at the library of the British Museum and happened in to my father's office because it was close by. People of all professions drifted in that way.

I cannot pass over this period — my boyhood — without some further reference to the British Museum, because during my entire life on the stage I have been drawing upon the characters that I met or observed during that time, and I am doing so still. I knew the smell of the British Museum almost before I could walk. When my mother wanted to get rid of the children she sent them into the Museum. I am writing these lines in Chicago, Illinois, U. S. A.; if a sudden cyclone should come and carry us clear away, and drop us through the dome of the British Museum, and I should hear the Chicagoans say, "Where are we?" with my first sniff of consciousness, before I opened my eyes, I should say, "Friends, we are safe. This is the Museum." I should know it by the smell — not a bad smell, but very museumy and quite British.

It was a safe place to send a small boy, because there

THE AUTHOR'S PARENTS

were terrible men with long wands and black cloaks and eagle eyes placed in every corner to correct the manners and behavior of all visitors, young and old.

Of course it was not at this early age that I registered my impressions of character studies. That came when I entered my father's business at the age of sixteen or thereabouts, and during the year that I remained in his office. My father was a very popular man. He was familiarly known as "The Duke of Bloomsbury" — mainly I suppose because he dressed exceedingly well, always wore a monocle and never appeared to be doing any work. As a matter of fact he had spells of close application to his business. He started three local newspapers, any one of which might have become a considerable property if he had had the faculty of sustained application. This he unfortunately lacked. As soon as he had the thing going, after infinite labor and pains, he lost interest in it and allowed it to decline and finally to disappear. He was credited by his business associates with wasting an inordinate amount of valuable time in the society of a lot of useless hangers-on of the British Museum, a certain literary group of that great and wonderful Reading Room. But he loved their society and they had a great regard for him, partly for himself and partly because he could always be depended upon to lend them half-a-crown in an emergency — and that emergency was continually arising. To him and his cronies, the old tavern days so dear to the heart of Doctor Johnson had not yet passed away.

The Museum Tavern was a regular meeting place

for a picturesque and fascinating literary fringe — men who got a hand-to-mouth existence with their pen and lived Heaven knows where. Some of them were men of fine education, many of them brilliant writers; most of them "ghosts" forced into the shadow by the inexorable power of rum, brandy or whisky. The literary ghost is one whose name never appears; his efforts are frequently printed as the work of some other author who has sufficient commercial ability to command publication.

The ghost would apply himself diligently to the production of some amazingly good article for the sum of half-a-guinea, and having drawn the money would appear in the Museum Tavern and would refuse to fade away until the final sixpence had been consumed. Of course there were others more successful, who were part of the Tavern group, but the majority were of the derelict type who might have been prosperous literary men but for their uncontrollable desire for that particular kind of social intercourse that is stimulated at frequent intervals with potent liquor.

I had no idea then that I should ever use these characters on the stage, but they fascinated me and I used to steal into the Tavern like an alien spy and watch them from a corner seat, and without my being aware of it, they all fell into a pocket of my memory. And afterward, when I went on the stage, I used to find them popping up and begging for reincarnation. In a play called "The Elixir of Youth", of which Leonard Merrick was part author (as far as I know this was his only attempt at writing for the stage), I was cast for an old professor. When I came to study the part, at once there jumped up from my Tavern memory bag Mr. Oldfield.

Mr. Oldfield was not a regular habitue of the Tavern, but he would turn up there at intervals. He was a thin, diminutive Englishman of advanced but uncertain age, who had lived in Paris most of his life. I remember that he was supposed to have cut some figure in the French Revolution. I have a hazy idea that his business with my father was the printing of a revolutionary newspaper called *La Lanterne*, which, if my memory serves me right, was carried over to France in a balloon. He spoke perfect English but with all the volubility and extreme gesture of a Frenchman. He had a habit of trying to speak right in your face, and as he was very small this kept his head continually up in the air. If you turned to the right or left he jumped round you from one side to the other and always seemed to be about to climb up you and settle on your shoulder like a marmosette. I reproduced these peculiarities to the best of my ability in playing the professor.

Mr. Limpenny too I used once in a one-act play, and hope to use him again. He was a delightful person. Tall and erect but very frail. He was sixty or so, had a fair mustache and a lingering remnant of hair that had once been fair. He was seedy, very seedy, but so well brushed that he looked as though he had been carefully varnished. He had beautiful long white hands, of which he was obviously but pardonably proud, for there was very little else that could be calculated to excite his vanity. God had given him his hands. Just who had given him his clothes he had probably ceased to remember. He was never known to wear an overcoat or gloves even in the severest weather — possibly because he never possessed either.

Although he was unmistakably a man of culture, he had a pronounced "Oxford accent" or what is known in America as an English accent. If I met him he would extend a white hand and say, "And how is your deah fathah?" for all the world as though he had not borrowed two shillings of him an hour before. Once I met him when I was walking with my mother, and introduced him, and ever after that he would say, "And how is your deah mothah?"

He always appeared to be dressed for a wedding — in a top hat and a frock coat (dating back to the days when they were still called "Prince Alberts")—with a white handkerchief sticking jauntily out between the middle and the top buttons. This handkerchief was not intended for use; for such emergency another, less virgin, appendage was concealed up his sleeve.

His outstanding peculiarity in costume was that he always carried another frock coat, folded and thrown airily across the left shoulder, much as the gathered ends of the cloak were worn in earlier days. As far as I know nobody ever discovered why he did this; my own theory was that it served to cover a shameful spot on the shoulder of the coat he was wearing. Any character actor will appreciate my desire to elaborate so delightful a character.

Some years ago, when Mrs. Fiske produced Ibsen's "Rosmersholm" I got a great deal of credit for the way I played Brendel. As a matter of fact I don't think I deserved it, for it was almost a photographic reproduction of one of my British Museum group. It was no other than Bill Trafford brought back to life.

Bill Trafford was more than sixty; he was the husband of a teacher of singing. He wore a broad hat and a flowing mustache; every gesture of Bill's was broad; he looked as though he had been a magnificent tenor in his day — but of course he had never had a day. But he was grandly optimistic. His day was coming — it was always coming. Great schemes for revolutionizing music — for the invention of instruments needed for generations in every orchestra — for the building of magnificent schools of music.

"Arliss," he said to my father one day, when I was present at the Tavern, "Arliss, you now have the opportunity of being able to say to your children in years to come, 'Children, I once had the privilege of lending Bill Trafford a shilling.'"

My father murmured something to the effect that it was possible he may already have availed himself of that opportunity many times.

"But you don't understand, my dear Arliss," swept on Bill, "you see me now in this common pothouse asking you for a shilling — begging for a shilling. In a week — a month — three months perhaps, you will see me rolling along in my carriage and pair! You ask me why? How?"

My father said he didn't.

"I will tell you," went on Bill, "you, old friend, shall be the first to know it. I have discovered, in the utmost recesses of the vast depths of the Library of the British Museum, a hitherto unpublished and unknown score of the great Mozart, a mine of music, a wealth of melody, passed over, unrecognized, unobserved, by all my brother artistes, who with equal opportunity have lacked the application, the industry which, thank God, I possess, and which has led me to this discovery. A shilling, dear Arliss, till Monday."

This was not a story invented as a device to extract the shilling; he really believed every word he uttered. And so he went through life; nothing ever came of anything, but he was an optimist to the end. Meanwhile, of course, his wife worked unceasingly and the rent was paid.

With such a wonderful character in my mind it was not difficult to play Ulric Brendel.

How often in these later years I have wished I could pass a half-guinea over to these men and say, "I owe it to you. You have earned it for me many times."

I leave these characters with regret, but there are so many of them, and I find it difficult to curb my inclination to introduce them one by one. They really form a large part of my stage equipment.

II

HIS OWN DRAMATIC SOCIETY

From the moment of my meeting with the Soutar boys, my time was entirely given up to preparation for the stage. Not, I am bound to confess, the kind of preparation that includes dancing masters, fencing masters, professors of music, rhythm, poise and such tuition, which I am given to understand is so necessary to fit one for the stage; nor did I, I am ashamed to say, spend hours of study with my Shakespeare. My studies were pursued not in an attic, but mainly in a cellar — or rather a half-basement.

The Soutars lived in the district of Clapham Common, within the four-mile radius of Charing Cross. In the basement of the house was what was designated by our elders the "Stage-room", but was facetiously dignified by us with the title of "Theatre Royal." It consisted of a platform (the stage) with proscenium wings and a real curtain on a roller. There was only one scene: this we periodically renovated with new wall paper, and it had to serve equally for the prison cell of the hero, or the gilded cage of the unhappily wedded heroine. For footlights we had to use candles. On one special occasion we did get a length of iron pipe with holes in it, and enlisted the services of an amateur gas fitter to connect it with the main service pipe. That night we had a grand illumination, but unfortunately the device was discovered above stairs

25

and in the middle of our drama the lights were suddenly put out and the entertainment brought to an unceremonious end. The next time we risked this maneuver with the gas pipe, we had a row of lighted candles behind the gas, so if the gas went out the performance might proceed without further interruption.

Our seating capacity was small, but sufficient, for it must be confessed that our great difficulty was to get an audience, and we frequently had to resort to bribery to avoid playing to empty benches. I have since discovered that this is a difficulty not unknown to professional managers and one which is overcome in much the same way. We could seat eight comfortably, but we seldom succeeded in getting a full house. Often we only had one, but we made an effort to get at least two, for we found it was easier to work on the emotions of the crowd, than on a single individual. And how we worked! How tremendously we acted! An audience of four would stimulate us to great heights of dramatic intensity. Proving that everything is a matter of comparison. I doubt if I could do my best to-day to an audience of four, even if they were willing spectators. Our company consisted of:

LEADING MAN	*Joseph Soutar*
CHARACTER ACTOR	*George Arliss*
COMEDIAN AND STAGE MANAGER	*Henry Soutar*
HEAVY MAN (VILLAIN)	*Fatty*
LEADING LADY	*Alfred Scrimshire*

Alfred Scrimshire had to be the leading lady because he was small and lisped. He was to be educated as an engraver. I have lost sight of him since those days, but I have many times seen his etchings prominently displayed in the windows of Fifth Avenue art dealers. Poor Fatty passed away at an early age. Henry, after some years in the theatre, left the stage and retired to country life on a small income. Joseph is now a recognized London actor, known as Farren Soutar.

Here, in the basement, we went through all the motions and emotions of a stock company — only more so, for we changed the bill every night; perhaps not every night, for there were certain days when we were not able to get together, but we seldom repeated a performance. You see, we were very temperamental. We had to be. Our method of production demanded it. We would meet at six P.M. for rehearsal of a new play — possibly a three-act play. Perhaps four acts. It made no difference to us. And the curtain would rise on the public performance promptly at seven. It was intensive work, but it was done. First of all, somebody had to have an idea. It generally fell to the lot of Joseph or myself to have the idea; we were prepared for that. This is how it was done.

The company assembled on the stage and amid breathless excitement Joseph would say, "I've got an idea. The play's called 'Brought to Bay.' (We always got a good title.) The first act is in the country, Dora's Cottage. You're Dora, Alf. George, you're Dora's father. I'm engaged to Dora. My name's Gerald Travers. I'm a young farmer. I shall

27

wear leggings. We are talking over our wedding which is to be to-morrow. Dora and I are both very happy, but you seem to have something on your mind, George. You shake your head every now and then, when we talk about living in this pretty cottage. You can wear that wig you wore in 'The Miser and His Gold.' After a bit I say, 'Well I must go and look after the cattle,' and I go off. Then you, Alf, ask George, your father, you know, if there is anything the matter, and you shake your head again, George. When just then Fatty comes in. Fatty's the villain. His name is Geoffrey Belding." (Fatty being quite fat and small and looking rather like an overgrown baby, always had to wear a black cloak and a slouched hat in order to assume the weightiness necessary for a villain.)

"You come in smiling, Fatty, and you say, 'Good morning, Miss Dora,' and then you turn to her father and say, 'Well, Mr. Franklin' (that's your name, George), 'have you spoken to her?' And you shake your head again, George. Then there's a big scene where it turns out that Fatty has a mortgage on the house and that he's going to turn them out unless Dora consents to become his bride. You refuse him, Alf; say you are betrothed to me and would rather die than become the wife of another — like the speech you did in 'Greater Than Life.' Then Fatty says, 'We shall see,' takes a little bottle out of his pocket, puts a few drops on his handkerchief — I can lend you a clean handkerchief — seizes her, puts it over her mouth, says 'My men are waiting outside

with a carriage,' and drags Dora off. You're too old
to defend her, George. You're supposed to be about
fifty, but you cry out, 'Help, Help.' I rush on with
my riding whip and my leggings and say, 'What is the
matter? Where's Dora?' And you say, 'Gone.' And
I say, 'Gone, where?' You shake your head, and I
say, 'Speak, speak.' And you say, 'Geoffrey Belding.'
And I say, 'Curse him. Henceforth I devote my life
to finding Dora, and running her betrayer to earth,'
and you are left alone saying, 'Dora, my little Dora.'
That's the curtain on Act I."

I have since discovered that this method of production was by no means original. I have it on excellent
authority that the smaller professional companies,
which used to play in booths through the villages of
England, were in the habit of taking the press reviews
of London productions of such plays as "The Lights o'
London" and "The Silver King", following the story
as nearly as it could be gleaned from the criticisms,
working up to the main situations by means of entirely
impromptu dialogue and composing in this way a
four- or five-act drama, lasting from two to three
hours. The "team work" in these entertainments
must have been truly remarkable; the old mummers
would roll off long bravura speeches good for number-
less rounds of applause, speeches borrowed from
Shakespeare or any other author they had at one time
committed to memory.

It will be seen that the plays which we produced
at our Theatre Royal were not of the highbrow order.
They gave no food for meditation on the problems of

life. But in a crude way they reflected the drama of that period.

I have often deplored the passing of the stock companies which gave the actor such valuable opportunity of playing many parts, but I am of opinion that such companies in a metropolitan center, when they were composed of actors of distinction, were very narrowing to the dramatist. The stock companies in the west end of London had passed away before my time, but the pleasant custom of holding together settled groups of actors for certain theatres still remained.

For many years in my recollection there might be seen at the Adelphi Theatre (the home of melodrama) the same leading man, juvenile man, heavy man, second heavy, comedian, character actor, leading lady, chambermaid and first old woman. I believe several of these actors had long contracts with the management. The Adelphi was the most important theatre for melodrama. The consequence was that when an author was moved to write a play of that kind, he at once thought of the Adelphi and of the Adelphi Company. And so, whatever his plot might be, he felt it necessary to weave it round an impeccable hero and heroine, an entirely unscrupulous villain, an irrepressible comic gentleman, an unbelievedly bright young woman, with a strong part for a character actor. The result was often an exceedingly good entertainment, but one which contained much that was reminiscent of the previous efforts of the same company. I believe I am right in saying that many of the successful authors of that period were not concerned

30

in writing plays that necessarily had any relation to real life, but rather devoted themselves to inventing a series of stirring situations through which the established company could most creditably disport themselves.

The Drury Lane dramas were designed, up to within the past few years, to afford the opportunity of presenting great spectacular scenes, but they almost invariably contained the stereotyped set of characters that I have mentioned.

Dramatists were more bound to the mechanism of the stage than they are to-day. Most melodramas had at least three scenes in each act: a "full set" followed by a "front scene", then another full set to end the act. The "front scene" was played well over the footlights in front of a "cloth" or a "pair of flats." The "cloth" was a painted scene let down on a roller and was generally an exterior, such as a wood or a garden. The "flats" were mostly used when an interior was necessary, and were pushed on from the side, meeting in the center, and then interior wings were pushed forward to complete the picture. The author knew that these scenes must be relatively unimportant to the main story, partly because an audience never gave its undivided attention to a front scene and partly because there was generally a good deal of noise behind, due to the setting of the "full set" by irreverent stage hands.

In those scenes the irrepressible comic man and the bright young chambermaid were invaluable. They had learned by experience never to be disturbed by noises back or front, and they could be depended upon to be so comic that they kept the people entertained while the big scene was being set behind. The author seldom brought on his heroine in these scenes, but if he did he contrived that the dialogue should be brief and the situation carried more or less by action.

"The exterior of the prison cell" was generally a front scene; but there you saw the hero brought on between two warders (hero in white shirt, open at the neck if in any way permissible) and the heroine weeping in his wake. She was generally accompanied by the low-comedy couple because they would inevitably be needed later on. She would break away from them and cling to the hero and say, "Is there no hope?" and he would answer, "None," and the warders would disentangle her and march the hero into the cell, and she would go off R. weeping, and that's as much as the author would give her in the front scene.

Then the low-comedy people, having allowed the heroine a respectful exit (in those days the leading lady always got a round of applause when she went off and it was the business of the other actors not to kill it), the chambermaid would say, "Poor young thing," and the low comedian would at one leap alter the tempo of the whole scene by taking an imaginary adversary by the throat and telling the chambermaid that that is what he would like to do with those warders if he could only get them alone: and then they would settle down into the acknowledged comic scene which lasts until Scene 3 is set.

32

This method of construction of melodrama went on with little variation for a long period. It is interesting to reflect to what extent the author was influenced and restricted by the physical conditions of the theatre.

And this was the kind of thing we were doing at our Theatre Royal with great gusto and to the limit of our ability. Although these impromptu performances continued until that tremendous day came when I became a real actor in the Elephant and Castle Stock Company, and although every moment was full of interest for me, I am afraid there is little worth recording. There comes to me the memory of one awful moment, though.

We had written a play, actually written it this time, and rehearsed it with an augmented company. Joseph and I wrote it. It was called "The Miser and His Gold." It was inspired by a long, gray, old man's wig which had belonged to Joseph's father, Robert Soutar. We gave a party — a large party including grown-ups — and we had programmes printed. We had some real actors and actresses in front to see us. It was a thrilling thing.

The Miser (I was the Miser) had the sympathy of the audience because he was saving his money for his daughter when she should marry. And the day comes when she is to be married. And you see the Miser counting out his money and putting it in bags, each bag marked "£500" in large letters on the front. And you see him put ten of these bags in his iron safe (an iron safe is easily constructed with a small packing case painted a dark color with a door that hinges and a piece of string on the door and a nail at the side of the case; you deftly wind or unwind the string to and from the nail while you are pretending to insert the cellar key) and as he gazes at the row of bags he says, "For her, all for her," and then I take my candle and go to bed. And then by the moonlight you see the villain (Fatty) come in through the window in a dark cloak, a slouch hat and steal all the money, and that's the end of that act.

And in the next act comes my big scene when I bring my daughter into the room to give her the money and open the safe and find the money gone — gone! It was a great scene as we wrote it. I go mad and jump out of the window. A tremendous mad scene. But, — it's terrible to think of it even now!

Henry was our stage manager, and like most stage managers, he knew very little of what the play was about, so after the second act in which the money is stolen, Henry had to prepare the stage for Act III. He saw these bags of money at the back of the stage, and as he had made the iron safe he concluded that they ought to be in it, so he put them all back again; and when I unwound the piece of string and flung open the door, and said, "Gone. Gone!" there they were — ten of them, all marked £500 in large letters, staring the audience in the face. Of course if I hadn't said "Gone, Gone" something might have been done: with our experience of impromptu dialogue, we might have reconstructed the play on the spot and the audience might never have known. But you see it

was one of my big moments, and I had to stagger
back and put my hands over my eyes in grief. And
I had braced myself for it, and as I opened the safe
door I staggered and put my hands over my eyes too
soon, so that when I said "Gone, gone" I didn't
really know that they hadn't, until I heard the awful
laugh from the front. Well, that was the end of the
drama for that night. It was a bitter moment for us.
It would have been impossible to pull the audience
together again and we knew it. Henry defended
himself verbally and physically with all the vigor
of an incompetent stage manager. But "The Miser
and His Gold" was never attempted again. No manuscript of the play is now in existence, but I rather
suspect that the audience was grateful to Henry.

During all this period of my association with the
Soutar boys, I was giving recitals, readings, entertainments — anything to be seen and heard — at
concerts, church meetings, working-men's clubs,
work-houses, anywhere. I was very partial to readings from American authors. A chapter from one of
Max Adeler's books which I called "The Editor of
the Patriotic Journal" was one of my sure-fire recita-
tions. The American humorists always appealed to
me. I think I am right in saying that the first story
I ever read was Mark Twain's "Celebrated Jumping
Frog." My father bought every book of Mark
Twain's just as soon as it could be got from the publishers, and I have a very vivid recollection of the
first arrival of "The Tramp Abroad" — published in
England by Chatto and Windus — and my keen delight

in it. As a child American men always attracted me. I used to think of Americans as tall, thin, kindly comedians. I suppose the reason I thought all Americans were funny and kindly was because of my very early acquaintance with the writings of Mark Twain, Max Adeler, and Bret Harte. This impression clung to me until I came to America in 1901 — and then I found it to be to some extent true. And what a wonderful moment it was for me when in course of time Brander Matthews placed me next to Mark Twain at luncheon!

I must have had a good deal of assurance in my early youth. I suppose I have some still or I should not be doing this. But I can't have as much now, because I should not dare to do the things I did then. I should be frightened to death to-day to find that I had contracted to give a two hours' entertainment on a Sunday evening at a working-man's club. But I did it then, and got paid for it: sometimes five shillings — sometimes seven shillings and sixpence and on rare occasion half a guinea. I had to keep these readings a secret, on account of their being given on the Sabbath; I've explained what Sunday meant in Museum Street. I called myself Mr. Augustus Buckland on these occasions, because my father knew a man named Buckland who was very entertaining. I used to steal away from home in a large overcoat, under which I had concealed a number of "props" and disguises for use in my entertainment. I did not dare to carry a bag because that would at once have called for explanation.

A working-man's club was a large, foul-smelling room, generally over a public house. It had a door one end and a piano and small platform the other and masses of working men in between, all smoking pipes and drinking beer. I always arranged to have a small screen behind which I made my changes. I suppose my youth and my assurance carried me through, for I always got safely away after I had finished. The British working man was, I think, a different man in those days. He was fairly contented with his lot and as an audience he was warmly appreciative and easily pleased. My most vivid recollection is of the thin, over-worked, patient and obliging pianist, who worked Heaven knows how many hours for a few shillings.

During this period my theatrical activities were many and varied. It must not be supposed that I was always paid for my exuberant efforts. Indeed such windfalls were few and far between. Sometimes I had to pay for the privilege of acting. I knew a man who used to write one-act plays "intended for amateurs." There seems to be a difference between such plays and those intended for the regular theatre. Perhaps the author knows it, and is modest enough to subtly admit in this description that they are not good enough for professionals. Or perhaps it is to assure prospective producers that there is nothing at all wicked in them. Those written by my friend were very mild indeed — terribly mild. And for fear they should never even be considered by the aspiring group for whom they were admittedly intended, he conceived the brilliant, but not entirely original, idea of producing them himself. By payment of a shilling I was allowed to play a small part; the larger the fee the bigger the part; but I could only afford a shilling part. We used to perform them at Percy Hall, Percy Street, Tottenham Court Road. The audience was not allowed to pay for admission because the hall had no license, but they paid sixpence for a programme as they came in. I suppose they must have been very religious people — people in the habit of going to church — for they always behaved nicely and stayed till the end. The programme was padded out with songs and glees contributed by the nobility and gentry of Tottenham Court Road.

Of course I was still acting in the basement at the Theatre Royal, but I think it was at Percy Hall that I made my first appearance in a play on any stage erected on the actual surface of the earth. I was always reciting somewhere. I recall appearing at Battersea for some fund in connection with the Great Western Railway (as compensation I was allowed a free pass for one journey to any station on the line) and on the same programme was a young man who sang a song — with a very red nose and a very funny get-up. He amused me mightily: as far as I remember there were no programmes so I asked his name and was told he was "a young fellow named George Robey." Mr. Robey is to-day the idol of the London Music Halls.

I wish I had more recollections of that kind: it is so interesting to have rubbed shoulders with famous people before they became anybody; and so gratifying to one's vanity to have observed talent hitherto undiscovered by others. But I have never had that sort of adventurous life. Nothing ever seems to happen to me. I have always been the despair of theatrical press agents. I have friends whose lives are made up of exciting moments. I know men and women too who cannot go out to buy even a newspaper without coming back palpitating from the effect of some startling experience; whilst I can go forth praying for adventure and the only thing that happens to me is that I lose my way — which I almost invariably do. I suppose I haven't a very vivid imagination. I should have made a hopeless newspaper man. I once went round with a reporter who was covering the police courts in the lower east side of New York, and after reading his reports I asked him why he didn't stick to facts instead of drawing upon his imagination and he said, "Why, if we reported facts all the newspapers would be the same, and all the reporters would be fired." It is a great drawback to a writer of reminiscences to have the kind of conscience that binds him to facts.

But in those early days, if I didn't have adventures I had my moments of exaltation — those moments when I was allowed to recite at concerts. Whenever you listen to a recitation and are bored almost beyond endurance, you may comfort yourself with the fact that you have done your one good act for that day, because you have given a tremendous pleasure to the reciter, by letting him recite to you.

About this time I formed an amateur dramatic society. I had been looking through an old scrapbook compiled by my grandfather. I suppose everybody's grandfather in those days made one of these scrapbooks. A massive and wonderful thing it was. Engravings of London Bridge — of Mr. Pitt — of Charlotte Corday; colored reproductions of Rowlandson — Hogarth's "Road to Ruin", cuttings from Punch; steel engravings from Arliss's Pocket Magazine, a very popular monthly or weekly, I forget which, published at the end of the eighteenth century by John Arliss, my grandfather's uncle (all my people had been printers and publishers for generations), jokes cut from newspapers, always with the point emphasized in Italics — which for the most part was very necessary. Recipes for coughs and colds — stanzas from Byron — how to take spots out of silk — and a thousand other treasures, one of which was a programme headed "The Pantheon Amateur Dramatic Society." This at once attracted my attention and I asked my mother if she could tell me why it was included in this cherished collection. She told me that my grandfather had once appeared as an amateur and that the Mr. Draper whom I saw recorded there was none other than my grandfather under an assumed name.

There had for some time been growing within me a craving to act before larger audiences than we were able to attract to the Theatre Royal, and the discovery of this programme, together with my experiences at Percy Hall, fired me with a desire to get up an amateur dramatic society of my own. It was really quite a good idea, because by founding it myself I could make myself president and general director and so cast myself for all the best parts. It opened up wonderful possibilities; we could play real plays, all thoroughly rehearsed, take public halls, and play to huge audiences.

The Pantheon Amateur Dramatic Society seemed to be a noble name and not to be improved upon. So I wrote to all my aspiring friends and told them that The Pantheon Amateur Dramatic Society was about to be formed and pointed out the advantages of joining early and being on the Committee. The idea appealed to them: a number of us got together and discussed finances. It was necessary to have printing; and then a deposit would have to be paid before a hall could be booked. So we decided on a five shilling entrance fee, and I think a shilling a week each during rehearsals. I appointed a treasurer — a man I was sure would be a very bad actor but a very good treasurer — and the thing started in real earnest. The first production was to be "Blow for Blow" (very popular with amateurs). The money was paid up to the treasurer and rehearsals began.

This was my first and only experience of an amateur society, and I was very surprised and disheartened when I found that my company was most difficult to get together for rehearsals. I had thought that there would be the same coöperation as I had been used to at the Theatre Royal, where nothing in the world mattered but acting. But here were people who

regarded the drama as a mere amusement and not as a
life or death occupation. And so the rehearsals
dragged on week after week: the shillings were paid
to the treasurer, but the play did not develop as
rapidly as I had hoped. It was unbelievable to me
that any one could want to do anything else if there
were a chance of rehearsing. But many of my company sacrificed art to parties and week-ends up the
river. The treasurer always came; and as the weeks
went by it was impossible not to observe that the
treasurer began to come out in wonderful new ties,
and immaculate gloves, quite beyond his station.

Well, it was all very unfortunate. I hope all bogus
managers are not as sensitive as I was. When the
time approached to pay for the printing and book
the hall, the treasurer was taken suddenly ill and
letters to him remained unanswered. He may have
recovered his health, but to this day we never recovered our money. This incident shattered the morale
of the Society; they began to lose such interest as I
had been able to inspire in them. I felt they regarded
me with suspicion, for which I cannot blame them.
"Blow for Blow" languished and finally the Pantheon
Amateur Dramatic Society took the count and surrendered without a single performance.

There is to me something pathetic about these
feverish efforts of young people who have a burning
desire to go upon the stage. The rising generation
of these sufferers write to me and beg me to tell them
what to do — how to get started on the stage — and
I am always unable to answer them with any degree

of satisfaction to myself. I generally tell them to attach themselves to some good school of dramatic art, not so much for the knowledge they will gain there of how to act — that depends largely upon their luck in receiving desirable instruction, and the chances of this are, I believe, against them — but more because they will be thrown with people who may be able, directly or indirectly, to squeeze them through that obstinate door that leads to the professional stage.

In my early days there were no dramatic schools, or if there were I never heard of them. There were those terrible institutions known as "elocution classes," from which, having once been infected, it probably took you years to recover. There were some Shakespearian companies "on the road" which the beginner might get into with considerable influence, and which turned loose upon the public, in the course of years of training, some of the worst actors on the English stage. Also a few of the best actors came through this channel, but that in my opinion was mainly because their mental constitution was strong enough to withstand the training.

Judging from the letters I get, the young people of to-day imagine that I strolled into a theatrical company, chose the parts that I thought would suit me best, and was immediately acknowledged by the manager as an indispensable member of the cast. Of course it was not at all like that: it was a hot fight all the time, using any tactics to get through and meeting with defeat at every turn. I had to go into my father's business for a year, and pretend that I liked it; and I lay awake at night wondering how I was ever going to gain the courage to tell him that I never meant to continue with it, that I intended to go on the "Stage" — a most terrible bombshell in a family in which as far back as William the Conqueror there had never been an actor, except at an occasional amateur performance. I had to steal away from the office an hour — sometimes two — before time, in order to attend a rehearsal of something; and that unheard-of proceeding had to be explained away. Mysterious young men and women would sometimes call at the office during the day and ask for me — seeking some information as to our next rehearsal or the choice of a play — and they had to be explained away.

But during this trying time I had one great consolation: my mother was on my side; she was in my confidence and helped me through many difficulties. My father was a great stickler for young men applying themselves entirely to their business. He didn't set a very good example at this time, but as a young man he had been an insistent worker. My mother was always for "letting the boys do the thing they want to do." My father's attitude was, "What nonsense! Wasting their time. I want them in the business."

Strange to say, when I finally broke away and he saw that my mind was set on the thing, my father became most sympathetic toward my work and did everything he could to help me along, and although my progress was terribly slow and must have been most discouraging to others he developed an unexpected pride in having a son on the stage: indeed on one occasion when he was in the audience he was so proud of me that his behavior brought about my dismissal from the company. I may speak of that later on.

Well, I knew that the longer I stayed in my father's business the more difficult it would be for me to leave it. So I resorted to strategy. I saw no possible chance of getting upon the stage, but I knew it had to come sooner or later and I wanted to prepare the way. I had a heart-to-heart talk with my father, and said that I thought it was a bad thing for a son to get all his business experience in his father's office; it kept him in the same old rut, whereas if he went into some other man's office for a year, he might get fresh ideas which he could bring back and adapt with great value to the home business. My father was at first shocked at the idea of my going away from him, but he admitted after some discussion that my reasoning was sound and eventually he agreed. I had no hesitation in this subterfuge, because I knew that if Fate decreed that I should never go on the stage, my suggestion was not a bad one, and the experiences I gained would certainly be useful. So I left my father's business and entered a wholesale firm. This made it easier for me to follow my theatrical peregrinations because my hours in business were shorter. And so I got deeper and deeper into the mire of amateur entertainments.

And soon something happened. I had been away for a summer holiday and when I came back and dashed over to the Theatre Royal, Joseph and his brother met me with the staggering remark, "We are going on the stage."

"We — who?" I said.

"Me and Henry," said Joseph. This was no time to worry about choice of words.

"When?" I asked.

"We start on Monday at the 'Elephant.'"

A dreadful feeling of desolation came over me. They were going into a real theatre, and I was left behind. I knew this was the end of the Theatre Royal; and the end of all pleasure for me in amateur work, for now anything but the actual professional stage seemed futile. I felt deserted — terribly alone, dreadfully unhappy. But I did not know at that moment how loyal my friends were. They opened at the Elephant and Castle Theatre on the Monday, but they never rested until they had pulled me in after them. Within three weeks I had started my "career."

Joseph and Henry had been taken on through the influence of their mother — Nellie Farren. But two raw recruits were as much as the management could carry and there seemed no chance for me. The two boys left no stone unturned, however. They discovered that their Aunt Harriet had in earlier days acted with the stage manager (George Skinner) at the Old Vic — in the days when the Old Vic was known as "The Home of Melodrama." So Aunt Harriet was badgered into writing to George Skinner, and using the memory of their early days as a lever to wedge me in.

But without success: he submitted that it couldn't be done. So one night Aunt Harriet (dear tender-hearted soul) took me down to the Elephant and introduced me to George Skinner and begged him to take me. That visit is as fresh in my memory as though it had happened last night.

Skinner said, "But my dear Harriet, I can't do it. I've just got those two kids of Nellie's on my hands. My work's hard enough as it is. This isn't a school for amateurs, you know, my dear. I want people who know the business."

"Well, George, let him just walk on."

"Oh, my God, Harriet, you talk exactly like an amateur. You know it takes a year to learn how to walk on."

"Not in a crowd, George, it doesn't. He can come on in a crowd and nobody will ever see him."

"We don't have crowds in this theatre, my love. We can't afford 'em. Each one of my supers has got to know how to look like half a dozen."

"But George —"

"Oh, God Almighty, Harriet, let him come. But he comes as an extra gentleman, remember."

I nearly swooned with joy. I knew that "extra gentleman" was merely a gentlemanly name for "super" but I nearly swooned with joy. I murmured something about doing everything I could for the management.

"My boy, when once you're in the theatre, you'll do everything you can for yourself." It was said savagely and it shocked me, if I were capable of

47

receiving any further shock at that moment — but I found it was terribly true.

"Let him come at ten o'clock on Monday."

Good, kind Aunt Harriet, I wish she had lived long enough to get a little greater satisfaction for all her trouble on my behalf.

III

AS "EXTRA GENTLEMAN"

THE Three Musketeers were certainly more picturesque, but they could never have been half as joyous as we three boys were when we first came together after the news of my being "taken on." To be in a real theatre together; to go to rehearsals; to hang about the stage door; to mix with the actors as one of them, and talk shop — it was gorgeous.

When that Monday morning came and I pushed open the narrow stage-door that swung back on a spring, my heart thumped and I suppose I felt very elated, for I remember thinking, "I am opening the door of an entirely new life: I may fail, but whatever happens I shall never regret it, because it is the only life I care to live." I had no particular ambition in the acknowledged sense of the word. I don't think I ever have had. I just wanted to be on the stage and play parts. I believe I'm rather glad that I never was ambitious. The lack of any special desire to set the world on fire has enabled me always to find infinite pleasure in the thing that I am doing. It seems to me that ambitious people must be terribly impatient of the struggle for their goal, and sorely tempted to scamp work which must seem to them relatively unimportant. As I look back, the only burning desire I have ever had was to get out of the "provinces" and become a "West-End Actor."

The Elephant and Castle was very far from being a West End theatre — I mean socially, not geographically. It was across the Thames on the Surrey side — "over the water." And any one who has lived in London will know that everything on the other side of the water is regarded by the West End with contempt. It was a prosperous district, but populated almost entirely by the hard-working classes — largely by a healthy, happy, overworked lower class. The streets were lined with the barrows of the hawkers and Saturday night was like a fair. Almost anything could be bought on the stalls — kippers and bloaters at bargain prices; potatoes almost given away; and cabbages fit for kings. Large clothing and boot stores thrived there — everybody seemed to buy boots on a Saturday night.

It was to this class that I made my first bow as a professional actor and it was from acting before such people that I really learnt my business. The prices of our seats compared favorably with those of the cabbages and potatoes and the kippers and bloaters. The lowest price was threepence and the highest one shilling and sixpence. There were sixpenny seats, and ninepenny seats and shilling seats, according to the location. Of course the one-and-sixpenny seats were the best. I do not remember ever seeing anybody eating fried fish in the one-and-sixpenny seats, even on a Saturday night. Whereas the threepenny gallery was a perfect orgy of food.

The youth of the district were great patrons of the drama and of hot chipped potatoes; and they liked to take them together. They seldom wore collars and were unencumbered by underclothing; and experience had taught them that a shirt open from the neck to the waist forms a convenient and warming resting place for a bag of chipped potatoes or a sausage or a piece of fried fish, and leaves the hands free to applaud as the actor directs.

There was a chivalry amongst the gallery boys towards the performers. They knew exactly when they were expected to applaud and they seldom failed. Of course the first entrance of the leading people was a signal for a burst of welcome such as a West End actor could hardly hope to get, even if he had been away to America for a year and had been shipwrecked on his way back. All exits of leading people required that the hands of the gallery boy should be free for action; if the actor made a quiet and unstrained exit that was a signal from him that the applause was not to be such as would interfere with the leading lady then on the stage; if he banged open the door with the flat of his hand (our doors seldom had handles; such falderals were reserved for the West End of London) that was a signal for great and resounding clapping and stamping.

These patrons of the drama seldom showed resentment for anything done by an established member of the company, but woe to the newcomer who took the place of some departed favorite and who failed to come up to their expectations. They would listen with terribly obvious patience for a long time and then some hardy regular Saturday-nighter would cry,

"We've heard enough." This was the password that let loose the sinews of war, and a vigorous fusillade of boos would almost surely follow. But on the whole they were patient and friendly. Large quantities of ginger-beer-and-beer were consumed and the popping of corks was so frequent that it ceased to be a distraction, either to the audience or to the actors. A hardy race of actors they were, in whose vocabulary the word "temperament" had no place.

And this was the stock company of which I had become a proud member. I believe it was the last of its kind to exist in England, a remnant of the old Sadler Wells, the Vic and the Surrey days. In comparatively recent years stock companies have been revived, notably in Birmingham and Liverpool, but they are very different. At the time of which I am writing the Surrey was also running stock under the management of George Conquest, but to the best of my belief the Elephant maintained its policy after the Surrey had given up. We changed the bill every week except on special occasions when a play would run for a fortnight, and at Christmas when we put on a Pantomime, which as far as I remember would run about eight weeks. At the time, this theatre seemed to me a bright and angelic spot just once removed from heaven. Actors to-day would regard it, I expect, as far more like the place to which I believe angels are condemned to retreat when they are once removed from heaven. It was in fact, I suppose, a dingy theatre; of course it was lighted by gas — all theatres were then; and Sir Johnston Forbes-Robertson assures me that in his opinion stage lighting has never been as good, never as soft and sympathetic since the introduction of electricity. But gas was an item at the Elephant and was used as sparingly as possible. I have never been able to understand why more theatres were not burnt down in those days. The flaming gas jets in the battens and in all parts of the theatre were protected only by inadequate wire frames and the flimsy sky borders seemed always to be in danger of catching in the flame. Yes, I suppose it was dingy. The stage and dressing rooms were kept fairly clean, but smelt of generations of old melodramatic actors — a fusty, lovely smell that sometimes comes back to me now at unexpected moments and makes me feel happy all over.

The company was composed mainly of good sound stock actors, who knew the business thoroughly. Many of them might have been very good actors; but from long experience in bad plays before primitive audiences they had come to accentuate the mechanism of the art of acting instead of concealing it. It was the revealing of the mechanics that taught the gallery boy when to take up his cue in the responses. These experienced and seasoned actors were very kindly and helpful to us boys. It is true they stole our ginger-beer-and-beer — a combination not to be despised as a beverage — but they did it in an open and friendly spirit. The boy who fetched refreshments had to pass the dressing rooms of all the other actors before he reached ours; he would be challenged as many as three times on the way. A head would be thrust out,

"Hi, boy, whose drink is that?" "Mr. Arliss'."
"Tell him I had a taste." This little pleasantry would
be overheard by the occupant of the next dressing room
with disastrous results to my diminishing refreshment,
and when the tin can reached me I was constrained to
receive it as a loving cup. But it was all fun to us,
and we were rather proud of such attentions from the
leading people.

It seems to me that there was a great spirit of
comradeship throughout the company. If there were
any petty jealousy or backbiting, I never saw it. Indeed throughout my experience on the stage I have
seldom observed any of those instances of jealousy
between actors or between actresses that we are so
frequently led to believe exist in the profession.
There is no more generous audience than that which
fills a theatre at a professional matinée to witness the
efforts of their fellow craftsmen.

At the Elephant we were with actors who were
unused to the presence in their midst of young gentlemen who had come to learn the business, and we
must frequently have got on their nerves; but they
were always patient and never made us feel self-
conscious or ashamed. There was one, George Belmore, a character actor of great ability, to whose
generous assistance I owe practically all I know
to-day about make-up; and the friendly hints of all
those people are standing me in good stead to-day.

The proprietor and manager was Joseph A. Cave,
generally known as Joe Cave. He was a little old man
with a thin face and a hooked nose, and a high color

almost exactly like the pictures of Mr. Punch. He couldn't have been as old as I imagined because he lived for some thirty years after this and died at the Charterhouse. He was an old-timer: it was said that when very young he made quite a stir as a child vocalist in a song with the refrain "I'm ninety-five." Curiously enough I think he was near this age when he died. He had owned and managed music halls, dance halls, and melodrama theatres, including the old Marylebone. He was a queer, doddering little figure and seldom came behind the theatre, except to grumble about something. When he was going to find fault he had a funny nervous habit of closing his lips tight and blowing air through his nose in a manner which might be described as the reverse action of sniffing; and simultaneously he would place the first finger of his right hand, slightly crooked, against the side of his large hooked nose and would always preface his remarks with the words, "My God, sir." His complaints were usually about the extravagance of his stage manager and staff. He would dodder in and look round and call, "Mr. Skinner, Mr. Skinner." (Blowing nervously through his nose and up would go his finger.) "My God, sir, what are those three lights doing burning there in that corridor — three lights, sir, three lights?"

"Must have light, Mr. Cave."

"Must have light, sir, but my God, sir" (pause for blowing and for beating finger against nose), "my God, Mr. Skinner, why three — why *three* lights? Do you think I'm made of money? Do you know what my gas bill is this quarter? Do you know what it is? No, sir. My God, sir, you don't know, none of you. You'll ruin me, sir, that's what you'll do."

Poor Skinner would turn off the lights with a snap and would say, "We do all we can to save your money, but we must have light and we must have scenery. You might as well know now you're here, the carpenter has just told me that he must have some more wood to build the mill scene for Mr. Roberts' new play week after next."

At this Mr. Cave's anger would become so great that for a moment he would seem to be in danger of an apoplectic stroke, and he would stand blowing through the inside of his nose and beating on the outside of it, until speech came to his rescue and he would pipe out, "Wood! Wood! My God, sir, he can't want any more wood. Do you know what I've just paid for wood, for the production of 'The Man Monkey' only last week? Two pounds, sir — two pounds, Mr. Skinner, my God, sir, for wood alone. No, sir, let him use that, sir. My God, sir —" and he would dodder away and be seen no more for perhaps a week.

The first time I ever saw him was one Monday night when he came round to complain about me. I had been in the company then about three weeks: of course I had not been entrusted with any speaking part. But George Skinner, who was really a good soul, would give to one of us boys the part of a messenger who brought on a note or any such solo bit that was available and that did not have words attached to it. Of course we had to come on in all crowds, and were continually quick-changing from Indians to miners and from miners to "gentlemen of the Court." We none of us liked to have the trouble of "blacking-up" for Indians or Africans merely in order to come on with the crowd; it meant a lot of trouble and no chance for personal distinction, so if we knew that the play called for the introduction of these dusky hordes, when George Skinner would say, "Three or four Indians come on here at the back," we would be missing — hiding behind the flats — in the hope that the regular supers would be assigned to this job. And then the voice of Skinner would ring out, "Where are those boys — they can black up and come on here? Where are the little devils?" And then Tommy Sullivan, the assistant, would dig us out and we would come sheepishly forward.

But the time that brought Joe Cave blowing round was when I was given the part of a clerk in an office. As the curtain went up I had to enter, hang up my hat, sit down at a desk, open an account book and remain silently writing while the play proceeded, until at a given cue I closed the book, took my hat and went out. I was just atmosphere. Of course such a thing as a dress rehearsal was unknown at the Elephant; when a boy of eighteen was given the part of a non-speaking clerk, it was supposed that he would come on as a clerk of eighteen and go silently off unnoticed.

But this was the first time I had ever been allowed to come on as a unit. I had a brilliant idea. I knew an old clerk, a very old clerk, who used to dress in a very strange way. I would make up like him. So when the curtain went up, a decrepit old man walked on, in a queer low-crowned top hat (that had taken me many hours to manufacture). He had on rusty trousers too long, and a seedy frock coat, buttoned up at the neck; took off his poor old hat and proceeded to hold up the play while he polished it with a large well-worn bandanna handkerchief, and as he hung up his hat it was perceived that the tips of his fingers were coming through his black cotton gloves. With much deliberation he removed his gloves, and having rolled them up with tender care he put them in his tail pocket; he then took out a large pair of horn-rimmed spectacles (an unfamiliar sight in those days), took a pinch of snuff from an old horn snuffbox, blew his nose and sat down to work. During all this business, which was received with great expectations from the audience, the principals who were waiting to come in were fuming on the side wing at their entrance being thus delayed: but the curtain was up and nothing could be done about it.

When it was time for me to go off, of course I went through all the same deliberate pantomime with hat and gloves and handkerchief, etc., entirely regardless of the dialogue proceeding, and went off to a distinct effort at a round of applause from some members of the audience.

It was then that Joe Cave came blowing round; he doddered up to Skinner and I could see that something had happened, so I kept out of sight; but I overheard the conversation.

"My God, Mr. Skinner, my God, sir, who told that boy to do that?"

"Nobody, Mr. Cave. I just told him to come on, that's all. How was I to know that he was going to give this exhibition?"

"But my God, sir, does he come on again?"

"No, he's finished now."

"Well, that's a mercy. He'd ruin the whole play, sir. The audience think by the way he's behaving that he's going to be the leading character, and my God, sir, he doesn't come on any more!"

"I know, Mr. Cave, but I can't be everywhere. I didn't see him before he went on. The young devil. I've a good mind to give him a damn good hiding. I'll see he doesn't do it again, Mr. Cave."

And then Joe Cave made an amazing remark and turned on his heel and doddered out of the stage door, and the doorman who watched him go out afterward said he distinctly saw him chuckle. The amazing remark was, "Let him do it his own way. Leave him alone."

Skinner was staggered, but those were orders and so I never received any formal complaint. Of course Skinner was right: I deserved to be thrashed; at least, I should have deserved it if my actions had not been the result of ignorance; I did not realize then that any bad actor can "queer" a good actor's scene by distracting the attention of the audience with comic business. There was nothing clever in what I did, and certainly nothing original; every young actor who attempts to play an old man uses a bandanna handker-

chief and takes a pinch of snuff. I was quickly bringing to pass Skinner's prophecy, that once in the
theatre I should do the best I could for myself. I was
attempting to attract attention to myself at the
expense of the play — an unforgivable sin on the
stage, but I really didn't realize my sin; and in this
case it did not much matter, because the principals, for
the remainder of the week, merely waited until my
business was over.

But as I was not corrected, I repeated the offense a
few weeks later, with the result that I was nearly
thrown out of the theatre. It was a very special
occasion: a visiting star was to come with his wife;
they played the two leads and our company filled the
remaining parts. The Star was a well-known provincial actor named Scudamore. The play (of which
he was also the author) was called "Rags and Bones."
The rehearsals were even sketchier than usual: the
two leading people having played their parts hundreds of times on the road, just mumbled through
their words and came to cues. So nobody really knew
from rehearsals what the play was about. At any
rate, a Sergeant of Police had to come on at the end
of the third act and arrest the hero for some crime
(which of course he had not committed) and as the
hero was regarded as a tough customer, the sergeant
brought another police officer with him. Our super-
master (Sydney) was the Sergeant. Sydney was a well-
set-up man who could always be trusted to say, "I
arrest you in the name of the lore", or "You'd better
come quiet, you know", or "'Ere they come; now,

boys, do your dooty." He was generally given parts of that kind, parts which required authority.

In this instance I was detailed as the other police officer — his assistant. He had to dash on, followed by me. His line, as spoken by Sydney, was "'E's 'ere somewhere; I'll search this room, you guard that door." Then he went off right, leaving me alone, and returned in a moment saying, "'E's not there, curse 'im: where can he be?" At which the hero came from somewhere and said, "You can save yourself further trouble, my men, he's here," or words to that effect, and he was immediately pinioned by the two officers: then there was a dramatic ending in which the heroine was included.

It will be seen that this at first glance does not seem to afford great opportunity to the second police officer. But in those days, having no words to study, and no interviews with newspaper gentlemen, and no social activities, I had a great deal of time to devote to the thinking out of "business" for my parts. Make-up and business were my only opportunity for distinction. Mine were thinking parts and I did a great deal of thinking. It came to me in the privacy of my bedroom that a nervous policeman would be a novelty and a great contrast to Sydney who was always bold. And knowing that I had but a short time in the act in which to make good and attract to myself the attention of the audience, it occurred to me in the course of further intensive study, that a red wig (which I possessed — a remnant of my Theatre Royal wardrobe) and a helmet much too small for me

61

would be of invaluable assistance. I look back with horror on that opening night.

Had I known that our entrance led up immediately to the great dramatic moment of the play I am sure I should not have done it, but the rehearsals had left me in the dark as to this and I thought of it only as a scene with Sydney. Nobody saw me before I went on, not even Sydney; I kept well in the background. My entrance was greeted with a roar of merriment from the gallery and when the amazed and dazed Sydney went off and left me alone to guard the door, I had the stage to myself and proceeded to exhibit great nervousness and an obvious desire to run away. And when the hero came on and said, "You can save yourself further trouble, my men, he's here," I made a frantic rush for the door in abject fright.

The gallery of the Elephant had never before seen the leading man overshadowed by a comic policeman: the novelty tickled their fancy and they shouted and stamped with laughter. The dramatic dénouement was finished in pantomime and the curtain came down to a riot of laughter. I knew then what I had done. I knew then just how the murderer feels when he gazes on the body that he has struck down by an uncontrollable impulse and deprived of life. It was a terrible moment. Skinner made a dash for me and I ran for my life to the dressing room. Who saved me I never knew: I rather think the star was magnanimous and begged the management to spare me. But I learned my lesson and I hope I have never since queered the other man's scene.

Almost immediately following this came the annual Pantomime which was produced under the personal direction of Joe Cave, and was, I believe, regarded even by the West End press as an exceedingly good specimen of the wholesome, old-fashioned children's pantomime. In this I was one of six demons in the Demon Scene: carried a "big head" in the Palace Scene, was the fishmonger in the first comic scene of the Harlequinade, and the Comic Swell in the second comic scene. I learned how to come up a star trap, to disappear through a "vampire" and to "take the leaps." I was never proficient at any of these accomplishments, but I knew how it was done.

The Clown was always the Czar of the comic scenes; the "producer" had nothing to do with that part of the entertainment. The Clown invented and produced these scenes and was entirely responsible for them. My duties as the Fishmonger consisted of continually looking surprised and indignant when I discovered that my fish had been stolen: the process of stealing being carried out with great secrecy (to which the audience was admitted with many winks and admonitions to hush) by the Clown and Pantaloon, either with their hands or their teeth or their feet — always a very neat operation. As the Comic Swell it was my part to look inane and to allow myself to be punched by the Clown in any part of my body that was likely to bring the most general reaction of delight from the audience. It was unfortunate for me that the harder and oftener he hit me the more the audience laughed, and in the hands of the Clown, I

63

was merely a means to that end. It was my part also to come down the trick staircase — which was a long flight of stairs that collapsed as soon as you put your foot on the top step, and brought you down on to the stage in a most undignified manner. To enjoy playing the Comic Swell one must have a youthful and generous spirit.

The "big head" such as I carried in the Palace Scene may require some explanation, for I believe it is a species of humor which is no more resorted to. It was a large papier mâché head about six or eight times as big as life size which you placed over your own head so that it rested on your shoulders and gave you the appearance of having an exceedingly small body. There was a procession of about a dozen of them — all very grotesque faces with large staring eyes — which marched down center in twos, turned right and left and stood at the back. To carry a big head was considered the very lowest form of dramatic art — lower even than the hind legs of an elephant, for it may be possible to put some character into them, but not into a big head.

To do myself justice I did make an attempt to gain distinction even with this crushing handicap. After much diligent labor I manufactured a winking eye to my grinning head. This was done by making an eyelid with wire and pink linen, and a piece of elastic to enable it to fly back; then attaching a cord to the wire frame of the eyelid, passing the cord through a small hole in the big head, and carrying it down inside the sleeve of my costume, so that I could hold the end in my hand and when I pulled the eye would close and when I released the cord the elastic would open it again. I thought that having walked down center, if I pulled the string just as I turned up left, the effect on the audience would be electrical. But though I pulled and pulled I never got the faintest response. Although it worked beautifully before I went on, something always went wrong at the last moment. I either pulled too soon or too late or else it wouldn't work at all. So it never made me famous.

As one of six demons I had little opportunity to display genius. We all came on and went off with the principal comedian, who demanded a monopoly on all laughs in scenes in which he appeared. I once took a chance, and warmed my hands at his red head while his back was turned and was terrified when I got a laugh. My fellow demons never gave me away, but the risk was too great for me to attempt it again.

In looking back at these early efforts I am bound to admit to a feeling of disappointment that I showed no spark of originality. My intensive mental exercises taken in my bedroom in order that I might invest my non-speaking parts with distinction and originality seem to have resulted always in the most obvious comedy or character business. Oh, but they were great days, those pantomime days! During the regular season we played only at night — six performances a week — but during the pantomime we gave matinées as well. And "between the shows" we three boys would career across to Lockhart's and dine.

Lockhart's was a sort of forerunner of Lyons in

London, or of Childs' in New York, but on a much cheaper scale than either of these popular places of to-day. For about sixpence we could get sausages and mashed potatoes and bread and a large cup of coffee; and we would eat and jabber and laugh and talk over the adventures of the morning — every performance was an adventure to us; and what I said to him, and what he said to me, and what we would have done with such and such a part if we had been playing it; and what a scream our low comedian had been to-day; and why wasn't he snapped up by the Drury Lane management for their pantomime next year! And how we were going to insist on George Skinner giving us some lines to speak after the run of the pantomime. And then back to the theatre a full hour and a half before we were needed, so as to be about the stage and smell it. Great days!

Sometimes we would make a wild rush, after we had finished, to get over to the Surrey Theatre to see Dan Leno. They were playing panto too, and finished later than we did, so we were just able to see little Dan in his last scene. He was so funny that the audience was in convulsions of laughter every moment he was on the stage. He was snapped up by Drury Lane the following year and became the greatest "Widow" the pantomime in London has ever known.

It was immediately following the run of the pantomime that I had my first speaking part. The play was called "Saved from the Sea." It was written by a little stout man named Roberts. Roberts was attached to the theatre as an author and wrote plays designed

for the Elephant just as Pettitt and Merritt, and afterwards Sims and Pettitt wrote for Drury Lane. Roberts
may have been better or worse than these more
popular authors: he probably lacked something that
they had, because I never saw his name connected with
any play outside our theatre, but it seemed to me that
he did exceedingly good work. He was always on
hand to patch an old play or write a new one. I
think his salary was thirty shillings a week. We
played every possible play and a great many impossible ones. "The Man Cat", "Sweeney Todd",
"Maria Martin or The Murder at the Red Barn",
"The Lady of Lyons", "Forsaken", and scores of
others. The manuscripts were kept pell-mell in a
large wooden box, together with the parts all written
in pen and ink and sewn together with thread — old
tattered parts, whose discolored pages had been turned
by many a hand that had long since made its final
gesture and had been folded on a breast that it would
beat no more.

Occasionally there were Benefits. It was an old
established custom in these stock companies for the
leading man to have a "Benefit Night" once during
the season. On these occasions he was allowed to
choose his favorite play and to sell tickets. All money
accruing from the sale of these tickets was his own.
The money taken at the box office went to the management. I believe that was the general arrangement.
The Comedian and sometimes the Leading Lady had
the same privilege. Our leading man (Tom Percival)
played "The Duke's Motto." The leading lady

(Augusta Tulloch) put up "Romeo and Juliet", in which I was not allowed to appear as she did not wish to take any risks.

Once Joe Cave took a Benefit for himself and played "The Shaughraun", making his "spectacular reappearance on the stage for this performance only as Con the Shaughraun." I appeared in this. Of course every one knows that there are two assassins in the play named Riley and Corrigan. They neither of them speak: I played one and Joseph played the other. Their business, as all the world knows, is to rush simultaneously with upraised knives from up right in a savage attack on Con who meets them down left and saves his life only by his quick action of catching the wrists of his would-be assassins one in each hand as the knives are descending on his breast. Well, of course, when you are playing with Mr. Cave, your duty is to rush at him savagely enough, but to keep your hand which holds the knife poised in the air until you are quite sure he has got hold of your wrist and then show your teeth — grind them if possible. You may have to keep your hand in the air for some time, because Mr. Cave, being old and short and the manager, must not be unduly hurried, but if you are a true artiste you fill up this time by hissing at him, thus maintaining the tension. But I didn't know this. And never having been entrusted with so important a moment before, and with the manager too, and never having spoken a line on the stage and being therefore a realistic actor, I got a piece of wood at the rehearsal to represent a knife, and when the moment came I rushed at him and the piece of wood had descended upon his poor old chest before he had even thought of looking for my wrist. And then he cried. The horror of the thing that might have happened to him if it had been a real knife overcame him. And then he shouted, "Mr. Skinner, Mr. Skinner, my God, sir, my God" (business of blowing through nose), "did you see that, sir; did you see it! This young man; did you see what he did, sir! My God, sir, he'd have killed me. Oh, my God, Mr. Skinner, don't let him do it. Where's Mr. Sydney? Let him do it." And so again I lost my chance and had to come on in the crowd.

But every now and then, just as soon as he could turn them out, we played "A Great and Original Melodrama in five acts by George Roberts." One of these was "Saved from the Sea." The cast was long so my opportunity came and at last I was given a speaking part. The scene was a deck of a boat; the sailors are going through a ceremony known as "crossing the line." King Neptune is master of ceremonies and directs the actions of the men. I was King Neptune — in long white beard. No young actor could ask for anything better than that: here was I in the center of the stage, giving orders to all the principals. It is true my long white beard was on a wire, but that didn't matter because it was supposed to be a false one and I had to double the Second Officer directly after. And all beginners will agree with me that the more stuff you have on your face the more important you feel.

Well, I was a great success. There's no doubt about
it. Joseph and Henry congratulated me and even
Skinner patted me on the back, and said, "Well done,
my boy." Of course it was not an opportunity for making any lasting impression on an audience. The beard
practically covered my face, and those wire frames always leave the actor in doubt as to whether he is
speaking through his mouth or his chin. But I spoke
all the lines and I felt that I was an imposing figure —
which I am quite sure I was not. But to be patted on
the back by the stage manager was the next thing to
being knighted by the King. I felt that I was made.
Unfortunately I had not had sufficient experience to
be prepared for the reaction that sets in on the second
night of a spectacular success. On Tuesday night I
went on the stage, all prepared to repeat my great
creation, when suddenly and without warning my
heart stopped beating and I was seized with a terrible
fright; my beard hung like a dead thing round my
ears and words refused to come. The entertainment
stopped, for the director of ceremonies failed to
direct. King Neptune was a drowning man. George
Skinner gave me a look that destroyed my last hope
of life and I was sucked completely under water. But
Skinner was not only the stage manager, he was the
low comedian, and when he was on the stage, he could
always be depended upon to turn defeat into success,
untoward tragedy into screaming comedy. If every
member of the cast had suddenly fallen dead about his
feet, he would have finished the play alone and
brought the curtain down to shouts of laughter and

applause. He belonged to the school of actors who never admit defeat in the face of an audience. And so he leaped in with "King Neptune means to say" etc., hoping that I might eventually come to life. But I didn't. I kept on my feet but I was dead. The curtain came down and the audience was quite unaware that anything had gone wrong.

Skinner was frantic and swore by everything holy that he would never again be saddled with a parcel of kids as long as he remained a stage manager. Well, I suppose he thought it over and with his experience realized that it was just the kind of thing that was likely to happen to a beginner on a second night, and I was forgiven and allowed to continue in the part. Of course I was firm as a rock after that, and by the end of the week I had regained my confidence and began to feel that I had really made a start in the business. Which as a matter of fact, I had. For from that time until I left the Elephant, I was entrusted with small parts that were of the utmost value to me in teaching me my business. I did not stay long enough ever to play important parts. And I was never, I think, taken to the bosom of the gallery boy. That fact was brought home to me one day by a chance remark which I overheard at the stage door.

The stage door was down a court behind the theatre. The actors would come out during rehearsal to smoke a pipe or a cigarette when they knew they had a few minutes' wait. There was nearly always a little group of three or four ragged boys, devotees of the drama and regular Saturday night patrons, standing

round at a respectful distance, watching every movement of their popular favorites and speaking words
of admiration to one another in an undertone. I had
always hoped for some recognition from these representatives of the masses, but hitherto I had received
only a cold and curious stare. This morning four or
five of us were gathered at the stage door before going
in to rehearsal, and I distinctly heard the leader of
this small gang behind me say, "See that tall one,
that's Teddy Vivian; the one with the curly 'air,
that's George Belmore; see that one in the gray
trousers, that's Tommy Percival." Then he edged
round and gazed at me for a long time, and said, "Who
that bloke with the eyeglass is, Gord knows."

This was a blow to me, but I accepted it philo-
sophically I hope. However, I was making headway:
I was at any rate gaining recognition from the management; that cannot be denied when I record that at
the end of a year when I left I was receiving three
times the salary that I got when I started. Would
that all actors could do that. And would that I could
ever have done it again. Yes, my initial salary was
six shillings a week: in one bound, soon after my
successful appearance in "Saved from the Sea" I was
raised to twelve shillings a week, and shortly before
I left, through some circumstance which I cannot
recall or even imagine, I was given eighteen shillings
a week. So my reason for leaving the Elephant was
not on the score of money. I was getting more than
half as much as the author of "Saved from the Sea"
and every member of the company agreed that I was

highly paid. But I felt I had got as far as I should ever get while I remained there. My goal was the West End. And I had come to realize that no actor would ever be taken directly from the Surrey side to the West. I didn't realize then how much I had learned in that short delightful year. It is true I played only small parts, but I took infinite pains in make-up and characterization, and much that I evolved from those little bits I have since been able to elaborate in the creation of leading characters. I am eternally grateful to the members of that company for their kindness and patience, and to George Skinner and George Belmore in particular, two kindly actors who have long since passed away.

IV

TO THE PROVINCES

I DECIDED that my next move should be towards the provinces where I could play big parts, thus crystallizing the experience that I had gained at the Elephant. I am amazed when I realize how little I knew about the business side of the profession. I thought that all provincial companies were on one level. That the English stage was divided into two distinct groups — London and the Provinces, neither group having any gradations of relative importance. So that when I decided to go into the provinces, I did not stop to consider whether I should get into a good company, or a bad company, because I thought they were all the same. How I came to be so foolish I don't understand, but so it was.

And then the question was how to get there. I had always been brought up in London and knew no country actors or managers. My idea was that what you had to do was to answer an advertisement in "The Stage", a newspaper in which country managers advertised in the "Wanted" column. So I answered an advertisement that read, "Wanted, a good sound actor. Play anything: for Irish repertoire company. Apply Auguste Creamer."

Then I had to carry the news of my intended desertion to my friends, Joseph and Henry: I knew it would be a blow to them that the trio was to be broken, but

74

I felt the time had come for me to get away. So I told them I was going to leave. In great consternation they said, "Where? Where are you going to?"

I told them I was going into an Irish Repertoire Company.

Joseph said, "Have you got your contract?"

I told him no, but I had answered the advertisement.

Then a great guffaw of relief went up from them both. "Why, you'll never get that. There'll be hundreds of actors answering that. You silly ass."

That had not occurred to me. I visualized the manager opening my letter and sending for me at once. So I said I'd keep on answering advertisements till I did get something. But my friends of the Theatre Royal felt they had me fairly securely.

Strange to say, I did get it. By return of post there came a letter telling me the terms and stating what clothes I should need and when I should open. I was to go to Doncaster and join the company there. I was to join in two weeks. I had no difficulty in arranging to leave the Elephant at short notice. George Skinner knew that I was trying to gain experience and made no effort to stand in my way.

It was the first time I had ever been away from home and I was covered with good wishes, and underclothing and handkerchiefs by an affectionate family. My mother made me promise that I would always wash myself thoroughly before leaving the theatre at night; that I would go in clean and leave without a trace of make-up clinging to me. I don't know what suggested this to her, for she had never met actors, and could not have known through personal observation of the unpleasant habit of some provincial mummers of carrying the marks of their calling so as to be plainly visible in the bright sunshine. I think she must have read about it. But I am grateful to her for that admonition. As I said good-by to my Elephant friends I felt that I was starting out into the world alone, and unprotected. I assured Joseph, my particular pal, that I would do my best to work him into the company as soon as possible.

I arrived in Doncaster and put up at the Woolpack Hotel. I had a charming room and some of the best food I have ever tasted — including sweetbreads for breakfast. I paid two shillings a day, board and lodging. I remember this distinctly because I have never known such value for money either before or since. I was much surprised to find some one to meet me at the station — a short, chubby-faced, fresh-colored man, who looked as though he really ought to be naked with two little wings sprouting. Instead of which he had on a very seedy yellow overcoat, which had possibly been some other color to start with, and boots of similar antiquity. A kindly-looking little man with a queer square-topped hat which seemed to have some difficulty in keeping its equilibrium on a head that was evidently not intended by nature for hats. He discovered me easily for there were few people at the station and I suppose no one else who looked as though he could "play anything." He approached me with a pleasant smile on his face and a number of parts in his hand. He told me he was the stage manager, and that he thought I ought to have my parts as soon as possible, so he decided to meet the train. He showed me the part I was to play next Monday: it was the leading juvenile in "Just in Time", a long part written in long hand on innumerable sides of paper. On each page there were two or three phrases underlined in red ink. I asked what that meant, and he told me that those were rounds of applause. The words thus underscored had to be spoken with such force as to compel the audience to respond. This was going one better than the Elephant. He handed me seven other parts, making eight in all. I asked when I should have to play the other parts, and he told me that I had to play them all next week. The company was going to Rotherham, where they changed the bill every night!

I was terrified. I had never had to study a long part, and had always had a week for each of my bits at the Elephant. But I refrained from showing any evidence of emotion lest I should expose my lack of experience. The advertisement had said "play anything", which I now realized meant, play everything. There were six long parts in six Irish dramas, and the other two parts were in farces. How I got through that week at Rotherham I don't quite know: but I put my back into it, sat up of course nearly all night every night, studying, and I think I spoke most of the lines, but there were moments when my Theatre Royal experience stood me in good stead.

When I went to rehearsal I felt that I was looked upon with a certain suspicion as one who did not belong there. The company was almost entirely made up of people who toured the provinces year in and year out, mainly through Lancashire and Yorkshire, Durham, Northumberland and the "smalls" of Scotland. Manchester was their center, and any one who came from London was regarded as a person who was likely to put on airs, and who must therefore be kept at a respectful distance. I was further removed from them by the fact that I was wearing a new suit, an apparition which was almost as strange a sight at rehearsal as a Roman toga might have been.

"Just in Time" was an Irish play in which the leading man and the comedian were always just in time to save everybody else from the villain. Each act, as far as I remember, ended with the words "Just in Time" which brought the curtain down to great applause. I noticed at my first rehearsal that everybody spoke their lines with an Irish accent, so I took it for granted that I had to do the same, and proceeded to do it. I remember about half through rehearsal, when I had got my courage, I thought I ought to exhibit a little spirit to show that I was an old hand — one of considerable experience. So I said, "By the way, I never asked you whether you wanted this part played with the brogue or without."

My Irish manager said, "Which is it that you're doing now?"

With some surprise I said, "With."

"Well, we'll have it without," said Mr. Creamer.

This was the first intimation I had that dialect parts were not to be my forte.

By the end of that first week, my hard study was over and I had no more all-night work. Within a short time, the company, which had held aloof from me, began to come closer and to warm up, and I found them for the most part, dear, kind, warm-hearted people. Of course they had realized at once my lack of experience and they helped me in every way in their power.

My advent was a Godsend to the leading man, because I had a top-hat. He had a frock coat but no top-hat. Hitherto, whenever he got married, as he did in several of our plays, he had to arrive at the church door without a hat. He had a bowler, but even in Rotherham he did not dare to wear that with a frock coat. But now he could swagger on resplendent. In some plays we both had to appear in wedding garb, and then a great deal of manipulation was required in order to double the hat. My clothes were always at the disposal of any one they would fit — that is any one who could get into them, for fit was not essential with us. Our plays mostly called for the appearance of soldiers and squires. There was only one officer's coat, and if you were the officer you had to wear it, regardless of the relative size of you and the coat.

I very soon learned how to make top-boots out of pieces of "American cloth" and how to turn them into coachman's boots, by the addition of a yellow bandage round the top; also how to make a period coat out of my every-day overcoat, by pinning a cape under the collar and round the shoulders. Arthur

Jefferson, who played the character parts (he afterwards became the manager of three or four provincial theatres), used to make everything. He made his own wigs and even his own grease paints, and from him I learnt many tricks of which I should otherwise have remained ignorant.

Both in this company and at the Elephant I linked up with a period of the stage the manners and customs of which had nearly passed into obscurity even then. Although the Elephant company was composed of far better actors than the Irish company, they had for the most part got their training in the old school and were still carrying on its traditions. Several of Mr. Creamer's company had been booth actors so they too brought with them the traditions of the immediate past, and even more distant past. In my first two years I always believe that I got a glimpse of the stage much as it was probably fifty years before my time. After these first years, although still in the provinces, I got into an entirely different atmosphere.

Auguste Creamer was a gentlemanly, dignified manager, a hard-working comedian and generally respected. My salary was twenty-five shillings a week. The leading man also got twenty-five shillings a week. Mrs. Creamer was the leading lady. The principal character actor and his wife got a joint salary of forty-five shillings; the second character actor and his wife got a joint salary of thirty-five shillings. So it was not an expensive cast and if some of the acting was not good I am bound to say it was very good for the money. And it is astonishing how far the money went. I made some fast friends and four of us used to live together. We lived well and our bill for board and lodging was never more than fourteen shillings a week each. Of course when the time came that business was bad and the management could give us only four or five shillings at the end of the week, it was not so easy.

I remember one Sunday we were to travel to the next town about three o'clock in the afternoon. We had had no salary and couldn't pay the landlady. I volunteered to interview her. I rang the bell and the others went out of the room. Presently the landlady appeared: she said, "You never ordered any dinner."

I said, "No, I know we didn't: we — er — we have ordered it in the next town." I lied to her but I didn't think she knew it.

Then she said, "Well, what was it you wanted?" And I told her.

I made a clean breast of it. I said we would send her the money soon and I passed over to her two new suits of underclothing as security. Her name was Mrs. Wogan: she was tall and bony; she took the news in silence and went off with my underclothing. I called my fellow lodgers in again and told them what had passed. We were very miserable: it is beastly not to be able to pay your lodgings. And she was a poor woman with a large family; some of them went out to work, but on Sundays they were always all together for the Sunday dinner in the middle of the day. We could smell it cooking. We sat talking over ways and means, and about one-thirty there came a knock at the door and the daughter came in with a tray on which there were four plates of roast beef, Yorkshire pudding, potatoes and cabbage, and a loaf of bread. "Mother said you'd better have this before you go; and she's put your parcel in your bedroom. She says you may want it."

It was one of those acts of kindness that you can never forget. We knew that somebody had gone short of their Sunday's dinner to supply four unexpected meals. Mrs. Wogan lived in Salford, but she has passed away, and I know she is now in heaven.

I feel I must say a word here for theatrical land-ladies. I was on the road in England for nearly ten years and during all that time I seldom encountered a dishonest or unpleasant landlady. As a class they are (or were then) hard-working, scrupulously honest and kindly disposed. They let lodgings exclusively to actors and took an interest in the gossip of the theatre. They seldom showed any desire to see the play, and would often decline an offer of free seats. If they did come they were generally very unim-pressed by anything they saw and by anything you did, in particular. More than likely, having seen the play, they would not mention it at all unless you approached them on the subject; then they would probably say, "Eh, it was very good," and that's all. If you yourself had been playing Hamlet, for instance, and looked for some word of praise for your performance, you would almost surely be disappointed. The most they would say would be, "Eh, you had a long part, didn't you; ye must be tired?" They looked upon the theatre rather as a workshop than as a Temple, and entirely without any sense of awe.

They always took a great interest in your visitors and your tea parties, in spite of the fact that such occasions meant more work for them. I remember one landlady's daughter being much concerned one afternoon when an unusual number of the company had called upon me for tea, and still another came. I rang the bell and asked for "another cup, please." The girl said in a stage undertone, "Well, you'll 'ave to 'ave a green 'un." It appeared that the party tea service had given out.

I recall once too being somewhat embarrassed when I was giving lunch to a non-theatrical friend; the land-lady had served the lunch and with a last look round she said, "There, I think you've got everything. The bell's broke but if you want anything just put your 'ed out of the winder and 'oller."

The only compliment I ever remember receiving from a landlady was one which came to me second-hand and was unexpectedly extracted by my wife. It was before we were married when she was playing in the "Guardsman", a comedy in which I was appearing as a bucolic old gentleman. Her landlady was, strange to say, amused at the play and said something about the funny old gentleman.

My future wife said, "That is the man I am engaged to."

"But, my dear child," said the lady, "isn't he rather old for you?"

"He's only twenty-six," said Flo.

"Twenty-six!" said the landlady scornfully. "Don't you believe him, my dear. He's sixty if he's a day!"

It is possible that I might have stayed longer with this company of Irish comedians if it hadn't been for Joseph. An exciting thing happened. Arthur Jefferson, the character actor, was leaving. I at once asked if I could have his parts and strongly recommended that Joseph be engaged to play mine. After some diplomatic interviews with Mr. Creamer and much telegraphing to London, this was arranged. Joseph was to have the standard Creamer wage of twenty-five shillings a week and pay his own fare from London. It was a great day for me when he arrived. I had been away for nearly nine months. Of course we shared diggings and after he had finished studying his parts, we would sit for hours talking over "old times" of the Theatre Royal. And here we were together again!

But as the weeks went by, it began to dawn upon me that Joseph was not popular with the Creamer company. It came to my ears that he was regarded by them as being uppish. I hadn't observed that he was uppish, but I had noticed he was moody. I would find him staring at me in deep thought. Now if Joseph was in deep thought there was something the matter with him. I knew that, so at last I said:

"What's the matter with you? What's the matter with the old gentleman? I get you a job — I drag you from obscurity in London to a coveted position on the road in Auguste Creamer's Company of Irish Comedians at a weekly salary of twenty-five shillings and yet you don't seem happy."

84

He said, "George, old pal, do you realize that I have been with you now for nearly four weeks and during that time I have had nothing to eat but Armour's canned corn beef?"

I said, "Don't exaggerate, you've had roast beef every Sunday."

"Yes," he snapped, "and cold beef every Monday, and hashed beef every Tuesday — and Armour's for the balance of the week."

"Well, what's the matter with Armour's?" I asked. "It must be nourishing — it's full of jelly."

Now Joseph has always been well fed: when we used to have our sixpenny dinner between the shows at the Elephant, he came merely for company and not from necessity: he was a massive youth, requiring much sustenance, and I knew that the Art which I was offering him was not filling the void.

"But," he said, "I am not thinking so much of the food" (liar!) "I am thinking of you and your future. You've been with this combination long enough."

"What?" I said. "Don't you like this company?"

"No," said he, "I don't. If Aunt Harriet saw one of these performances, she'd turn in her grave." (Joseph always got theatrical after he'd been in deep thought.)

"Don't be ridiculous," I retorted; "your Aunt Harriet is alive and well. How can she turn in her grave?"

"Well," said Joseph doggedly, "she would turn in her grave if she were dead. George, you've got to leave this show."

"What!" I shouted. "I may never get another job."

"Then go home and sit at mother's knee. It'll do you much more good. You're getting awful. I've been watching you and you're becoming a blooming old mummer. If you stay here another month, I know you'll be calling me 'Laddie.'"

That was a body blow and he knew it. We had always been suspicious of a colleague who addressed us as "Laddie." He generally turned out to be a fruity actor, very overripe. I had a great respect for the old-timer's knowledge of mechanics, but I objected to his method of applying them. I had a horror of becoming "old school." But I couldn't take this from Joseph lying down. After all I had done for him too. I snorted, "Oho, you West End actor."

"No," said Joseph with holy calm, "I am not a West End actor. But I'm going to be and so are you. Come 'ome, laddie."

I became really alarmed. This "heavy father" stuff from Joseph to me was something quite new; that had always been my rôle towards him. There must either be some truth in what he said, or else he must be suffering from some complaint brought on by malnutrition: in either case something had to be done. So after turning it over in my mind and avoiding his steady gaze for about a week, I decided to "chuck in my notice." And so we both left for London town.

I had been with the company for nearly a year. During that time there had been several changes in the cast. Some surprisingly good individual performances were given, and some terribly bad ones. The experience I gained at this time was most valuable to me. I acquired facility of study, confidence and self-reliance. I learned how to meet emergencies, how to cover mistakes and deficiencies due either to my own errors or to those with whom I was acting. By playing all kinds of parts I was able at the end of a year to form a fairly correct estimate of what my line of business was to be. I started with the conviction that I was intended for a low comedian. I fancied myself cutting all kind of humorous capers on the stage; but I soon began to realize that even a bad low comedian was much funnier than I was in such parts. I never believed that I could play a straight leading part, and there I was right, for I never have been able to. The experienced old actors round me soon discovered that if I was to be anything at all, I was to be a character actor or perhaps a light comedian. I have always considered myself fortunate in the chance that took me into this cheap repertoire company at this particular period of my apprenticeship. The experience I gained in one year might have taken me three or four times as long under other conditions. Young people to-day who ask me for advice are much surprised when I recommend them to try to get into some cheap stock company. The manager of a first-class company will seldom risk his reputation by giving a beginner a chance in important parts, while in a third-rate company one is bundled into anything and it becomes a case of sink or swim. There is no reason why the young actor should acquire the bad habits of the bad actors around him, if he doesn't stay too long in their company. Perhaps, but for Joseph, I might have stayed too long. But I should say twelve months is a fairly safe period.

I was very sorry to leave the friends that I had made. Mr. Creamer wrote me a letter couched in that pleasant phraseology which perhaps only an Irish comedian can acquire, in which he said, "Had you asked me for a reëngagement, I would have done so." Mr. Creamer is now living in honored retirement in Dublin, having reached the respectable age of eighty-six, which seems to suggest that the labors I have described are not to be regarded as killing work. I am sure he will not mind my saying that he was not without that unintentional humor in conversation, peculiar to his race. He described his wife, of whom he was very fond, in quite an unexpected way one day. She had been taken suddenly ill and he had come, tearfully, to a group of us for sympathy. He allowed himself to be quite carried away by his admiration for her: he dwelt on her virtue and her beauty, particularly her beauty, of which he was very proud.

"Ah, bhoys," he said, "she's lovely. Of course you only see her on the stage, dthressed up in clothes, and sometimes vile clothes: but if ye could see her as I see her, in the privacy of our chamber! Bhoys, she's a perfect Adonis."

V

THE WEARY ROUND OF AGENTS

I was now a full-fledged actor. Back in London looking for work. Once more Joseph and I hoped to get something together, but we knew that was almost too much to expect. The only thing to do was to go round to the dramatic agents. That was a weary business. Day after day, day after day, the same old round. My credentials were not such as to recommend me to the better managers. I soon discovered that; and I found I had an uphill course. The agents were mostly rude to struggling actors, or at best very aloof. They would keep groups of weary men and women waiting for hours in an outer office. Anxious, hopeful faces would turn eagerly toward the door as it opened to let an office boy in or out of the agent's sanctum. It would have been so easy for the great man to have come out and to have said whether or not he was likely to need any one of these actors, but for some reason he seldom did. I could never understand why. It may have been that he considered it looked more like business to have his offices filled with people, than to release them and let them go elsewhere. There was one, St. John Denton, who was a striking exception. He was always kindly and considerate to young and struggling people and I remember him with admiration and gratitude.

I was thrown into the stream of tired, out-of-work

actors. Up and down the Strand we walked, down Bedford Street and Maiden Lane, from one agent to another, always hoping to run up against some one in the street who might "know something." There was a little "pub" off the Strand where you could get a very thin slice of ham placed between a very thick roll for three half-pence and a glass of ale for two-pence, making a total of three-pence-half-penny. This was my pulling-up place when I had walked myself hungry. Of course, there was that other place in Bow Street; every one knew the ham-and-beef shop in Bow Street, but you could not get a good dinner there under eight-pence. A queer place it was; close to Bow Street police station. It had the reputation of providing the best cut of hot boiled salt beef in London for six-pence, potatoes one penny, cabbage one penny, peas pudding one penny. You stood at the counter and ate as you stood; there were no seats. It was frequented by market gardeners, clerks, actors, cabmen, and eminent attorneys who would dash in from Bow Street police court. You never knew with whom you were rubbing shoulders.

In the theatrical business perhaps more than any other the unexpected happens. I was going home tired and dejected when I chanced to meet a man who knew my father and who knew me by sight. He was a naturalist by trade. We spoke, and he said, "You are on the stage, aren't you?" I admitted that figuratively speaking I was, but for the moment I seemed to be a very long way off it. Then he told me that he had just left a customer at the St. Pancras Grand Hotel, who had come up from Cornwall, and was going to take out a theatrical company. He said, "Why don't you go and see him? I'll give you a letter."

I could not believe that after all my fruitless efforts in the heart of the theatrical market in the Strand, I was really going to get a job through a man who sold stuffed birds. But off I went to the St. Pancras Hotel with my letter of introduction and was at once kindly received by a pleasant, shy little man, with a lisp and an influenza cold. I could see at once that he knew nothing about the stage, and had no idea how a manager should behave, for he offered me whiskies and sodas and cigars and seemed very pleased to talk to me. It was all so different to any experience that I had had, that I felt sure there could be no business in it. And I wondered all the time why in the world he was taking out a company. He gave me a letter to his "director" and said he was sure everything would be all right.

The director was a rather handsome, clean-cut man with a firm blue chin; he looked as though he would be a good actor, but he wasn't. He was one of those men who drift about in our business without having any real excuse for being there: he had a small private income, and should have been perhaps a lawyer or a clergyman, and indeed he had probably been one or the other, or both in his time, but had always been attracted by the apparent glamour of the stage and was unable to keep away from it. He had never done anything, but he had a certain air of authority and seemed always on the very point of bursting upon the public. He had walked on at Beerbohm Tree's Theatre (then the Haymarket). He got that position, I understood, through a letter of introduction from some titled person. In his conversation he would generally manage to throw in an Earl or so. A story was told of him that when he was walking on with Tree he had tried in vain to get a small part that was vacant in the next production; he never gave up hope however; and one day when Tree was rehearsing the gentlemen who walked on, my director arrived late, leapt out of his hansom cab at the stage door and dashed on to the stage; he was told that he had held up the rehearsal; he accepted the blame with downcast eyes and with much modesty and reserve. It became noticeable that he continued to wear a heavy and ample fur coat throughout the rehearsal, and at last Mr. Tree suggested that he might do better if he removed it. My director then walked quietly up to Mr. Tree and with much diffidence and secrecy he explained that he had only just been able to get away from Buckingham Palace, where he had been summoned by Queen Victoria in connection with some State activities and that he was still wearing his Court Dress and asked that he might retain his overcoat during rehearsal in order that he should be less conspicuous. The story goes that he got the small part he was after and returned the Court Dress, including the fur coat, to the costumer and considered it money well spent.

Well, I settled the engagement. I learned from the director that it was to be a fit-up tour through Cornwall and Devon. A fit-up tour is one in which you play in public halls and not in regular theatres. You

travel with your own proscenium and fit it up where-
ever you play. It is, as a rule, an exceedingly poor
combination — just once removed from the booth —
but this was to be a fit-up de luxe as the manager had
plenty of money. We were to play "The Vicar of
Wakefield", a version written by William Farren, Jr.,
and I was to play Mr. Burchell. The whole thing
turned out to be little more than a rather high-class
amateur entertainment. My director played Doctor
Primrose and had a very good make-up.

The manager never came to any rehearsal and it was
still a mystery to me why he was sending out the company. It couldn't be for money, because he had a
large estate in Penzance and had given, I believe, a
Public Museum to the town. It was not until after
the first performance that the mystery was solved, and
that I realized to the full how inscrutable are the
ways of Providence. There was I, a dejected, dis-
pirited, out-of-work actor, met by a man who stuffs
birds, and sent on this most delightful tour through
Cornwall and Devon, all because a gentleman from
Penzance wanted to work the limelight. I had never
seen him since our first interview, and by the time we
opened I thought we had lost him altogether, when
lo and behold, I spied his little figure on the top of a
pair of steps, working what was then a most elaborate
limelight arrangement. To the best of my belief,
fit-up companies as a rule didn't have a limelight.
But we were all limelight. The play seemed specially
designed for limelight effects. We sang Christmas
carols by moonlight outside the Vicar's house, and

birds chirped to the rising sun in the early morn. I am
sure that Oliver Goldsmith could never have dreamt
that his simple work would be so enriched. The chief
influence this short tour (it was only six weeks) had
on my theatrical life was through the friends I made
in the company. Some of them were able to do me a
good turn later on and one at least I count amongst
my best friends to-day.

I venture once more to offer a word of advice to the
young. Make friends in your own profession, and
make an effort to keep them. If you have average
ability and the good will of your associates, you are
likely to find yourself out of work much more seldom
than the actor with ability above the average who
lacks friends. If you are a genius I suppose you are
sufficient unto yourself. But I don't know. I am a
little skeptical of genius in connection with the
theatre.

In this fit-up company there was one outstanding
figure that I always remember — the old lady who
played Mrs. Primrose. She was a lady of title, Lady
Emily Cadogan, but she acted under the name of Mrs.
Graham; a very charming woman without the remotest aptitude for the stage, who at the age of about
sixty-five had decided that she wanted to be an actress.
She concluded that ours was just the sort of company
of which she would like to be a part. She had lived
all her life in the most exclusive quarter of the West
End — Eaton Place, I think — and although not rich
she knew nothing about being poor, in our sense of
the word. It was pathetic to see her trying to be one

of us in little cheap lodgings. She found we did our own shopping. So she would do likewise. She would order her half-pound of steak or her chop and say to the butcher, "Be sure you send it home in time for early dinner," and sail out, entirely unconscious of the surprised face of the butcher, who in those little places was never known to send anything home except perhaps the Sunday joint.

The same thing would happen at the grocer's. "I want a pot of marmalade, please — how much is that — yes, sevenpence — thank you. Be sure to send it home this afternoon," and out before the little shop-keeper could recover.

She used to love to sit and hear us talk shop and listen to our theatrical stories and especially to little bits of scandal: she felt then that she was in the inner circle of the profession. In the daytime she always wore a wig, without any attempt to conceal the fact; sometimes it was a fair one, sometimes red; occasionally it would be a warm chestnut. I have called upon her and seen as many as four wigs in a row in various stages of undress.

This engagement was in the nature of a holiday for me, for I was playing only one part and my costume and wig were found by the management. I had no study and no needlework to do. It was brief and pleasant and led to other engagements which, though unimportant viewed in perspective, were of great value to me at the time.

The tour came to an abrupt ending after six weeks, owing entirely to the misconduct of the company. The fact was, nobody could take the limelight seriously except the little man who worked it and who incidentally paid us our wages — the "angel" who hovered on the top of the steps playing with calcium and blue mediums and white mediums and diligently sprinkling snow as required. It happened that the entire strength of the company had to sing a carol off-stage at the end of the third act, something about Hark, Hark, the Lark and some line concerning a Prickly Pear. One of the company mixed his lines one night and sang in a sweet and distinct alto, "Oh, Hark, Oh Hark, the Prickly Lark." A little thing like this may be safely depended upon to disorganize a company of actors; there was much muffled laughter but we supposed that the episode had passed unnoticed. We didn't know that the shy little man at the top of the steps was sputtering with rage at having his "scene" treated with disrespect. We failed to realize that the carol was merely an accompaniment to his solo on the limebox. So when the next night came and the company with one accord sang, "Hark, Oh, Hark the Prickly Lark" we were quite unprepared for the news that the tour would end next Saturday night. The little man never spoke but he delivered his ultimatum in writing to his director and as far as I know he never worked the lime again.

This sudden termination to her theatrical career was so great a shock to poor Lady Cadogan that she determined to run the play herself, in order that she might continue to play Mrs. Primrose. Several of the members seceded and there was an interval of two or three weeks for reconstruction of the company. I seized the opportunity to "work in" Joseph for the part of Squire Thornhill. I was told I might bring him along. I hurried to the Theatre Royal and found him at home.

I said, "Joseph, you were not grateful to me as you should have been for all the trouble I took to introduce you into the bosom of a company of Irish comedians. You not only treated that company with contempt, but you dragged me away from a promising Hibernian career and cast me upon the world to procure a precarious livelihood as best I could."

"How much do you want?" said Joseph.

"I am about to return good for evil," I replied. "I am going to give you another opportunity to distinguish yourself."

"Half a mo," he interrupted rudely; "is this this another tinned-beef tour? Because if it is — "

I said, "Wait. You can live on the fat of the land. You will receive two pounds five shillings a week — the largest salary you are ever likely to get and everything found."

"What do you mean — everything found?" said Joseph blatantly, "Food?"

"No, not food," I answered with restraint; "costume and wig. You treated my last friends uppishly; this time I am taking you into a company drawn from the very cream of London Society."

"Well, I'm glad there's going to be cream this time, anyhow," grinned Joseph. "Do we play at the Lyceum?"

"No," I replied firmly, "we do not play at the Lyceum because Henry Irving already has the theatre. It is a fit-up tour."

"Oh, God!" from Joseph.

"But a very superior fit-up tour," I continued. "Before you come back, you will probably have played before all the crowned heads of Europe."

"All right, old pal," said Joseph, "I'll come. But I say, you do find 'em."

Of course he was really delighted, but we were neither of us of a demonstrative nature. We had the time of our lives for the next four weeks, by which time Lady Cadogan's finances had given out. She went back to private life in Eaton Place and we returned to swell the ranks of the unemployed.

My next manager was the baggageman of this company. He was a crusted, elderly actor of the old, old school. In "The Vicar of Wakefield" he played an old gypsy and looked after the baggage. He was raised to the position of manager by a young lawyer with money and a passion for the stage, who decided to run a company and who made him the figurehead.

(Advice to disgruntled actors:

Do not complain of the advent of the "monied amateur" into our ranks. He is frequently the means of supplying nourishment to impecunious actors who would otherwise be wandering empty and unemployed.)

My new manager was a fruity old actor if ever there was one; off the stage he would speak like a human being, but once before the footlights, he immediately became a professor of rhetoric, pointing out to the audience, in every sentence, the great difference between the common way they spoke compared with the beautiful cadences of his own delivery. He would improve the English language, where necessary. The word "wear" sounded hard and unmusical to him, so he always changed the pronunciation to "were" for stage use. Thus he was able to say to me, "Go! You disgrace the uniform you were," without offending his ear with the harsh sound of the original word. He always said, "I pledge you my hoath," because he felt he could get more soul into it by the addition of initial h.

The young lawyer was a very pleasant man. Heaven knows what put the stage into his head. He was unfitted for it in every possible way. He would therefore probably have been a bad advocate in a court of justice. He was a bachelor and cared only for four things in the world — billiards, boiled eggs, tobacco and the stage. I believe he always had boiled eggs for his dinner and supper, and I think probably a pipe for his breakfast. He liked to play juvenile parts, although he was extremely plain; he had a heavy under jaw and protruding lower lip which was possibly most useful and agile when negotiating boiled eggs, but which did not respond readily when called upon to assist in the formation of words.

I am perpetually surprised at the number of people who drift on to the stage handicapped by some kind of impediment in their speech. I recently listened to a scene on the stage between three people, each of whom

99

lisped in a more or less pronounced degree. Of the young men and women who come to me for advice as to their stage career, seventy-five per cent have badly formed mouths — jaws that seem to have no freedom of action. I don't observe this peculiarity in the trained nurse, or the young lady that hooks up my wife's frock, or the girl who asks me, "What is the next article?" or the young person I sit next to at lunch who doesn't desire a career. It seems unfortunately to be reserved for those people who have a craving for the stage.

During this tour we put up a number of plays and I was enabled to mature my experience considerably. "The Ticket of Leave Man", "The Shadows of Life" by Arthur Shirley (quite a good drama of its kind) and "The Captain of the Vulture" were our chief attractions. Business with us was never very good, and sometimes it was awful. Whenever there was less than twenty shillings in the house our lawyer financier would have the audience dismissed and say, "Let's play billiards."

This was no doubt very bad for my art, but it was a lark, and I liked it. Although this tour was full of pleasant incidents there is nothing worth recording, except perhaps that my father was the innocent cause of bringing my engagement to an end. We were playing at Hammersmith, a cheap district of London similar to that of the Elephant. The Lyric Hall where we appeared was then the only dramatic house. Since then many imposing places of amusement have been built there. It was the end of the week, Saturday night, and we were doing "The Captain of the Vulture." In this I had to play the lover in a fair tie-wig and pink tights: Nature never intended me for those parts and the tights merely accentuated this fact; the evenings when we put up this play were always distasteful to me. At the end of the last act my old friend Eric Scott, who played the Captain (who had disappeared for seven years and was believed to be dead), came on and claimed his wife at the very church door just as I had finished getting married to her. It was a most impressive moment. I was all decked out in colors, and he had on top-boots and an old blue pea-jacket. Unfortunately on this particular night my friend Eric when dressing had forgotten to do up his braces, and as he wore a very short coat, they hung down behind him, plain for all folks to see, and added greatly to the gaiety of Hammersmith. The people on the stage were convulsed and the angrier Eric became and the more he flung himself about, the more the braces swung up into the air, and the curtain eventually came down to hilarious applause. We took a couple of curtain calls standing in a row as usual, and the play being over the audience prepared to go, when there began an insistent applause from a certain section of the house, which the rest of the audience took up, as audiences will. Our manager directed us each to go in front of the curtain separately and receive the congratulations of the public. While the persistent clapping and banging of sticks on the floor is going on, I will avail myself of the advantage vouchsafed to authors and moving-picture writers of cutting back to an incident that happened earlier on that Saturday.

My father was walking with a friend when suddenly, with the assistance of his monocle, he closely scruti-nized a man who was coming toward him, and as they came face to face he said, "Isn't your name Hender-son?" The man said it was. My father had an ex-traordinary memory for faces and he reminded the startled stranger that they went to school together forty years ago. They chatted and Henderson, it transpired, had become a most important figure in his own country town. In fact he put on a good deal of "side." They were passing Carrera's, a little tobac-conist's that has since become famous as the makers of Craven Mixture, but was then a little shop about the size of a sentry box. Although well known to con-noisseurs of tobacco and cigars, it was quite unknown to Henderson from the country. He said, "Here, have a cigar with me, you fellows." The three went into Carrera's and the man from the country said, "Give me three of the best cigars you have." The man be-hind the counter got a stepladder and reached for a box on an upper shelf, from which they each took a cigar and the big man from the country flung a sovereign down on the counter with an air. The man behind the counter, after a moment's pause, said, "Another shilling, sir, please." The cigars were seven shillings each. That was probably one of the greatest shocks that Henderson ever had. I suppose after that the schoolmates began bragging about their families and my father said, "I've got a son on the stage; he's playing at Hammersmith to-night. Come over and see him." And they all three went.

We will now return to our hero in the pink tights listening to the applause of the audience after the play, with knitted brow. Everybody had been on but me and I had point blank refused. The banging and stamping continued, and unsuspected by me, my father and his friends who had started all this were saying, "Why don't they let the boy come on: it's a shame: everybody else that we didn't want has been on. Let's have the boy."

Meantime my manager was shouting to me to take a call. I remember I said, "No. I've been making a fool of myself before these people for three hours and I'm not going to add to it by one second."

"But they're calling for you."

I think my reply to this was "Rats", and I returned to my dressing room. My champions in the audience eventually lost the coöperation of the masses and had to give up as the house emptied. Ten minutes after I reached my dressing room, I received my two weeks' notice from the management for insubordination. It was not until I arrived home that night that I discovered that it was my father who had lost me my job.

This was the only time I ever lost an engagement through insubordination. But I was once discharged for incompetence. My manager was an Irish-American comedian who for some years toured the English provinces in a play of his own composition. With a lack of modesty, which I am sure was quite unintentional, he always worded his advertisements, "J. P. Sullivan in his own beautiful romantic Drama entitled 'Leaves of Shamrock.'" I was engaged for the heavy part — the villain. My predecessor in the part had formerly been a ringmaster in a circus, during which time his principal duty had been to go through the mechanical process of "feeding" the clown. This is even more important in a circus than feeding the lions, for a lion, I imagine, could sustain life longer without beef, than it would be possible for a clown to survive who was not adequately fed with lines.

To those who are unacquainted with the technical terms of the stage, it may be well to explain that a "feeder" is one who sacrifices himself for the good of others. He is called upon to be more than human. As a rule it is his duty to speak his lines with such point and inflection as will enable the other man to score off him and make him look ridiculous. Mr. Sullivan was an enormous man with a tremendous voice, and when I got on the stage with him I felt very much as poor Daniel must have felt in the lions' den, including the sensation of imminent danger of being eaten alive. I realized what an advantage it would have been to me if I too had once been a ringmaster. Mr. Sullivan had a voice that would, I imagine, have been most valuable in keeping together the Children of Israel in the Wilderness; being an Irishman, he would probably not have been called upon to perform this duty, but his voice was evidently intended by nature to reach far greater crowds of people than it was possible to get into the Theatre Royal Rochdale, or the Court Theatre Wigan.

In "Leaves of Shamrock" he played the Wild Irish Bhoy with red cheeks and gray stockings, and he always scored off the villain. But in order to take full advantage of the gift with which Nature had endowed him, it was necessary that he should have a villain who shouted his lines at the pitch of his voice, so that he, the Wild Irish Bhoy, could "top" him, and with that wonderful organ of his shout him down into insignificance. My predecessor, the ex-ringmaster, had a voice that could rise above the clatter of the circus, but it was as a child's compared with Mr. Sullivan's. My inclination is, I believe, to be what is known as "subtle." Too much so, very often; there is a danger of being so subtle that one becomes ineffective. I have many times had cause to be grateful to my old friend Herbert Budd, who used often to watch my scenes and say, "Look out, George, don't be too damned artistic."

At any rate, I was far too subtle for "Leaves of Shamrock", and within a very short time I was given my notice with the explanation that I was "not strong enough for the part." As Mr. Sullivan has the distinction of being the only manager who has dispensed with my services on the score of incompetency, I have dwelt upon this in order to show that he was perfectly right. However valuable I might have been to some one else, I was entirely wrong for him, as my method killed every scene in which I appeared with him.

This was one of a number of short engagements that followed on the heels of my "Vicar of Wakefield" and "Captain of the Vulture" tours. At the termination of each engagement came the sickening feeling that I should never be able to get anything else to do — the walking round and round to agents' offices, the deadly depression of going home night after night with no prospect of work, and then the delirious delight of settling something and studying parts, and rehearsing in all kinds of holes and corners before going on tour.

These rehearsal periods are full of pleasant memories for me. The sudden reaction from despairing inactivity to days filled to bursting point with hours of study, of artful manipulation of wardrobe to fit new parts, of chatter with fresh and hopeful members of one's own profession, discussing what we have done and what we hope to do; of the little private rehearsals in corners and the joy of discovering in a scene some new piece of business or some illuminating inflection that you had not suspected was there! That whole period of buzzing activity leading up to the moment when you all meet at the railway station and leave London for your opening town has always been exhilarating to me.

It is still; but now it is tempered with the pain of grave responsibility. In those early days of my provincial experience I was merely a supporting actor, and I knew that if I were reasonably competent that was all that was looked for from me. If I succeeded in giving a little more than that and gained some recognition from the manager, I had the satisfaction of knowing that I had gone farther than was expected.

It is very different to that feeling which seizes you when you know that everything is expected of you: that perhaps the success or failure of a play and the season's work of an entire company may depend upon you alone. To one who has always shunned responsibility that is a paralyzing consciousness.

After my secession from the "Captain of the Vulture" company, brought about as I have explained by the over-exuberance of my too paternal father, I had another period of hunting for work. I believe the out-of-work actor in England to-day frequents the district of Charing Cross Road and Shaftesbury Avenue, leading up to Piccadilly Circus. But in those days it was always the Strand. Having been to the agents, he crawled along the Strand from Wellington Street where stood (and still stands) the Lyceum Theatre in which Henry Irving and Ellen Terry were then playing — both in their prime, the unchallenged leaders of the English Stage; he crawled along the Strand to Bedford Street, always hoping to hear news that might lead to an engagement. Down Bedford Street on one side, up Bedford Street on the other, across the road and down the Strand on the opposite side of the way as far as Waterloo Bridge, which is opposite Wellington Street; cross the road, and up the Strand again from Wellington Street.

There were houses of call — public-houses — between Bedford and Wellington Streets, frequented almost exclusively by people connected with the theatre. First "The Wellington" at the corner; a little farther the "Marble Halls" — the name given by the

actors to the Adelphi bar in appreciation of its somewhat pretentious architecture — then the "Bodega"
in Bedford Street; and on the other side of the Strand
there was "Miss Barnes'." There was also Romano's,
but this was reserved for the more opulent actor. In
these public-houses might be met the actor who was
in work and who seldom refused to relieve the distress-
ful thirst of his less successful associates; although, to
be just to my own profession, I record with satisfaction
that the majority of actors who went into these
saloons did not frequent them because they wanted
drink, but solely for the purpose of seeking work.
I don't know any class of society more industrious
than the actor if he is given the opportunity of plying
his trade. All he wants to do is to act — to work.
And he is willing to work hard — much harder than
the "working man." The more he has to do, the
better he likes it, and the happier he is. That is my
experience of the profession.

But the actor out of work is a depressed and desolate
fellow. And he has reason to be. What is his position? It is quite unlike that of the man who makes a
specific thing and can give ocular demonstration that
he makes it well. He has not the advantage of the
painter who can show his work and be judged on the
spot. The ability of the majority of the great unemployed in the theatre is entirely unknown to managers.
The actor who faces a manager or an author knows
that first of all his general appearance must suggest
the part for which he is applying; and because he can
show evidence that he has successfully played such

and such parts, that doesn't prove that he can be relied upon for this one. Has he sufficient sense of comedy for the first act? Will he have the necessary repose for Act II? Can he carry that tragic moment in the third? Nobody can say. It is all a toss-up whether he gets the part or not and in most cases the decision is against him. Pity the poor actor who is out of work! He must try to look bright and cheerful and prosperous, no matter how often he is attacked by the pangs of hunger.

There is so much that is pitiful in the actor's life. What can be more pathetic than the "juvenile" actor who is getting old! The desperate effort to maintain his youth — the touching up of the hair that is beginning to go — or worse still, the terrible toupe when the hair has gone; the pulling in of the waistcoat to disguise the slipping chest; the jaunty air, no longer springing fresh and spontaneous to the fore, but dragged out for duty when it should be peacefully sleeping.

And what of the women? They depend upon their physical attraction far more than the men. If a woman looks the part exactly, directors will often take a chance on her ability to act it. Can you wonder at actresses coming out "looking like the devil" in their anxiety to look beautiful and secure the part. They know that they must "strike twelve" as they walk into the manager's office; and so often in their eagerness they go a trifle too far and they only strike one. It is pathetic.

I remember a young friend of mine, a quiet, pretty,

dark girl, leaving a director's office in the depth of disappointment: she had failed to get a part for which she was capable but she was told she didn't look it. She suddenly got an idea: she hurried home, put on a fair wig and a picture hat, raced back to the office, sent up another name, and blew in as a dashing blonde and got the part on her appearance alone.

Of course, when actors and actresses become known, conditions for them are likely to be entirely different — but then how many in the crowded ranks become known!

It must not be supposed that managers and casting directors are stony-hearted creatures who turn actors away and are entirely unconscious of the pain they are inflicting. On the contrary, more often than not they are most sympathetic; I know a number of them who would give much to be relieved of this undesirable duty.

VI

"THE VERY MAN"

WELL, I had been going through my share of these
unpleasant experiences, when I saw my old friend,
then my young friend Alban Atwood, coming towards
me in the Strand, waving his arms and his walking-
stick frantically in the air, in a manner which denoted
that he had terrific news to impart. I had first met
Alban Atwood during my association with "The
Vicar of Wakefield" tour. He was one of those
fortunate men who are never downhearted: to meet
him was to imbibe a stimulant. He was always full
of ideas; great schemes for the future; he was ever on
the point of getting an engagement that would lead
him to the very pinnacle of fame, and he always
wanted to carry me up with him. He had that generous nature that desires that all his friends shall share
his success. Every time you met him something
amazing had just happened to him or some tremendous
project was on foot. He is the same to-day; and perhaps some time the thing will really happen.

This morning when I met him in the Strand he was
in a state of excitement bordering upon apoplexy. I
was just the man he wanted to see; he dragged me
hurriedly towards Bedford Street. "Come on, George.
We shall just catch him at the Bodega — friend of
mine named Innescourt — Henry Innescourt, taking
out a summer tour, all seaside places; splendid oppor-

tunity; you're just the man for him; ask two pounds ten a week." I endeavored to make some enquiries as to the financial status of Mr. Innescourt, for I had doubts about a manager who made his engagements in the Bodega. But Alban assured me that was all right. "He has guarantees everywhere. Safe as the Bank." So I was introduced to my prospective manager in the Bodega. He was a tall man with shifty eyes which were always making an ineffectual effort to look honest. He had a nervous habit of brushing aside his moustache with the back of his hand. This habit I afterwards discovered was acquired through the necessity of clearing away the drips of his last glass of beer or of preparing an unimpeded entrance for his next glass. The lapse of time between these two operations being as a rule negligible, he continued the motion from habit even when through the exigencies of a professional career beer was unobtainable. Alban thrust me forward and said, "Here is the very man you want."

Mr. Innescourt wiped his moustache and questioned me closely as to my capabilities, and at last said, "Well, I will engage you; you play a young man — a nice young man, good family and all that. Well dressed. None of your white waistcoats and summer trousers and blue serge coats, you know, but good clothes, first-class cut. I pay well — I'll give you two guineas a week — and I want the best in return." So I settled. That was my first introduction to Mr. Innescourt. The last I ever saw of him was a few weeks later when we locked him in his dressing room and called through the keyhole that we meant to keep him and starve him until he decided to give us some money. I never saw him after that because when we went back some hours afterwards, we found that he had dropped noiselessly out of the window, having first thrown out his most valued props, and had taken the train to London.

But I am getting ahead of my story. We rehearsed for ten days in London. "Our Girls" was the play, written by H. J. Byron. When the time came to leave London we all met at St. Pancras Station. There were eight of us including Mr. Innescourt, and we had a carriage to ourselves; we got comfortably settled and were very merry as actors always are when they start out on tour. The ticket collector opened the door and said, "All tickets, please." We pointed to the manager.

Mr. Innescourt said, "It's all right, Collector, it's all right."

The official said, "Who's got the tickets?"

Our manager brushed away some imaginary drop of beer and said, "Mr. Bosworth — Mr. Bosworth of Derby — he knows all about it."

The railway man turned impatiently away and shouted to the head inspector. "Here, no tickets," and passed on to the next carriage. In a moment the inspector came along and said, "Who is it hasn't got a ticket?"

Our manager turned his honest eye upon him and said, "Me. I'm going to Bridlington. How much?"

"Sixteen and fourpence," said the inspector.

So with the assistance of two shillings borrowed from our leading lady, Mr. Innescourt gave him the money — the price of one ticket; the door was slammed, the whistle blew and off we went. Eight people with one ticket! It was not a very honest act of Providence, but it was one of her most momentous interventions. So now we knew what we were in for; we knew that our manager hadn't got a sou.

Mr. Bosworth of Derby was an official of the Midland Railway Company, who frequently arranged for theatrical companies to "travel on their baggage." This practically meant that the luggage was pawned with the railway company, who took the actors to their destination and held the baggage until the fares were paid. Our manager had apparently not been able to get this satisfactorily arranged before starting and had hoped to bluff it through. It was obvious to me that my new suit which I had obtained through the good credit of an indulgent father was in imminent danger of becoming the property of the Midland Railway Company before I had even a chance to wear it. When we reached Bridlington, Mr. Innescourt borrowed money from the local manager and we opened.

But our tour was a series of financial disasters. Our houses were always poor. "Our Girls" was an old play in which the public took no interest. To do him justice, our manager made every effort to get the people in. We traveled from town to town, sometimes "on our luggage" and sometimes on money advanced by the theatre manager. When we were at a very low ebb, Mr. Innescourt had a brilliant idea for recuperating his shattered fortune by giving a monster matinée for schools at reduced prices. He got a directory and found that there were fifteen schools within easy distance, with an average of two hundred pupils in each school. If they all came this would be three thousand souls — little souls, but paying ones. He took us all into his confidence in this scheme and warned us that we must not expect more than half the number; but fifteen hundred at sixpence and threepence would bring a tidy sum. So the date for the performance was fixed and he interviewed the master or mistress of every school, and came back with the good news that he had been always most courteously received.

It looked so promising that the company held a council of war, excluding the manager, and decided that Mr. Innescourt could not be trusted to play fair and that we would therefore take the money ourselves as it came in and divide it at the end of the performance. Our low comedian was a little Jewish gentleman, a keen little man, and particularly keen on having what was due to him. We agreed that he was the best man to take the money; he would be quick and perhaps correct in giving change; at any rate he would be quick in taking the money. He pointed out that on an occasion like this the ordinary box-office methods would be useless. A crowd of three thousand children would not be easy to deal with. So we got a table with a large drawer to it and arranged that when the rush came, he would just sweep the money into the drawer while another member of the company passed the children in. Our little Jewish friend rehearsed it for us, showed us exactly what he was going to do and the quick movement of his hands and arms as he swept the imaginary coins off the table was so convincing that we could almost hear the money rattling in the drawer. Mr. Innescourt of course resented our high-handed action in taking the money, but accepted the inevitable.

And the time came. Two o'clock; that was the time arranged with the schools. The children seemed to be a little late — five minutes past — ten minues past two and they hadn't begun to come. Mr. Innescourt said that was quite easy to understand; they would have to go home after morning school, and have their faces washed, and their hands; and put on clean collars and say good-by to their mothers and all that sort of thing. But when twenty past two came and nobody arrived, we began to get really anxious. But Mr. Innescourt said it was quite obvious to him what had happened. When morning school was over, they had been sent home for their dinners and to get washed and told to come back again to the school, so that instead of being allowed to tear in all anyhow, they would be marshalled in classes of a hundred or so each, every class being headed by a master to keep them in order. At 2.30 Mr. Innescourt said he would just go round the corner and look and see if he could see any coming in the distance. At twenty minutes to three two little girls and three diminutive boys in large straw hats and wide-open eyes arrived, holding hands. Our Jewish money-changer immediately became very businesslike and called "Pay here, pay here!" and got his hands all ready for the sweeping movement.

The little girls said, "We want to go in."

"Yes, my dears," said the cashier, "Pay here. Threepenny or sixpenny seats?"

"Threepenny."

"Well, pay here and pass along."

The children looked at one another, rather dazed, and the eldest girl said, "We've paid."

"Paid?" said our Minister of Finance. "Paid? Who did you pay?"

"The gentleman round the corner," came the chorus.

By the time the low comedian had dashed round the corner, Mr. Innescourt had retired to an obscure pub where he remained until he had consumed the funds, and when he reappeared he made no effort to conceal the satisfaction he experienced, after our elaborate preparations to exclude him from the profits, in having taken and disposed of the entire proceeds of the matinée. No other patrons either large or small having appeared upon the horizon by three o'clock, we had a whip round for the five threepences due to the audience and dismissed them with a kiss. After this we dragged along for another week or perhaps two, and then our low comedian, with a sidelong glance at our manager, suggested that we should "throw up the sponge"; the subtle allusion to his beer-drinking propensities did not pass unnoticed and the suggestion was immediately agreed upon. As luck would have it, on the last few nights we did quite good business, but no money was forthcoming from the management. In this theatre we were not able to take possession of the box office, so we resorted to persuasion and threats. Our manager insisted, however, that all the money he had received had already been dissolved in paying other debts and that he had nothing for us. As I have already briefly recounted, Mr. Innescourt passed out of my life by way of the first-floor window, and that was the end of that.

This was followed by several short engagements, none of which opened up any prospect of advancement, but they gave me valuable experience in the playing of varied characters, and I made some stanch friends. Joseph and Alban Atwood were always trying to edge me in to any company with which they were associated. Alban had succeeded in getting an engagement with Clarence Holt in a play called "New Babylon." He wrote me that he had made a phenomenal success in a light comedy part, and that he was trying to get me into the company. There were many characters in that play: one was a comic Jew and when the part was about to fall vacant, owing to the comedian getting a better offer, Alban went to Mr. Holt and said, "I know the very man you want."

"What's his name?" said Holt.

"George Arliss," promptly responded my friend, with the air of one who was at least introducing Henry Irving.

"Never heard of him," said Holt, and that chance

was mercifully lost to me, for I should have been hopeless in the part.

Shortly afterwards the young juvenile part, that of a lad of eighteen, fell vacant in the same play, and as soon as Alban heard of it he went straight to Mr. Holt and said, "I know the very man for this part."

"Name?" said Holt.

"George Arliss," said Alban, as though he were presenting a nugget of gold to the manager.

"Don't want him. I've got somebody," said Holt.

Within three weeks it happened that the part of the aged sea captain became vacant, and my optimistic friend knocked up Holt out of his afternoon sleep and said, "I hear Barclay is going."

"Yes," said Holt, "the damn fool's leaving me."

"Well, I know absolutely the very man for the part."

"Well, who is he?" said Holt.

"George Arliss."

"God Almighty," shouted Holt, "is that the same —— man — what kind of an actor, in God's name, is he?"

"He's great," beamed Alban.

"Well, he dies in the first act, anyway," said Holt. "Send him along." So I was engaged. Those are the friends a struggling actor needs, and should always strive to keep.

Clarence Holt had made a great success and a considerable amount of money with this play. Under the management of Holt and Wilmot it had had a long run in London and had, I believe, netted them some thirty or forty thousand pounds. After Wilmot's death Holt continued with this drama and, to the best of my belief, played it in the English provinces until he died at an advanced age. I think he was not a large man but he appeared large; he was an autocrat of the most terrifying type. In his manner, his speech and his pose he was everything that is typical of the old-style tragedian. He looked down upon his company from the dizzy heights of his own superiority. He was well known throughout the profession as having a greater vocabulary of bad language than any actor on the stage. With this vocabulary he enriched his most casual conversation and when in anger he could invest this language with a power of expression that no man was ever known to successfully compete with. It is impossible therefore to report faithfully any conversation with him which one might like to repeat. It could and would be done, perhaps, by some of our very up-to-date authors, but they are fortunately not old enough to have had the opportunity of hearing and passing on to their insatiable public that rich but unrecorded verbiage of which Clarence Holt was master. When he spoke no dog dared to bark. When he entered the stage at rehearsal, the bones of his company turned to water and his assistant stage manager all but fainted. At his anger every one trembled. At his most faintly humorous remark every one laughed. At night he had a black imposing moustache. In the daytime he had sometimes a black one and sometimes a white one; it was the same moustache, his own, but it responded to

treatment according to the temperament of the tragedian at the hour of his toilet. I was inexperienced
enough to be blissfully unconscious of the majesty of
my new manager, and so I went light-heartedly to the
first rehearsal. The company assembled but Mr. Holt
did not arrive; so the stage manager took my scene —
only one scene, culminating in my death from apoplexy. Everything had to be done in the same way
as it had been done for twenty years, at the first
production. I remember asking if it would matter if
I was standing during a certain speech instead of
sitting; the stage manager looked startled; apparently
nobody had ever before made any suggestion during
the last twenty years, and when he had recovered
he said, "Mr. Holt always has you sitting."

About this period of the rehearsal I became conscious that something terrible was happening in the
theatre; there was an unnatural hush, and I seemed
to detect a trembling of the building, much as one
imagines the moment preceding a serious earthquake.
I looked round and saw standing behind me the unmistakable figure of Mr. Holt. He had on a large fur
coat, a large white muffler, a large broad-brimmed hat,
and a large black moustache. He looked long at me
and was obviously considering whether he should kill
me at once and so rid the earth of one more useless
encumbrance or whether he should let me live, and
allow Nature to take its course. I was relieved to find
that he decided on the latter and more merciful procedure. To the evident surprise of every one, he with-
drew the hand from underneath the first button of

his overcoat, extended it towards me and said fiercely but in courtly language, "Welcome to my company." The company gave a smile of relief. The tragedian then swept the stage with a fierce eye that made the company feel that perhaps they ought not to have smiled at all, and said, waving to his subordinate stage manager, "Let him proceed." So I proceeded.

I hadn't been frightfully impressed at the time, because of my ignorance of really great tragedians, so I continued to rehearse, without, to any great extent, losing my nerve. I asked the little stage manager if I might do this or that and was always nervously told, "No." Meanwhile Mr. Holt was pacing the stage behind me. Presently a large white thing flashed through the air and struck the stage manager. It turned out to be Mr. Holt's muffler with which for some reason he had decided to dispense. I continued with my rehearsal and the heavy measured tread went on behind me, back and forth with frightful regularity, but with a suggestion of increasing horse power. In the middle of one of my speeches, the large fur coat that I had last seen on Mr. Holt came hurtling through the air, missing me narrowly and falling into the arms of the stage manager, who with uncanny foresight seemed to be expecting it. I concluded that Mr. Holt was feeling the heat. I looked round and saw him now in a black frock coat which was tightly buttoned and which was deftly designed to suggest, in spite of all opposition, the place where the waist line should be. His hat was firmly on his head and though he continued his walking exercise, his head was turned towards me, and he glared furiously at me — as though I could help his being hot!

It was a beautiful day outside, bright and sunny, and as I continued with my rehearsal, I was surprised to hear unmistakably sounds of distant thunder. Evidently a summer storm. Nothing is more disconcerting at a rehearsal than thunder. I noticed that it seemed to affect the members of the company too, who were sitting about the wings; they all looked most uncomfortable. Presently the volume of thunder increased until it suddenly came crashing about my ears, and then I saw to my surprise that it was all coming out of the body of Mr. Holt. He strode down to the footlights with a mighty "Stop!" He stood before me in his shirt sleeves, pale with fury; he had discarded his frock coat in an almost futile attempt to avoid spontaneous combustion. He now removed his monster hat and crushed it on the prompt table with all the strength of his mighty right hand, and pointing an accusing and soul-destroying finger at me he said:

"I see what you are, sir. You're a —— modern actor! That's what you are, sir. That's not the way to act, sir. That's not how I act. If I offer a lady a chair, sir, I don't say, 'Will you kindly take a chair, Madam.' (Mr. Holt assumed for this a mincing manner of speaking.) I say, 'Sit down, damn you.'"

Here he raised the roof several inches with his voice and ruined the prompt chair with one stroke of his right arm. Then amidst a deathly silence he strode away and proceeded to walk round the stage two or three times as though he were giving some sort of demonstration of a circus exhibition, but never for a moment taking his furious eye off my person.

It now began to dawn upon me that it was my fault, after all, that Mr. Holt had got so hot: that it was due to my method of acting; and as I watched him circling round me with his fixed and hungry eye seeking blood, I thought of my days in "Leaves of Shamrock" and prepared myself for a struggle for life in the arena. My surprise then may be realized when he suddenly came upon me, not a ravenous bloodthirsty animal, but a limp and weeping creature. He placed his hands upon my left shoulder and wept; he became a mother to me. He begged me, with tears welling up in his eyes, to be a better actor. To be like him; or as near like him as it was possible for mortal actor to be. I promised I would. I was so glad to find myself still alive that I promised him everything, and before the rehearsal was over I was dying of apoplexy with all the strength of an expiring whale.

At dinner that afternoon I asked Alban whether my predecessor was leaving to go to another engagement or whether his health had broken down. Alban said, "Don't you worry; he was very likely thinking you were great. That's just his way."

My engagement with Clarence Holt was chiefly remarkable for the acquisition of a collection of stories about the old tyrant, none of which am I able adequately to repeat. I always regret that I was not present at the rehearsal during which Mr. Holt was endeavoring to teach a child of five to say, "Oh, Mamma!" with expression. The story was told me by my friend Herbert Budd. The child had only one way of saying, "Oh, Mamma!" and that was in a childish treble without the faintest semblance of meaning whatsoever. And Mr. Holt took her on his knee and kissed her and caressed her and said, "My dear, darling little child, God's blessing to its parents, listen to me, and say after me, my dear, darling angel child: now, 'Oh, Mamma'." and he spoke the words with much feeling.

She said, "Oh, Mamma" in a piping treble.

Mr. Holt's circulation stopped for a moment but he had himself well in hand and with infinite patience and kindness he embraced the child warmly and placed some feverish kisses on its lips and brow and continued, "No, no, my own — my dear, darling, little maiden: not that way. Let me explain to you; I wish you to express not only surprise, but disgust and horror at your mother's actions. Now, surprise and horror, darling child, 'Oh, Mamma!'"

The child, entirely unimpressed by the efforts of the gifted actor, repeated the words rather more inanely than ever.

Mr. Holt, with his left arm round the child, clutched the seat of his chair with his right hand, closed his eyes and gave himself up to silent prayer for several minutes. Then with his eyes still closed, he roared, "Again, 'Oh, Mamma!'" in a tremendous voice that shook the theatre.

The unconcerned tinkling, "Oh, Mamma" came from the little girl, and with one bound Clarence Holt sprang into the air, and — holding the child on high prayed fervently to God to stay with him and prevent him from taking this little one's life. His prayer was heard: the child escaped, and Mr. Holt lay back exhausted and did not recover until he had used every word of the language which he spoke so fluently.

Mr. Holt was not over-generous in his ideas of salary, so no aspiring actor stayed with him very long. In course of time Alban Atwood left, and I should probably have gone soon after, but for the fact that I was able to introduce Joseph into Alban's place. I must confess that my efforts were not making Joseph's life a bed of roses, but whenever he and I were together life was pleasant for us both. I knew, however, that by staying with Mr. Holt I was doing no good, so when I heard of the possibility of a part in a new play by Paul Merritt called "Round the Ring", I made a desperate effort to get it. I stood little chance unless I could interview the manager, Mr. Cobbe, and he was in Leeds, so I traveled all night, and spent all my savings in getting to Leeds, but I settled the engagement and got back in time to play in "New Babylon" the following Monday.

I remember my interview with Mr. Cobbe very vividly. He was a large, kindly man. I took a letter of introduction to him from a fine old actor named John Maclean. Mr. Cobbe said, "You're not tall enough, my boy."

I said, "I look tall in top-boots."

He laughed and said, "I should want you to do the assistant stage management. Have you ever done it?"

I said, "No, but I know how."

He laughed again and said, "Well, I'll engage you. Sign your contract; you're signing for the entire season. I've never seen you act and I don't know what you can do. But I'm signing everybody up for the season. If you're no good you can hold me to this agreement, but I warn you, we shall make it damned uncomfortable for you if you do."

I recall the first night of "Round the Ring." I was most anxious to make good. The author was a very fat man with a very thin voice; he sat in a stage box and laughed uproariously at all his funny scenes. But I was playing a serious part — a very serious part. I did a murder. I was wearing a new front tooth which I had recently had put in, in place of an original one that I had recently had knocked out. I was also wearing a black wig which was too small for me. I had it in my wardrobe; it was made for somebody else, but it saved me the expense of buying a new one. I got on very well until I came to my big scene and then in the excitement my tooth came out and my wig came off simultaneously, rendering me mentally and physically incapable of proceeding until I had darted behind a friendly wooden settle and collected my thoughts, my hair and my tooth. This is the only outstanding recollection I have of that season, except that it was in this company that I first met Herbert Budd, who became my valued and stanch friend until his death. After this I did some odd jobs that are rather hazy in my memory and then I joined the Stock Company of the Theatre Royal Margate. Margate being a very popular and very healthy seaside town, a great many schools and academies for young people were organized there and amongst them was the Academy of Acting run by Miss Sarah Thorne.

I have always regarded Miss Thorne's School of Acting as better than any that has since come under my notice. There may be similar establishments to-day, but I am unaware of them. The nearest approach to it is, I believe, that run by Miss Jessie Bonstelle in Detroit, Michigan. Miss Thorne ran her school in conjunction with a regular theatre that was open to the public all the year round. Her method was to engage about half a dozen experienced actors and actresses for the leading parts, and use her students for the rest of the cast. So that the pupils were continually playing before a paying audience; and if any young man or woman showed unusual ability there was always the chance of promotion to better parts. The plays were constantly being changed so there was opportunity for varied experience. The great advantage this school had over similar institutions was that from the beginning the students were in the atmosphere of a regular theatre and were facing a regular audience that had paid for admission. In one's preparation for a career on the stage good teachers are of some value; but the entire staff of the most proficient academy would be unable to teach in a year certain valuable knowledge that one can learn from an audience in a week. The regular audience that has paid for its seat is, in my opinion, the great teacher and the almost infallible critic.

VII

IN THE OLD COMEDIES

I ARRIVED at the Theatre Royal Margate on Monday morning with my bag in my hand, having come straight from the railway station. A nice girl afterwards told me that I was wearing a brown suit and a pair of brown boots. This record of my apparel has no significance beyond the fact that the nice girl noticed it. Perhaps I should mention how it was I happened to go to Margate at all. Well, I was dining in their charming flat in Victoria Street, Westminster, with a young married couple whom I had recently met in the provinces where we were fulfilling a "special engagement." The most special part of this engagement, from our point of view, had been our successful effort to get our salaries from a manageress who was unwilling to part with them. There was a class of manager then as there is to-day — and ever will be — who considered that the actor should at all times be willing to share the losses, without ever participating in the profits. I have always regarded theatrical management as a most hazardous undertaking, but I have never been able to understand by what method of reasoning the manager should expect the actor to "stand by him" in times of adversity when the most he (the actor) can ever hope for in days of prosperity is his bare weekly salary. In the present instance business was bad, but we knew the manageress had money, and the fact that she had sprained her ankle and interviewed us in bed, where she looked quite at her best, did not soften our hearts sufficiently for us to forgive her her just debts; so having given her fair warning we struck after the second act on Saturday night, and refused to allow the curtain to go up on Act III until we were paid. As it was her own theatre as well as her own company, of course she had to pay up.

Well, I had formed a friendship with the young married couple, and when we came back to London they asked me to dinner. Obviously it needs to be explained how it was that a young married couple who were willing to go into the provinces to act for a very small salary should have a charming flat in Victoria Street, Westminster. The truth is, it was a wedding present from a rich relative of one or the other. The rent was paid in advance for a period of three years. Surely a most practical wedding gift. During dinner we reviewed our adventurous pasts and speculated on our unknown futures.

Suddenly my host said, "By Jove. Have you ever played in the 'Old Comedies'?"

I said I hadn't.

"Ah, that's a pity. I saw Sarah Thorne yesterday in Margate and she's looking for a man to open next Monday."

"Well," I said, "why couldn't I do it?"

"No, it's no good," he answered, "you'd have to play Sir Anthony Absolute in 'The Rivals' next Monday, Old Hardcastle in 'She Stoops' on Wednes-

day, Old Dornton in 'The Road to Ruin' on
Saturday."

Of course the prospect of this didn't worry me, and
the upshot of it was that I got him to wire at once
to Miss Thorne, telling her he had found "the very
man." I settled the engagement (two guineas a week)
and my friend, who felt considerable responsibility,
told me that I mustn't let on that I hadn't played in
the Old Comedies before. I told him they were bound
to find out when it came to rehearsals.

"No, they won't," he said; "I was with Sarah for
two years, and I know all the business. I'll go
through the parts with you before you leave, and
put you up to all the tricks. When you rehearse with
Mrs. Hardcastle, all you have to do is to say, 'I
suppose we do the old business here' — and that sort
of thing, and they'll never know you haven't played
them hundreds of times before."

So that's how I happened to be standing on the
stage of the Theatre Royal Margate when the nice
girl noticed I was wearing a brown suit and brown
boots. I felt very strange and much alone. I didn't
know a soul there and the whole atmosphere was very
different from anything I had experienced before. In
place of the crusted mummers that I had been in the
habit of meeting, here were groups of young men and
women full of life and spirits. The young girls were
mostly fresh and pretty. Many of the young men
had long hair and queer ties, proving at once that
acting was an art worthy of the serious attention of
an *Artiste*. There were others with short hair. I found

afterwards that the short-haired ones were as a rule the better actors. This was perhaps not so much due to the length of their hair as to the way they approached their work. If you approach your art as an artist you are very liable to remember the artist at the expense of the art. But on the whole there was a freshness and youth about the theatre that was most exhilarating.

I was soon welcomed and put at my ease by the actors who, like myself, were there on a salary. There was the stage manager, Charles Daly, an elderly man who seemed to have borrowed youth from his surroundings. There were Charlie Rock and Frank Gillmore, both young men, but with a good deal of experience. I was conscious that I was being looked over by all the "pupes", as the pupils were generally called. I was "the new man" and had to stand the test of comparison with the man whose place I was taking. I was introduced to everybody and seemed to be regarded as fairly acceptable — except perhaps by one girl who seemed to look at me with somewhat unnecessary contempt. A nice girl too. But perhaps that was my imagination, or just her way.

That first week was very trying. You can't "wing" the Old Comedies — especially when you are supposed to have played them many times before; they have to be studied letter perfect. My brain came nearer to snapping than ever before or since. I sat up in bed in the middle of one night, wide awake, but unable to recall who I was or where I was. I knew that I was going mad. I caught hold of the side of the bedstead and was subconsciously aware that if I could keep hold of myself for the next five minutes I was saved, but if I let go I was lost. My eyes were starting out of my head and I held myself down for five or six minutes. I knew that I was either Sir Anthony Absolute, old Dornton or old Hardcastle, but which, or where I was, I could not tell. Gradually my brain collected itself, and I became normal; but it was a terrible moment; a long, long moment which I can never forget.

I got through rehearsals fairly well. Miss Emily Thorne (the mother of Frank Gillmore) was Mrs. Hardcastle, and when I reached the scene where my friend and sponsor had told me to say, "the old business I suppose," I said it, and Miss Thorne laughed quietly and patted me on the cheek and said, "Yes, I'll show it to you." She was on to me from the beginning, but she never gave me away. Emily was the sister of Sarah, and of course Frank Gillmore was Sarah's nephew. The Thornes were a well-known theatrical family. Tom Thorne, a brother, was lessee of the Vaudeville Theatre, London, for many years, with David James (who was a relative, I believe, of David Belasco), and together they produced the famous comedy "Our Boys" written by H. J. Byron, which ran in London for something like three consecutive years, and has been played in various parts of England almost ever since.

I was terribly nervous all that first week, but on the first night of "The Rivals" I noticed out of the tail of my eye that that girl who was so supercilious towards me was dressed for the part of Lucy, the Maid. I was told that this was the first part that had been assigned to her. And while I was thinking of nobody but myself, I couldn't help observing that she was darting about from one to the other of her girl friends who were also making their first appearance, telling them how well they looked, giving their frocks or their hair a little improving touch, dashing to her dressing room to get a puff or a piece of ribbon for them. She seemed to be a great favorite. I was surprised at this, because she certainly had not been encouraging to me. She had very pretty arms though; you couldn't help seeing that.

During my season at Margate we produced many plays but we continually repeated the old comedies. I became very fond of them and it has been a great disappointment to me that I have never been able to do them since. If I were a millionaire I would produce all those charming old plays, one after another. It seems a great pity that the present generation has practically no knowledge of "The Rivals", "The Road to Ruin", "The Clandestine Marriage", "She Stoops to Conquer", and many other delightful plays. "The School for Scandal" is occasionally produced, but seldom satisfactorily. The great obstacle in the way of these revivals is the expense. The casts are long and the plays must be well acted and good actors come high nowadays. Then the public is not likely to rush to see them immediately; they may have to be coaxed and all theatrical managers know that with the tremendous overhead charges of a theatre coaxing is expensive. And so I shall probably never do them again.

At Margate "The Road to Ruin" was one of our most frequent revivals, and somebody told me that that girl with the nice arms used to sit in front every time we played it, and that she was heard to remark that my performance was the best of the whole lot. This surprised me very much for she had never even spoken to me except to nod good-morning. After the first few weeks my experiences there were very pleasant. Frank Gillmore and I became the greatest of friends and eventually we lived together. We took long walks and during these excursions we would go over all our scenes and get letter perfect, and arrange bits of "business."

Then one of the girls fell in love with me. It must not be supposed that I merely imagined this: it was true. Nor must I be accused of bragging about it. There was nothing to brag about. It was inevitable that somebody must fall in love with the new man; it had to be done. Somebody was always falling in love with somebody in that company. The "pupes" had a great deal of leisure time, and without love life for them would have been terribly dull. And when I came, most of the young men were already engaged — not really engaged, but just snapped up for the time being. There were more girls than boys. The girl that was in love with me was a little girl in a large hat. I knew nothing about her passion for me until one day much to my amazement I received an invitation to tea from the supercilious girl with the nice arms. Of course I did not connect this in any way with love. I concluded that she must be giving a tea party of such large dimensions that it was impossible to leave me out. There were always tea parties going on. Tea and love went hand in hand. Sometimes the tea was responsible for the love and sometimes the love for the tea. In this case it was the latter. When I got there I found there was nobody to meet me but my hostess and the little girl with the large hat. My hostess was so gracious to me (it was the first time she had really spoken to me) — oh, so gracious; but unfortunately she had to say good-by because she must go out at once as she had some shopping to do. This struck me as strange, considering she had asked me to tea, but she floated out and left me alone with my lover. I afterwards found out that my hostess was a born matchmaker and when she discovered the little girl's state of mind, she felt it her duty to bring things to a head. Unfortunately I was far more innocent than I am now. I was blissfully unresponsive, and most of my remarks were directed towards the solution of the problem of why the other girl had gone out, and how long it would be before she came back; so when she did come back and said good-by to me again and said that she was so glad I'd come, and so sorry she had had to go away, and bowed me out of the front door, she discovered of course that the whole thing had been a frightful fiasco. Shortly after that the little girl in the large hat jilted me.

All sorts of distinguished people would come to see

Sarah Thorne's Company from time to time. London actors and actresses were apt to send their sons and daughters to Sarah to learn the business. Before I joined the company Ellen Terry would come down to see her son Gordon Craig, who was a pupil at the time. I believe Irving was even known to witness a performance. Irene and Violet Vanbrugh had both been "pupes"; so had Granville Barker. We never knew who might be in front.

Frank Gillmore and I were asked to so many tea parties that we felt we must make some return. We therefore gave a supper party on Sunday evening: such things were of course a matter of arrangement with the landlady, and ways and means had to be considered; this was quite a large party for us. The little girl in the big hat didn't come; she was indisposed. The other one came: I was half afraid she wouldn't, because she had always been so standoffish. But everybody liked Frank Gillmore. We had supper and music and games. Frank sang and she played his accompaniment. She turned out to be quite a brilliant pianist. I was surprised. She was really an awfully good-looking girl; a dark girl she was with brown eyes. She had on a red dress trimmed with black braid and a lace thing at the throat with a little ruby brooch in the shape of a crown and underneath the lace was a little diamond star that just sparkled every now and then as the lace moved. Most effective! As I said, she played for Frank; and Frank kept on singing. I was living with Frank and I hadn't even known that he could sing. But now he not only sang things that he knew, but he "tried over" things with her, an operation which always seems to bring the pianist and the singer so intimately together. It is useless for Frank, now that he is in a position of trust and importance, to try to deny that he behaved in this way, because I can bring witnesses to prove it.

We also played that game in which two people go outside into a dark passage, while the others think of something, and the two remain in the dark passage until they are called back and then they proceed to find out by ingenious questioning the thing that the others have thought of. Frank went out and she went with him. I thought of something immediately — almost before the door closed upon them, but it was not accepted by the others, and there were all sorts of discussion as to what was the best thing to think of, and a lot of ridiculous laughter and wandering away from the matter in hand, while those two were kept outside for what seemed to me an interminable time. And then when they were called, they had to be called twice. I didn't understand that at all. After that I suggested games where we all stayed together and I was quite glad when the party was over.

Sometimes, at night, after the play, I would take a walk by myself by the sea. The place was always very deserted at that time and you heard nothing but the regular swish of the waves as they spent themselves quietly on the sand. One night I saw a girl in a long light-gray coat and a hat with a little red feather in it. She was walking by herself too. And as I was passing her, I saw that it was the girl with the nice

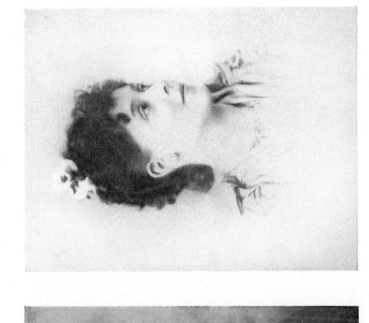

FLORENCE MONTGOMERY

The supercilious girl at Margate, who afterwards got caught in the rain

MRS. GEORGE ARLISS

As she appears to-day

arms — the girl who had played Frank Gillmore's accompaniment, you know. And so we walked together. And really she turned out to be an awfully nice girl. Quite different from what I thought. Not a bit supercilious now. I was surprised. We had a lovely walk. I found out that she was not so frightfully gone on Frank after all. She liked him, of course, but not so terribly. Her name was Florence Montgomery. I don't know that I ever saw the sea looking so nice and placid, and the moon too. I took her right home to her door and when I got back Frank had gone to bed. I met her several times after this quite by accident, walking alone. It is strange how you may walk about and never see a person at all, and then, when you once get to know them, how often you sometimes run against them.

Well, about this time, much to every one's surprise, Sarah Thorne gave a party on Sunday night. This was, of course, a real supper, lots of courses and everything very superior. Everybody was there and Sarah sat at the head of the table, very affable and motherly. And at the end of the supper Sarah got up to make a speech; you might have heard a pin drop for no such thing had ever happened within the memory of the oldest "pupe." She said how happy she was to see all these young people about her and how proud she was to know that they were all ladies and gentlemen. She said she always felt a great responsibility, particularly in the case of the young ladies, because when they were brought to her by their parents or their guardians they were left as it were as a sacred trust.

She had heard of instances of young gentlemen allowing a too strong friendship to spring up between
themselves and young ladies with whom their professional studies might bring them in contact, but she
was sure that no such thing would be likely to happen
between her young ladies and gentlemen. Particularly
she felt secure in those actors of experience that she
had been fortunate enough to gather round her (here
she looked at me). She was sure that these gentlemen
would realize that they were there to set an example,
and that none of these gentlemen would take advantage of their position to captivate the affections of any
young lady sitting at this moment at her board.
(Here she looked at me again: and everybody looked
at me. Heaven knows why.) She said that if unhappily there were any danger of such a condition, that
with her words to-night the danger would be passed.
(Here two or three young ladies exploded and looked
at Florence Montgomery and everybody tried not to
look at me.) Sarah sat down with the final remark
that she was happy in the knowledge that a gentleman
could always be trusted. After the party broke up and
the people left for their lodgings, hilarious laughter
might have been heard on various street corners of
Margate.

My experience at Margate was varied and valuable.
We were continually producing something different.
Not new plays but interesting revivals. Sarah was
seldom seen in the theatre but Charles Daly, the stage
manager, was one of those men who seemed to know
the traditional business of every play that was ever

written. When we did period plays we used to go and dig out our costumes from a large box at "The Towers" — the name of Miss Thorne's house where she gave instruction and where many of the pupes boarded. When the plays were modern we did our best from our private wardrobe.

We rehearsed every day — bright, pleasant rehearsals. The stage door was down a narrow opening which was christened "Repetition Alley", because we used to walk up and down there and study and hear one another's parts. It reminded me of the stage door of the Elephant and Castle, but everything else was so different.

The pupils were sons and daughters of prosperous business men (the fees were not inconsiderable), of well-to-do actors, of lawyers, authors and clergymen. All stage-struck members of the family. Some of them became famous, some quite the opposite. Some married well, left the stage and were miserable. Some married badly and were very happy. Which reminds me:

It can rain terribly in Margate; simply pour. One afternoon it was coming down in sheets of water. I was out in it and being close by I made a rush for the stage door of the theatre and dashed in. The stage always seems very dark in the daytime as one comes in out of the street: for a moment you can't see anything, but I heard some one just ahead of me say, "Huh! talk about cats and dogs," and then rattle all her clothes much as a dog shakes itself when it comes out of the water.

I said, "Hullo, you been caught in it too."

"I'm wet to the skin," she said, and I said, "So am I," and then I saw that it was Florence Montgomery. It was a curious thing that that theatre should have been absolutely empty except for us two. There is generally somebody doing something — a stage hand prowling about, or a property man polishing furniture, or cleaners sweeping up. But it happened that at this particular moment there was nobody else in the theatre at all. Anybody who has ever been in an empty theatre in the daytime will know that there is a queer unearthly quiet about it, a calmness and a hush that suggests intense seclusion. And almost any girl, wet or dry, finding herself quite alone in this large stillness, would be glad if somebody she knew suddenly appeared to, so to speak, protect her.

As my eyes grew more accustomed to the light I noticed she looked very pretty and rosy; I suppose she had been running. I had never before been alone in a theatre with somebody who was wet through. And as I looked at her, a tremendous feeling of sympathy surged in my bosom. There she was — wet through! And I could do nothing for her. I couldn't lend her anything because I was wet through myself. Of course there were lots of clothes in the dressing rooms, but you don't think of those things at a time like that. Even her hands were wet: you had only to touch them and take hold of them to know that; and her dark hair, all damp over her brow. Perhaps if she took her hat off, I suggested: in fact I helped her to take it off. And when I smoothed her hair back I found it was still wet: what could one do? Anybody would have been moved at such a moment. Well, Sarah, you may not think I behaved like a gentleman, but I think I did. In fact, I believe that is what gentlemen are for. I asked her to be mine. Whether I should have asked her to be mine at that moment if she had been dry, I shall never know, and from a practical point of view I ought not to have done it anyway, I grant you that, Sarah. If I had met a modest little house and asked it to be mine, or a modest little fortune, there would have been some reason in it, but to take a modest girl, just out of the rain, and ask her, when she must have known that she had to make up her mind quickly or run the risk of pneumonia, was perhaps hardly a fair thing to do, considering I had absolutely no worldly goods with which her to endow. But if I might be allowed to give advice to young actors of my age (I think I was twenty-three then) I should say give it a trial. It may not be easy to bring about these conditions — the combination of rain and an empty theatre; because even if you rented a theatre for the day, it might not rain. But if it can be done, results come quickly. I should imagine that in my case the whole thing didn't take more than four minutes, but there she was, at the end of that time — mine for ever. She told me only yesterday that I went down on my knees to her, but I don't believe that: and if you can get your girl thoroughly wet through I don't think you will find that necessary.

And now at last, having something in the world to work for, it happened, as it so often happens in our profession, that very shortly afterwards I hadn't anything in the world to do. Sarah Thorne used to run a pantomime at Christmas, and although I had had some experience in this work, as recorded in my Elephant days, I felt that my talents did not lie in that direction. And so my season at Margate came to an end; my assets due to this engagement being some valuable experience in the Old Comedies, a girl who believed in me, and the unswerving friendship and affection of Frank Gillmore.

VIII

ACTOR-MANAGER

JUST what I did during the next few months I cannot remember, but it was in the early part of the following summer that an unlooked-for thing happened to me. An old lady, a friend of my family, gave me fifty pounds. It was a great deal of money. In fact I didn't know another actor who had fifty pounds, or who ever had had so much money at once. But there it was, in notes. It was given to me to help me in my profession, and I felt it a grave responsibility.

I had never had any desire to become a manager, because as I have already hinted, I abhor responsibility. But with fifty pounds and no engagement, it seemed to me my bounden duty to become an actor-manager. I hadn't much idea how it was to be done and I was beginning to weaken in my resolution, when Fate took a hand in the affair and directed my eye to an advertisement in *The Stage* which read: "Wanted £50 to finance established Company in a high-class melodrama. Apply by letter to Blake, Chancery Lane." Giving, of course, the number of the house which I have forgotten. Fifty pounds being the exact amount which I possessed and also by an uncanny coincidence the precise sum which Mr. Blake required, and "High-class Melodrama" having been up to that time my chief experience on the stage, it seemed obvious that this was to be my opportunity.

Knowing that I was probably the only person in the profession, with the exception of the London managers, who had fifty pounds, I did not hurry my decision. I thought it over very carefully. At last I wrote to the advertiser, which resulted in my meeting him in Chancery Lane in a small room which smelt as though it had once been occupied by a solicitor. It was chilly and devoid of furniture: it struck me as being an excellent place in which to do a murder, and I was glad I hadn't brought my fifty pounds with me.

But Mr. Blake was a nice little man with dark and luminous eyes, eyes which if listed in a sale catalogue would inevitably have been described as "once the property of a Spanish prima donna." He was not well dressed. He seemed to me rather shabby, except in the matter of shoes, which were of brilliant patent leather and suitable for dancing. His appearance, however, did not surprise me; I had not expected to find him opulent or why should he need my fifty pounds? And I was familiar with the presence of shiny patent leather shoes in company with otherwise drab apparel, because it was a fashion often affected by so many juvenile-leads of my acquaintance when they went to interview managers, particularly a manager who had advertised for an actor who must "dress well on and off the stage." The patent leather shoes under these circumstances were intended by the juvenile-lead to convey the assurance that at any rate he knew how to dress like a gentleman. But as I have said, Mr. Blake was a nice little man. During our partnership, which was the result of this interview, I found him always pleasant, hard-working and scrupulously honest. After the tour was over, I never saw him or heard of him again, but I should say that if he is still living he is probably a prosperous merchant in the city. At the time I met him I believe he was a picture-frame maker in a small way in the Southwest district of London. How he ever became connected with the "High-class Melodrama" I never knew.

However, at this interview, it transpired that the melodrama was a sort of going concern. It had been on tour but had had to be withdrawn, owing to lack of funds sufficient to contend with depressed theatrical conditions. But the scenery was intact and the company could be reassembled at almost a moment's notice. Having assured myself of the facts, I struck a bargain to throw the weight of my finances into the concern, together with my valuable services and the firm of Blake and Arliss — fifty-fifty — at once sprang into existence. I look back with interest on this experience because it is the only time I have ever been my own manager. The play was called "In Face of the Foe." It had had a long and chequered career in earlier days under many minor provincial managers. Every manager rewrote the play, and I largely rewrote it again. I believe it had been lying dormant for many years when my partner discovered it in some way unknown to me. It was a military drama. And as there were several bloody encounters before the very eyes of the audience, between hordes of Arabs led by the Arab chief on the one side, and the strength of the British Army led most properly by the leading man on the other; and as we could not afford more than six supers in all, a considerable amount of ingenuity was required on the part of the producer in order to make these battles convincing.

Although my capacity for giving good advice to the young on the art of acting may very likely be questioned, I venture to declare that no one dare challenge my ability to give counsel to the youthful manager who is preparing to produce a military drama with six principals and six supers. I speak with authority, having had the actual experience. For battle scenes, a clear and open stage must be steadfastly avoided; the reason is obvious. As you have not a lot of men to fill up your stage, you must have a lot of something else. Rocks are useful — rugged, rocky scenes — large rocks behind which a number of imaginary men may hide. But good rocks are expensive to transport. I recommend tents — military tents: a lot of tents. The advantage of a tent over a rock is first that it can be easily rolled up, so that in the baggage car it takes up little more room than an umbrella; and secondly that whereas a rock has only an outside, a tent has also an inside. It can hardly be denied that if a large number of British soldiers were inside tents which were not open to the audience, the audience could not see them, and if the audience cannot see them it is not necessary to have the men. The same argument applies to Arabs lying flat on their stomachs behind the tents, awaiting an opportunity to spring. The very nature of an Arab is secretive; the great characteristic of a first-class Arab is his ability to creep along the earth at night — or even in broad daylight — and never be seen. Those are the kind of Arabs we had in "In Face of the Foe." If the tents are cleverly arranged together with a lot of red limelight carefully manipulated, it is quite surprising what can be done with even one Arab.

Or course there must be tension; and there must be an occasional burst of laughter from a tent. But when it is your own company, it is astounding what a number of different noises you can make off stage. At a given moment you can say off stage in a deep voice, "God, it's hot." And a super puts his head and hand out of one of the tents as though he had said it. But as I say, tension must be created in the audience. I used to do that too with "In Face of the Foe."

Naturally, I played the villain. I used to come on left, looking suspiciously about me and say, "Curse these Arabs: they creep about like flies — not a step but what you are conscious of eyes peering at you —" and so forth. That at once acquainted the audience with the fact that the stage was infested with Arabs, which they could very nearly see, but not quite. Then when I heard the honest laughter of the hero coming from one of the tents I said, "Yes, laugh, Captain Hilton, surrounded as you are by your young lieutenants — laugh, Captain Hilton, the idol of this crack regiment" (with a sweeping gesture). So the audience was at once introduced to the entire regiment.

149

Of course, the actual battle required considerable skill in management. At the first shot heard off stage, the entire British army would naturally come out of their tents. But with us Captain Hilton was too quick for them: he alone sprang out and shouted, "Keep to your tents, lads, let no man move till I give the signal." I would warn young managers that the signal having been given, considerable discretion has to be used as to the exact moment for lowering the curtain.

Later in the play when it comes to the interior of the palace of the Arab sheik, pillars may be used to effect results similar to those obtained on the battle-field with tents. A lot of pillars. They will all lie flat in the baggage van and take up very little room. If the action of the play necessitates the actual onrush of Arabs or British soldiers, the only thing to be done is to turn out the lights completely and have a lot of noise. In the event of this emergency, however, it is advisable to have some one on the stage say, "Curse this darkness." This will allow the audience to realize that you know it's dark, that there has been no untoward accident at the switchboard. I consider the information which I have imparted here most valuable. It took me three months to acquire it in its full maturity. I learned many things during my term of management with "In Face of the Foe."

Although we boldly described our play as a "High-class Melodrama," I am bound to admit that the validity of that description was open to argument. And I should hardly have dared to say, even at that time, that we had a high-class company. My business manager and my soubrette were of the highest class for they were none other than my old friend Alban Atwood and my own girl, Florence Montgomery. Of course Joseph would have been with us if he hadn't been otherwise engaged. But he had now entered the ranks of musical comedy under the management of George Edwardes. I don't think Alban was a really good business manager, but he had about him an air of prosperity and a keen sense of humor, both valuable attributes in times of adversity. Florence Montgomery, young and bright and keen, seemed sadly out of place amongst the other members of the company, all over-ripened in the service of Melodrama of all kinds. These were members of the original company as it stood before I became connected with it.

I have always been impressed by the loyalty and diligence of the actor, but I did not know before what stanch friends this class of actor can be when fairly treated. We did some terrible business but we struggled through; we always paid our way and never owed the company a penny of their hard-earned salaries. But how they worked! There was nothing they wouldn't do to help things along. Our Arab sheik, for instance — who in our play was quite unlike the sheiks of the moving pictures, except that he was amorous — was fat and past forty; but what a worker. He perspired until he sparkled in the limelight at every pore, in his efforts to make the play go. But that was not all; he felt that we were not sufficiently advertised in the town; so unknown to us he got up early one morning — or went out after the play at night, with a paste pot in one hand and a bundle of printing under his arm and proceeded to "fly-post" the town. He belonged to the earlier days when fly-posting was one of the duties of the actor.

Provincial managers would advertise for a good, sound, character actor, "one not afraid to use the brush." Which meant that he must go out with a paste brush and a pail of paste and do some fly-posting. "Fly-posting" is the act of posting bills on all available spots on which it is possible to paste a bill. Thus, a respectable householder wakes up in the morning and finds pasted on the side of his house a bill announcing that "In Face of the Foe" is playing every evening at the Theatre Royal. If, however, your fly-poster pastes a bill on a hoarding that is the property of a firm of bill posters, or if he covers other people's advertising matter posted on their own property, he immediately comes within the law and is liable to fine or imprisonment.

Unfortunately our sheik was too ambitious. He fly-posted everywhere and the next morning my partner found himself in the Police Court. Why I was not also arrested, and how we got out of it, I cannot recall, but I do know that it was a trying and undignified experience for a manager of a "High-class Melodrama."

The old and mellowed actors were always coming to me with suggestions for working up the business and were ready to do anything in the world to help. They would willingly have "paraded" but that would merely have exposed the weakness of the "strength" of our company. It was summer time and the heat was unusual for England; we did poor business everywhere: it was a mighty struggle to pay our way and my partner and I often had barely enough money to live upon. At last we gave up and I had to borrow another fifteen pounds to pay the final salaries. It was a hard experience, but looking back upon it, I feel that under the circumstances we deserved some credit for keeping a Stirring Military Drama going for three months on sixty-five pounds.

If the comic papers reflect the popular idea, one is led to suppose that the public visualize a theatrical manager as a man with a large cigar and a very limited allowance of brains who lives a life of luxury and license secured to him by the honest labor of his employees. I have never known that kind of manager, but judging from my own experience I should be inclined to say that whatever luxury, or leisure or license he may get, he thoroughly deserves it. At any rate I was very glad to climb down from my exalted position and accept two guineas a week to play a small part in a farcical comedy.

My new manager was Fred G. Latham and the farce was "The Grey Mare." I believe I got the engagement through the good word of my friend Herbert Budd. I remember being sent to see Fred Latham at Drury Lane Theatre. He was then the right-hand man of Sir Augustus Harris and he afterwards told me that he engaged me not because he knew anything about me, but because he thought I looked as though

I could act. But Herbert Budd was one of Latham's early acquaintances and I am of opinion that he put in a word for me. I cannot too strongly accentuate the value of making and keeping friends in the theatrical business. Whatever success I have attained has been largely due to the efforts of my friends. Fred Latham was running touring companies on his own account and I stayed under his management for two or three years. He was eventually instrumental in getting me my first London engagement — but that did not come until long afterwards. Under Latham I played in several plays, including "The Late Lamented", and "A Woman's Revenge."

In this last play I think I began to make some real headway and to come under the notice of provincial managers. I had a good part and it is likely that I played it well, because I copied Charles Cartwright who created the part when the play was first produced at the Adelphi Theatre, and Cartwright was, in my opinion, the best villain on the English stage. Without any further apology for giving advice to the rising generation, I would recommend all actors if they have seen a part played beautifully, and if it falls to their lot afterwards to play that part, I say I would counsel them to avoid trying to be original, unless they have very, very good and sufficient reason. In fact, I would go a step further and tell them to copy the other man to the best of their ability. If the actor who does this has a personality and a power of his own, such attributes will not be stifled, but will break through in spite of himself and enrich the performance. If he is lacking these qualities, then his performance will be so much better for having borrowed from the man who has them.

The leading man in "A Woman's Revenge" was Henry Neville, a sterling, dashing actor of the old school — the best of the old school. I remember his asking me once why I hurried a certain speech in a way that was inconsistent with the rest of my performance; I told him that I found those particular lines so stupid and badly written that I was ashamed every night when I came to them and that I tried to get them over as quickly as I could.

He said, "My boy, never do that. Whenever you have a speech to deliver that is particularly awful, always give it out as though you considered it the finest piece of literature that was ever written and the public will accept it."

This was valuable advice. An audience has instinct very like an animal. Let them see you are afraid and they are likely to turn and snap at you; face them boldly and they will eat out of your hand. I say this with reservations: I do not mean that they will be deceived by the boldness of ignorance, or that they will necessarily resent the nervousness that comes to you through a realization of your responsibilities.

From this time forward I was spared those hopeless intervals of inactivity. I had very little trouble in getting work. I don't wish to convey the impression that I was in the least sought after. I have always regarded with envy those actors who are continually finding themselves in the position of having to refuse innumerable "offers." Such keen competition has never been exerted in my favor. I have seldom caught anything worth having that hasn't required a certain amount of effort to land. My engagement following "A Woman's Revenge" was one of the very few exceptions.

I have mentioned that Nellie Farren was the mother of my friend Joseph. She had been the star of the Gaiety Theatre during the days of John Hollingshead's management, when Terry, and Royce and Kate Vaughan were all members of that same historic company. When Hollingshead passed on and George Edwardes took over the reins, Nellie Farren still remained the backbone of the Gaiety with Fred Leslie as her chief support. But Fred Leslie died (I think he was under forty) and Nellie Farren was stricken with an illness from which she never recovered, and there being no one to fill their places the character of the entertainment was considerably if not radically changed. At the time of which I now speak "The Gaiety Girl" had scored a tremendous success and was being played both in London and the provinces. I had no sooner finished my tour of "A Woman's Revenge" than Joseph excitedly announced that he had just heard that Eric Lewis' part in "The Gaiety Girl" touring company was going to be vacant and "George, why shouldn't you have a shot at it?"

Eric Lewis' part was that of an old Judge called Sir Lewis Grey who not only sang, but did a certain amount of dancing. I had never sung a note since I

AS SIR LEWIS GREY IN "THE GAIETY GIRL"

used to be lifted up on a chair to sing "The Friar of Orders Grey" to long-suffering aunts and uncles, and I had never been able to dance without feeling sick.

I said, "But he has to sing — and dance."

"Never mind," said my fellow veteran of the Theatre Royal, "you'll be all right. You can sing quite well enough for that." (He had never heard me.) "I'll get Eric to go through the music with you and I'll teach you the steps. George Mudie is playing it on tour, but he's leaving. You can sing quite as well as he can. I'll get Mother to give you a letter to George Edwardes."

I was staggered and unnerved at the thought of playing in Musical Comedy; such an idea would never in my wildest dreams have come into my head. So I at once went to talk it over with Florence Montgomery, thinking that she, being a sympathetic soul, would also be shocked and unnerved. But she wasn't in the least.

She said, "Certainly you must do it. I'll teach you the music. You can sing all right. (She had never heard me.) Get your letter from Miss Farren and go and see George Edwardes. You're bound to get it. And ask seven pounds a week."

"How much?" I gasped.

"Seven pounds. You'll get it all right."

Florence was always an optimist. I had never got more than three pounds ten at this time, even for parts that I could play, and to jump to seven pounds for something that I was utterly unsuited for seemed to me to be flying in the face of Fate. But I got my letter from Miss Farren and found myself trembling in the presence of George Edwardes.

He was a busy man, interested in various London productions, and he took very little concern in his provincial companies. He read the letter, looked me up and down, glanced again at the letter, said, "She says you're the very man." (I made a quick mental calculation of how many different kinds of parts I had applied for concerning which my misguided friends had applied that same term of recommendation.) "So I suppose you are. How much money do you want?"

"S-seven pounds," I stuttered.

"All right, sign your contract and see Sydney Elliston. Good-by." And I found myself stumbling down the narrow staircase that led from his office at the Gaiety.

The thought uppermost in my mind was, "He never asked me whether I could sing." If he had I don't know what I should have done. I am not sure that I could have lied about it. I know, if I had, that I couldn't have done it convincingly. But here I was, flung into the maelstrom of Musical Comedy, without ever having done anything to deserve such a fate. I rushed back to Flo: she congratulated me, and I felt like a criminal. And then they all started to work on me. Joseph, who was very nimble on his feet, and had inherited from his mother the very soul of burlesque, jumped and leaped about in an effort to inspire me with the spirit of Terpsichore. Flo labored with me at the piano while I sang with her and at her and away from her, and she never once gave up in despair. Eric Lewis told me everything he knew about the part, and Sydney Elliston regarded me as a living mystery.

Sydney Elliston was the permanent stage manager for George Edwardes. He knew every song and every dance and every bit of business that had ever been done in any of the George Edwardes' productions, and he could do them all. So when it became necessary to rehearse any one who was to join a touring company, he could go through all the parts with them in London and then send them away ready to appear with the company on the road. And I knew he was wondering all the time why in Heaven's name I had been chosen. I remember that after we had rehearsed together for some days, he suddenly stopped and looked at me curiously and said, "Have you signed your contract?"

I said, "Yes."

He sighed and went on with the rehearsal. The Gaiety Theatre appeared to be run on a very lavish scale and nobody ever seemed to be in a hurry about anything. After my rehearsals had been going on in this way for about a fortnight I asked Elliston how long this was to continue and when I was to go. I said that I felt we had now come to a point when these rehearsals were not doing me any more good. He raised his eyebrows and agreed with me. He said, "You had better see the Guv'nor" — George Edwardes was always called "the Guv'nor" at the Gaiety. So after a few hours of waiting I managed to get admitted to the Guv'nor's office. He hadn't the remotest idea who I was or what I was talking about, having entirely forgotten the whole incident of my engagement. After some difficulty I made him understand.

His brow cleared and he said pleasantly, "Oh yes, I remember; you were going to take George Mudie's place on tour. Well, that's all settled now; George Mudie is going to continue. He isn't leaving."

For the moment I couldn't think of anything more definite to say than "Oh!"

"No," said the Guv'nor, "he was going, but I'm giving him a bit more money and now he's stopping. So you won't be needed."

"But," I said, "I've been rehearsing the part for the past two weeks — here, on the Gaiety stage."

"Yes, I ought to have told Elliston," said the Guv'nor, "but it was only settled a few days ago. But everything's all right now, so of course we sha'n't want you."

I now became angry and very firm. Why shouldn't I be? He didn't know whether I could sing or not! For anything he knew, I might have a magnificent voice. So I could speak sharply to him. I said, "Look here, Mr. Edwardes, I'm not a novice doing this thing for fun. I'm an actor. I get my living on the stage. I've signed a contract with you and I've been rehearsing for a fortnight."

Mr. Edwardes ran his hand wearily over his brow and said in a calm voice, "My boy, what is it you want to do?"

I said heatedly, "I want to join the company of 'The Gaiety Girl' now playing at Newcastle, and I want to play the part I'm engaged for — Sir Lewis Grey."

"Well, my boy," said Mr. Edwardes, getting up from his chair and leading me by the arm gently but firmly to the door, "go and do it; but for Heaven's sake don't worry me about it."

So I went to Newcastle. I arrived at night during the performance and went in search of the manager of the company. I found him in front of the house, a pleasant man named Lockwood. I said, "My name's Arliss."

He said, "Yes," and waited.

I said, "I have come down to play Sir Lewis Grey."

He evidently thought I had been drinking for he laughed merrily and obviously considered the matter closed. I decided that if this was the way they did business in musical comedy it was not at all the way I conducted my affairs when I was manager of a "High-class Melodrama", and that I wasn't going to put up with it. So I told him the whole story, and his eyes opened wider and wider with surprise as he assured me that nobody there had ever heard anything about any change in the company.

I said, "Well, here I am."

Lockwood was most sympathetic; he said, "Of course, my boy, you're all right. It's not your fault. You'll be paid, but you'll just be paid for walking about until we get this matter settled."

I told him that I had no intention of walking about.

I had been engaged to play the part in this company and I was going to play it. I knew that Mudie had a three years' contract with Edwardes so that I was not doing him out of his job. I proposed that I should open next Monday.

Well, I opened on the Monday and George Mudie went to London. The part was a purely artificial musical-comedy Judge and I daresay I gave a sound artificial performance, as far as the acting was concerned, but my vocal efforts left much to be desired. My singing was always bad, but that first night it was terrible. I had a wonderful entrance preceded by a chorus of some thirty men and girls; they had to bow me to the centre of the stage, where I at once executed a most difficult recitative which was in its turn followed by the magnificent chorus. I use the word executed advisedly. I wabbled all over the scale without ever hitting the right note. The most horrible thing about it was that my ear is really very good. I knew exactly the awful thing I was doing, but I couldn't help it. My nerve had deserted me. I had the right note in my head, but it wouldn't come out.

The chorus turned pale under their make-up: they didn't laugh — the moment was far too awful for that — they just paled and prayed, "Oh, God, make him finish on the right note for us at the end." The conductor pounded away at his baton with Herculean strength, as conductors do when they are trying to bring an erring singer back to the path of rectitude. I could faintly see his violent movements; he appeared to me to be digging my grave in the orchestra pit, and I am sure he devoutly wished he had been. But wonder of wonders, I finished on the right note, and the chorus came in with oh, such a reassuring swing! They seemed to me to be trying to convey to the audience, "It's all right now. Don't go. The worst is over." But it wasn't. I had three verses of a song to sing after that, the memory of which I prefer to black out. I was always able to conceal my nervousness from the audience, more or less, so the people in front on this occasion thought I was merely a fatuous ass who imagined he was a vocalist. After the first night I wasn't so bad but I was never too good.

The chorus became my stanch supporters; they regarded me as their special responsibility and they always tried to cover up my deficiencies. Although I was afterwards in plays with music this was my first and last experience of a large musical-comedy chorus. I found them earnest workers, orderly, and admirable in many ways. If all the chorus girls behave as well as these "Gaiety Girls" they are surely as a class grossly slandered. I don't know what their morals were, but if there is a distinction between virtue and respectability, as applied to chorus girls (and I hope there is), these girls were at any rate highly respectable.

By a merciful dispensation of Providence, George Edwardes never paid a visit to this company during my time, and so I kept the engagement until the end of the tour. What would have happened if he had seen me I don't know. I looked very smart, so perhaps he might have kept me. They used to say of the

"Guv'nor" that the first consideration with him was what you looked like — your clothes: that he would visit his companies on tour and say to his manager, "Get rid of that man; he can't act; look at his trousers." Whether this was true I don't know, but that was his reputation. It is a fact that he furnished every stitch of clothing that was worn on the stage, including modern dress of all male principals down to their collars and ties and shirts; their hats and shoes and even their socks. Although I met with nothing but kindness in this company, I am bound to say I always felt a little out of my element, and so it was with considerable relief that following this I found myself back in the legitimate and once more under the management of Fred Latham.

Mrs. Patrick Campbell had but recently finished her spectacular triumph as Paula in "The Second Mrs. Tanqueray" and was now playing in Pinero's next play, "The Notorious Mrs. Ebbsmith." Fred Latham had secured the provincial rights of this play and was sending it on tour, headed by his wife, Cynthia Brooke. He offered me the part of the Duke of St. Olpherts then being played by John Hare (afterwards Sir John Hare) at the Garrick Theatre, London. This was a decided step forward for me; it was a most important part and of course I accepted it without hesitation. I could not know then that the Duke of St. Olpherts and Cayley Drummle (in "The Second Mrs. Tanqueray") were to be the two parts responsible for my very warm welcome some years afterwards by American audiences.

Pinero was at the height of his popularity. Many of his best plays were yet to be written ("His House in Order", "Mid-channel", "The Thunderbolt") but "The Second Mrs. Tanqueray" had placed him at once in the position of leader of all British dramatists. As a writer of parts for women he was unrivalled, but he also wrote extraordinarily good men's parts. The Duke of St. Olpherts is perhaps my favorite character. It may not be the best part I have played, but it is the one that most strongly appeals to me, and which seems to me to fit me without any tailoring. Pinero's characters are always consistent; they maintain their individuality from beginning to end, which accounts in a large measure for the personal successes scored by so many actors in Pinero plays.

As soon as I had settled with Fred Latham to play the Duke I went to the Garrick Theatre to see Hare's performance. In my opinion he was superb. I copied everything he did. I should have been very foolish if I hadn't. Whatever originality I displayed in my performance was by accident rather than design. It occurs to me that this is the last time that I ever had the opportunity of borrowing from another actor; since then I have always played in revivals that I have never seen or else parts of which I have given the original performance. There is one exception and that is old Heythorp in "Old English." But I had already studied and formed my own idea of this part before its production in London and when I saw Norman McKinnel's splendid performance, I realized that I had conceived the part from such a different angle that it would be physically impossible for me to follow his conception.

On second thoughts I cannot give Sir John Hare the credit for all that might have been good in my performance of the Duke of St. Olpherts: a certain part is due to a dream that I had at a critical moment. I regard dreams generally as useless and meaningless. I have seldom had first-hand information of a dream that has been of any real value to any one. The exception that comes to my mind is that of "The Green Goddess." William Archer told me that he dreamt the story of the play almost exactly as he wrote it. That was a useful and most lucrative dream. And then there was mine. Considering how serviceable my dream was to me I can't see why Nature, or whatever it is that is responsible for dreams, couldn't have repeated the experiment. During a considerable number of years I have given it ample opportunity to practise on me; for I not only go to bed at a reasonable hour, but when I am playing I always take an afternoon nap. As there apparently have to be such things as dreams, it seems to me that in my case at least a great many favorable chances have been lost. Still I am very grateful for this one dream.

We had been rehearsing "The Notorious Mrs. Ebbsmith" for about two weeks. I was most anxious to make a success in it because I knew that if I was ever going to be any good at all, this was the kind of part in which I ought to show some promise. So I had worked very hard. But the nearer we came to the opening night, the farther I seemed to get away from the part; the character seemed to be escaping me. In the early rehearsals I had done well; but now I was losing my grip. I was very unhappy about it but I didn't know what was the matter; the more I tried the worse I got. After the dress rehearsal which was two nights before we opened, Latham came to me and said, "What's gone wrong with your performance? You've lost all your humor and your manner."

Of course that didn't help me. Well, that night when I was asleep, a lady appeared to me. She didn't seem to be either an angel or a fairy, but she was in some sort of robe and she carried something that was neither a staff nor a wand; it appeared to be a sort of cane. And she said in a very matter-of-fact way, "I'll tell you what's the matter with you, you're handling the part in the wrong way. You're holding it like this," and she took the cane firmly in her hand and shook it vigorously. "You should be holding it like this." And she took the end of the cane between her thumb and her middle finger and allowed it to swing easily of its own volition backwards and forwards like a pendulum.

I didn't wait to dream any more; as far as I can remember I didn't even thank the lady. I woke up at once and I knew that I had the solution of my difficulty. I had been trying too hard: I had been forcing the character before me, so to speak, instead of allowing it to swing easily with me. Ever since then, whenever I catch myself over-accentuating a character, I remember the lady of my dream, and at once I mentally take the character between my finger and thumb and let it swing. The immediate result of that nocturnal visitation was to give Fred Latham a most welcome surprise when he found that all the ease of manner which he had missed at the dress rehearsal was miraculously restored at the first performance.

IX

"WEST END" AT LAST

It was during this tour that I wrote a farce which I called "There and Back." It was never a spectacular success and the only remarkable thing about it was that it was accepted by the first manager to whom I read it and that it ran in some form or another for nearly fifteen years almost without a break. While on this tour I lived with my friend H. A. Saintsbury, who was playing the part of Lucas Cleeve, originally played by Forbes-Robertson in London (and I think one of his most artistic creations). Saintsbury was a man who was always writing plays. It was no uncommon thing for him to finish one in three weeks. I decided that I would endeavor to profit by this good example, so I wrote a one-act farce which I called "Widows' Weeds." Having finished it, I read it to Saintsbury. He was very encouraging and said, "You've really written the last act of a three-act play. Why don't you tack a couple of acts to it and make it into a full-length piece?" He gave me some valuable hints as to how he would set about this with the result that I did it, and the "Ebbsmith" Company played it for me for copyright purposes at the Theatre Royal, Birmingham. I eventually read it to Frank Curzon and he took up the English rights. He was unable to produce it for some years, but he paid me a sum annually in order to hold the right to production.

Just when I had grown to regard this payment as a settled annual income he decided to produce it.

Charles Hawtrey and Arthur Williams played the leading parts. Hawtrey's part was afterwards taken up by Robert Loraine. The Shuberts bought it for America and it was produced at the old Princess Theatre with Charles E. Evans and Charles Hopper as the stars. My wife played in this production and scored a decided success. Later it became a musical play under the title of "I Loved a Lassie", and later it returned to its original form of a one-act farce and was toured for many years by Charles E. Evans and his wife Helena Phillips under the name of "It's Up to You, William." In this form it was still running in England when the Great War broke out and since then it has been done only spasmodically. It will probably be played many times in the future; for the central idea is funny and capable of being written up every ten years or so.

(Advice to mature actors about to write their Recollections:

> Do not attempt to be modest. If you are by nature bashful or shy, try to get over it or else lay aside your pen. Referring to the Oxford Dictionary, which I always use to find out how to spell "reminiscences" and to discover which is "principle" and which is "principal", I read Egotism: "Too frequent use of 'I' and 'Me'; practice of telling about yourself."
>
> Now that is the very essence of the contract; to talk about yourself is what your publisher asked

you to do when he first approached you; you agreed to do it, so don't be half-hearted about it. If you are going to be reserved, then the only thing to be done is to get some one else to write the story of your life for you — some admirer. But if you do this, I warn you, he will lay it on so thick that he will make you look far more ridiculous than if you did it yourself. The Oxford Dictionary, under the head of "egotism" continues: "Self-conceit, Selfishness." Don't let that deter you. For whatever you do, there will always be the people who will say, "Did you ever read such a conceited book in your life?" And it is just possible that the more you exert your effort towards modesty, the more conceited you will appear.)

It might be supposed that with the experience which I now had and the not inconsiderable success that I had made as the Duke in "The Notorious Mrs. Ebbsmith", visiting all the important provincial theatres, I should have had no great difficulty in getting at any rate a small part in a West End production. But as a matter of fact I seemed to be as far from my goal as ever. I don't know how much initiative the London manager has to-day, but in those days it seems to me that when he was casting a play he never looked beyond the four-mile radius. I don't think a manager would even have taken a cab and driven to a suburban theatre in order to see or discover new talent. The man who broke into the West End did it either through his own tremendous exertions or

else through the efforts of some "friend at Court."
A West End manager never knew anything about an
actor until he was thrown into his lap. And so for
three or four years after this I still continued to travel
through and through the country in all kinds of
plays, skirting the West End area, but never getting in.

And at the end of each tour I would walk up and
down the Strand, stopping sometimes and reading
the casts outside the theatres, long casts very often,
biting my lips and making a mighty effort to keep
back the lump in my throat as I asked myself, "What
is the matter with me that I'm not taken in?" I had
no difficulty now in securing provincial engagements,
but I had been born and bred in London, and I knew
that I had not "arrived" until I played in the West
End. My chief consolation during this period was
that I was able, in several instances, to find a place for
Florence Montgomery in the same company with
myself. She had developed into a very charming
actress and her advice and companionship were of
great value to me.

Following "Ebbsmith" I played in the provincial
company of the Drury Lane drama, "The Derby
Winner." Then I went under the management of
Alexander Loftus. With Loftus I appeared in several
plays with songs and dances. I had learnt by this
time that it was not at all essential to know anything
about music in order to be in a musical play. With a
good part and plenty of assurance one could always
worry through. I do not wish to convey the impression that my work at this time was in any way irk-

THE DUKE OF ST. OLPHERTS
IN "THE NOTORIOUS MRS. EBBSMITH"
One of Sir Arthur Pinero's most notable plays

some to me. I enjoyed every minute of it and it was only when I stopped to brood over the fact that I had had more than my share of provincial apprenticeship that I became discouraged. My association with Alexander Loftus was exceedingly pleasant and I have never regretted it.

Loftus was one of those men who never had any money, but could always get it. That type of man seems to be active at all times in the theatrical world. How he does it has always been a mystery to me. I asked one man to enlighten me as to his method of procedure and all he told me was that he could whistle money off the trees. The wilder the scheme — the more obviously doomed to failure — the easier the money seems to come. I was never able to get any, except the sixty-five pounds which I have already accounted for. I once tried to get "backing" for a plan I had worked out to establish a possible National Theatre in America, but I failed hopelessly. Perhaps I may speak of that later. To do my friend Loftus justice his schemes were always sane, and he often returned a profit to his investors.

At last my chance came. I heard through an agent that a new play from America was to be produced at the Vaudeville Theatre by A. and S. Gatti in conjunction with Charles Frohman, in which there was a small part which might suit me. At this time Sir Augustus Harris had been dead some years and Fred Latham had severed his connection with Drury Lane and had become the general manager for the Gattis. So I hurried over to Latham's office and told him what

I'd heard. He shook his head very decisively and said I wasn't a bit like it. I told him that I could play any part. He said he knew I could — any part but this. He said this had to be a big man — large all over; it had to be done just the same as it was done in America; that Frohman had sent over a producer and that he knew exactly what he wanted. For the sake of our earlier association he would like to do something for me but this part was out of the question. He said he was seeing Frohman's producer next morning and everything would then be finally settled and so there would be no chance for me. He smiled at me and waved me warmly out of the office.

Whether my lady friend with the wand was hovering about me that night I cannot say. I have never been very pushing and in a general way I am the kind of person who takes "No" for an answer. But the next morning, contrary to my nature, I decided that I would go to Latham's office again on the off chance of seeing Frohman's representative myself. My old friend Herbert Budd was now Latham's assistant. I arrived at the office and told him what I had come for. He said that Latham was at that moment in conference with Mr. Frohman's representative. He said, "I'll take you right in."

(Advice to young actors:

Always keep your friends.)

Latham was obviously surprised at my sudden entrance, but he didn't say a word to me; he looked at me curiously and then said to Herbert Budd, "What's the game, Herbert?" as Budd went out.

I said to Mr. Frohman's representative, "My name's Arliss. There's a part going in 'On and Off' that I think I can play."

Latham kept quiet; I knew I couldn't count on his help, but I also felt sure that he wouldn't oppose me if the other man thought I was possible.

"What part?" said the producer. "Brumaire," said I.

He smiled broadly and shook his head. "You're nothing like it."

"Why?" I asked rather vaguely.

"He must be a big man," said he.

"Why — what's he do?" I pushed.

The American was kindly and told me in a few words. Latham sat like a Sphinx.

I said, "Well, if that's all he does, why does he have to be big?"

"He's always been played by a big man in America," said the American.

"But America's a bigger country," I tried being comic.

"No, sorry," said he. "You won't do."

I have always admired Fred Latham's voice; it is rather rich and well-modulated; I have often thought it a pity that so good a voice should be lost to the stage. But it has never sounded so musical to me as it did at this moment when he suddenly said to Frohman's representative, "You don't know what you're talking about. Give him the part. He can play it on his head." I was amazed at this sudden and unaccountable change of front since the day before.

"But he's not the type," said the producer.

175

"Type be damned," said Latham. "He's the very man."

It seemed to me that whenever my friends were recommending me for a part for which I was eminently unsuited they always said I was "the very man." The battle now shifted entirely from my shoulders to those of the two managers. The more the American resisted the harder Latham insisted, and by degrees he waxed so enthusiastic about me that I began to think that whoever got me had a bargain. I found myself rather in the position of Joe Weber, when in the old days of Weber and Fields, Sam Bernard and Lew Fields made a wager as to who could shake Joe Weber the harder and little Weber mildly lent himself to the experiment.

No one can deny that Fred Latham has a pugnacious side to his character which is sometimes valuable in argument. At any rate in this instance he won, and I signed my contract and got the part. I afterwards asked Latham why he did it. He said he didn't know — he just felt like it.

Well, I was now at last within the charmed circle of the West End, and having once got in I never went out again until I walked out of my own accord. I played the part in "On and Off" during the entire London run. Of course it didn't really need a big man. All that was necessary was a decent character actor.

These restrictions so often imposed by authors and managers are seldom necessary. There are parts for which certain physical developments are practically essential and there are parts that absolutely demand a

special type of man. I am inclined to defend the
manager who insists on types, although fundamen-
tally I believe him to be wrong. But there is something to be said on his side. There are some parts
that may be considerably enriched by being played
by a man of a distinct type. In these instances a
mediocre actor of the required model may easily be
mistaken by an audience for a good actor; and on the
other hand the really good actor who is miscast may
be regarded by an audience as mediocre. But it is my
opinion that given six distinct parts in six different
plays, each part of varying type, if, on the one hand,
all these parts were played by one sound, versatile
character actor, and on the other, by six separate
actors, each chosen for his type, I say it is my opinion
that were it possible to make a mathematical calculation of the total percentage of excellence on the six
performances, the result would be found in favor of
the one sound, versatile character actor. My grounds
for defence of the manager is that it is easier to find
the six type actors than the one versatile character
actor. So long as plays continue to run two or three
years, just so long shall we continue to condemn
actors to remain types. But if ever repertory should
become fashionable, then the range of all actors must
surely expand, and I believe there would develop some
great leaders — so badly needed.

I was now in the West End at last, and I was very
happy! I remained at the Vaudeville Theatre some
two years. It seemed that I should have little difficulty in remaining in London. This security was due

to my backbone of experience. I found that I had not spent nearly ten years in the provinces for nothing. As Latham had said, I could play these small parts "on my head"; I had a considerable advantage over most of those actors who, by influence or by chance, had started their career in the West End of London and who at the end of ten years had not played more than a score of parts at most.

Having settled down in the Vaudeville Theatre, my mind turned pleasantly, but not at all lightly, to thoughts of marriage. As I have said I was never of an adventurous spirit, and neither was Flo. It was a long time since that day at Margate when Providence rewarded us for having shown sufficient intelligence to come in out of the rain — almost at the same moment. We had frequently agreed since then that love in a cottage would be exceedingly pleasant, and all that we could desire, but that love in theatrical lodgings was not to be trusted. I had seen so much of poverty in my years on tour, of poorly paid actors dragging their wives — and sometimes their babies — round the country, poorly dressed and under-nourished, men and women who had taken the chance and regretted it ever since, that I had come to the conclusion that Providence was all very fine on occasion but that it was not above temptation. I had a great respect for Love and I did not intend to subject it to the indignity of having to fly out of the window. If it had to go, I desired that it should be able to go respectably out of the front door, and if in great haste, call a cab.

MRS. GEORGE ARLISS

The girl with the nice arms

We had waited, faithful, but single. But to wait longer, we thought, was to be overcautious. So I began to go through those preliminary proceedings of interviewing clergymen and acquainting myself with the marriage service and such details as I suppose make all men feel appropriately ridiculous. Flo said she wanted me to be married in a brown suit and brown boots. I asked her why, and she said that was what I wore when I first arrived at Margate. (This was how I knew she'd noticed it.) I commended her eye for beauty, but told her it couldn't be done — not by a West End actor. I told her that if I attempted any such thing Joseph, who was to be my best man and who was nothing if not dressy, would be carried out of the church in convulsions with the ring in his waistcoat pocket, and then there could be no wedding at all. So in the end she had a lovely new dress and I had a lovely new suit, and Joseph looked a picture in his gray trousers and his tail coat with a white flower in it, and we were married in the prettiest church on the prettiest day that ever was seen. The church was Harrow Weald and the day was September 16, 1899. I was acting at the Vaudeville at the time and I have been acting ever since, so our honeymoon is still to come. We have not yet decided where we will go. We sometimes think of taking a voyage round the world. I have been told there is nothing like travel to finish off your education. I am not fond of traveling. When I want to be finished off, we shall probably take it.

My long engagement at the Vaudeville Theatre was

exceedingly pleasant. Although I made no particular success, I knew that I should never have to be a "provincial actor" any more. Then came my momentous association with Mrs. Patrick Campbell, momentous because it resulted in my coming to America. Mrs. Campbell was an exceedingly popular star and had now become an Actor-Manager, having leased the Royalty Theatre for, I believe, a term of years. At this time she was about to produce "The Fantastics", a very charming translation by Constance Fletcher of Rostand's "Les Romanesques." Her stage manager was Ian Robertson, a brother of Forbes-Robertson and of Norman Forbes.

All the Robertsons seem to me to have a curious way of giving you to understand that they really don't know anything about theatres, or what's going on in them, or the people who are acting in them, while in reality they know all about them. Ian wrote and asked me to see him about a part that might suit me. I called at the Royalty and he received me very pleasantly and said, "Oh, yes, Mr. — er — Arliss (all the Robertsons feel for names) — sit down, won't you? — Well — er — somebody told me that you'd been doing some quite good work at the Vaudeville; of course it seems perfectly ridiculous but I don't know a bit what you've been doing at the — er — er Vaudeville, in fact, I've never been to the damn — er — theatre since those two old fellers, you know, James and What's-his-name, played 'Our Boys' donkeys, years ago. Well, Mrs. Campbell is going to produce a play called 'The Fantastics.' It's from the French, you know, 'Les Romanesques', written by that old feller — at least as a matter of fact they tell me he's quite a young feller, who wrote that thing — er — 'Pelleas and Melisande.' No — that was that other feller, wasn't it — this is Rostand. Yes, Rostand, that's the feller. Well, somebody thought you might play one of the parts; there seem to be two old fathers in it who have scenes together about their son and daughter and all that sort of stuff. I really don't know much about the damn thing; as a matter of fact, it isn't really finished yet — I mean Miss Fechter's — Fletcher's — Constance Fletcher's version. But as far as I know, you would have to play a perfectly ridiculous part of some sort of an old man, but the point is, do you think you can do it?"

The upshot of the interview was that I told Ian I thought it would be better if he made further enquiries from the person who had suggested me to him. And we parted. I grew to like Ian exceedingly. I liked him for his interest in his work and I was always amused at his assumption of boredom at everything and everybody connected with it. After our interview he probably told Mrs. Campbell that I seemed to be a perfectly ridiculous feller who wouldn't say anything about what I had done or what I thought I might be able to do, but that he had no doubt I shouldn't be worse than anybody else.

Anyhow I was accepted and there followed the most interesting engagement I had yet had. I remember that my contract said, "for six performances, with full salary for all over." The custom of signing for seven performances, or for half-salaries for matinées, was just creeping in. The Saturday matinée was firmly established, but as far as I remember the midweek matinée was quite unusual. The beginning of my association with Mrs. Campbell was a disappointment for me, because she had revived Sudermann's "Magda" as a stop-gap while "The Fantastics" was in preparation, and much to every one's surprise it caught on so tenaciously that it ran for some sixteen weeks instead of the three or four that had been anticipated.

As this was quite unexpected and I was on the salary list all the time, I consented to understudy the part of Schwartz, then being played by that fine old actor, James Fernandez. This was my first and last experience of understudying. I afterwards played the part on a preliminary tour of the big towns in England, which Mrs. Campbell made before sailing for America. I am very proud to have had this opportunity of playing Schwartz to her Magda, for I consider her performance in that play one of the most magnificent I have ever seen.

X

OFF TO AMERICA

DURING my active association with Mrs. Patrick Campbell, I found her a most ardent worker. In spite of the many social functions with which her name has been associated, she seemed to have no real interest outside the theatre. She was always planning great schemes for new productions and special matinées, many of which she carried through with success. A great deal has been said about her sharp tongue. I was closely associated with her for more than two years and I never knew her to say anything with *malice prepense*. She had a quick brain and perhaps a too keen sense of humor. If a neat repartee came to her mind she could not prevent it from tripping on to her tongue, even if it carried with it an undesirable sting. She was always sorry, however, the moment she knew she had given pain and was the first to apologize — or to make extravagant presents to her victim. But she would do it all over again the next day. The story of her reply to George Alexander when she was playing Mrs. Tanqueray and he was playing her husband at the St. James' Theatre must have been told many times. But I'll tell it again. George Alexander, of whose ability as an actor Mrs. Campbell had no great opinion, was at that time her manager; something happened during the performance that angered him and amused her. At the end of the act he sent a message, with his compliments, "Would

Mrs. Campbell kindly refrain from laughing at him on the stage." Mrs. Campbell immediately sent her compliments to Mr. Alexander with the reply that "she never laughed at him on the stage; she always waited until she got home." I submit that any one who had the wit to think of this retort at the moment would find it very difficult to withhold it. In the theatre she never assumed majestic or "managerial" airs, but she liked to have her own way and she never gave up without a prolonged struggle.

I remember a long argument we had on the subject of make-up. She arrived at rehearsal one morning with the startling news that she had observed that all healthy men in real life had blue chins, and she made the request that from now on all the gentlemen in her company should make up with blue chins. We pointed out to her that we were playing men of ultra smart society, and that if we did as she suggested the effect would be what is known amongst actors as "a dirty shave." She said that was nonsense. It would just look manly. "All you men coming on every night with pink chins look like little girls! It throws the whole play out of perspective. Makes me feel as though I were placed amongst you as a chaperone." So that night we all came on with blue chins. I never heard exactly what happened, but I believe her manager came round from the front of the house and told her she appeared to be surrounded by burglars and that she had turned a drawing-room comedy into a crook play. Anyhow, we were told we needn't do it any more.

My first performance with Mrs. Campbell was in
an unimportant one-act play which she put up as a
"stunt" during the run of "Magda" called "Mrs.
Jordan." Then came the long-delayed "The Fantastics" in which I played one of the two fathers. Gerald Du Maurier played Strephonal (I think it was
Gerald who first suggested me to Ian Robertson) and
Mrs. Campbell played a slim young man in knee
breeches, looked a picture and acted charmingly. It
is a delightful little play, but too short to be a commercial possibility. I should very much like to see
it played again. I remember that just before the first
performance Mrs. Campbell surprised me by telling
me that she loved a first night. I have never known
any other actor who approached a first night with
pleasurable excitement. Personally I could pick out
several tortures designed by the Spanish Inquisition
to which I would rather be subjected.

During this season we did a number of interesting
plays. There was a one-act play by Max Beerbohm
called "The Happy Hypocrite" in which I played
the Vendor of Masks — an effective bit. "Max"
used to come sometimes to rehearsal. I don't think
he ever said anything, but he wrote these directions
to the actors which were passed to us with the parts.

VAGUE HINTS FROM THE AUTHOR TO THE COMPANY

I hope the artists who are to honour me by inter-
preting my little play will acquit me of any desire
to teach them their business if I make a few sugges-

185

tions about the performance. The little play is not quite like anything else that has been done on the stage — not (I think) quite so good as anything that I have seen done on the stage — and so my suggestions are necessary, in order to make sure that the actors and actresses may know what the author has been driving at. In other words I want to tell them what to do. How they are to do it I don't profess to know. That is *their* business, not mine.

"The Happy Hypocrite" is a fantastic allegory, a fable with a moral. The fable aspires to have been written prettily and charmingly. The interpreters ought, therefore, to remember that the first requisite is that they should act as prettily and charmingly as possible. Let them move and pose as gracefully and speak with as much unction, as they can. They need not persuade the audience that they are real people swayed by real emotions. They are nothing of the kind. They never could exist in real life. They must justify their un-reality by being altogether delightful. Those of them who find that they have anything beautiful to say must say it beautifully. And those who do not find, in what they have to say, anything they can persuade themselves to think beautiful, must be all the more careful to say it beautifully, so as to trick the audience into the belief that I have succeeded in my endeavour to conform with beauty. Without a general effect of beauty, the play will be quite a deadly little affair. So let the actors and actresses concern themselves primarily with "style" in their acting. Sincerity may go hang.

Also, let the "style" be as fantastic as it can be. Let there be no fear of exaggerating the characters and emotions which I have brought into the play. Let there be a great deal of over-acting. Let Lord George Hell be a monster to the eyes, let Jenny Mere

be such a paragon of childish innocence as never was
seen before, let Le Gambogi suggest a greater lack of
principle than ever was displayed by anyone. And
so forth. Let everyone be, in fact, a caricature. Yet
always a caricature done with a sense of beauty, not
less than with a sense of humour.

As I have suggested, the characters in this play
never could exist in real life. They are caricatures.
But they are caricatures with a date to them and a
locality. The date is 1815 A.D., the place London.
Therefore, the actors and actresses ought to reproduce,
in caricature, the manners of the Regency. These
manners were not the mincing manners of the Eighteenth Century. They were florid, rather; florid and
full blooded and high-spirited — the manners of the
Tom and Jerry period. Lord George Hell, Count
Hesseldorf and Captain FitzClarence must behave in
an elaborately full chested manner. La Gambogi
must keep feminine pace with them. The Hawker of
Masks may be uninfluenced by the fashionable manners of the period. He is but a comic rustic, with a
dash of mystery. Jenny Mere, also, of course, is a
creature apart. All she has to do is to be girlish.

As to my notion of what the various characters
ought to look like.

La Gambogi ought to have a very blonde wig, with
dancing ringlets. It ought to be obviously a wig.
She ought, also, to be obviously rouged. She ought
also, to be fat and to speak with a more or less
Italian accent. Age: about 40.

Jenny Mere ought to have light brown hair, and
no figure. Age: 17.

The Hawker of Masks ought to have a red wig —
a small uncurled wig of an inferior kind. Age: about
50.

The other three men ought to wear the regular wigs

of the late Georgian period — brown wigs with elaborate masses of curls, and without any pretence to an appearance of growing hair.

Count Hesseldorf ought to have whiskers, a moustache, and a tuft on the chin. Age: about 30.

Lord George ought to have a bibulous and libidinous face — beetling brows, a loose mouth, a complexion of various crimsons and (if the actor wish to show himself a master in the art of make-up) bloodshot eyes. (I am, however, willing to waive the blood-shot eyes.) The saintly mask which he afterwards assumes should be a mask of a very smooth white face with very red lips, the eyelashes as definite as a doll's, the eyebrows drawn upwards like those of an ecclesiastical martyr. As sinner he ought to look about 45 years old. As saint, anything between 17 and 17½.

Any other hints that may be needed I shall be as delighted to give as will (perhaps) the actors and actresses to receive them. I trust that the hints I have given are clear and helpful, and I doubt it. At any rate, they are well meant.   MAX BEERBOHM

I have never seen Max Beerbohm since, but at that time he always seemed to me to be immaculately dressed and groomed, and looking as though he had just stepped out of a bandbox. With "The Happy Hypocrite" we played a "Society Drama" called "Mr. and Mrs. Daventry" written by another immaculately dressed author, Frank Harris. But whereas Max Beerbohm remains in my memory as looking very small and very clean-shaven, with very smooth and rather retiring hair, Frank Harris comes back to me as flamboyant with ample black curly hair and moustachios complete; the whole set in a massive fur-lined coat suggestive of wealth and the Continent.

Mrs. Campbell warned me that there was no part for me in "Mr. and Mrs. Daventry", but she afterwards suggested that rather than be left out of the cast I might like to play a small part of an Irish servant. I read it over and accepted it; I decided that it would at any rate be a good contrast to the part I was playing in "The Happy Hypocrite." I suppose my brogue had not matured since I played Irish parts with Auguste Creamer, for after the dress rehearsal Mr. Harris requested that I should make the part an English valet and give up my feeble attempt at an Irish accent. This I declined to do, and whatever nationality my accent suggested, so it remained until the end of the run. This part proved to be a surprise; it "stood out" and assumed an importance that was quite unexpected.

Every now and then we meet instances of a small part finding great favor with an audience, although during rehearsals it has been practically passed over by both author and producer and regarded by the actor as quite insignificant. In these cases the actor generally gets all the credit, it being conceded that such a result is due entirely to the artistry of the performer. As a rule this is not strictly true. It will generally be found to be open to argument as to whether this success is not at any rate partially due to the way the part is placed in the play; it may be its strong contrast to some other character that will throw it into prominence; or the part may break a too painful tension at the exact moment when relief is required; the very presence of the character on the stage may enhance a situation in some quite unexpected way. There is probably more credit due to the actor than to any one else, for he at least has made an effort, whereas when these surprises come, it will be found that the importance of the character has been entirely overlooked by the author and that the value which it brings to the situation or to the scene is the result of accident on his part and not of special constructive ability. The player of small parts generally gets either too much or too little praise. There are the small parts which we know in advance are good parts; the little bit of which we say "The actor who plays that will run away with the scene." Often when I have been in the audience I have heard people say of an actor who plays one of these showy bits, "In my opinion that is the best actor in the company," while a man with a "thankless part" who is an infinitely better actor, may pass unnoticed. There is a great deal in the old saying that "good parts make good actors."

My part in "Mr. and Mrs. Daventry" turned out to be one of these unexpectedly useful high lights; my scenes were mainly with Gerald Du Maurier and Mrs. Campbell. As soon as they saw the possibilities of the part they did everything they could to help it along. This desire amongst actors to help one another to success is the rule rather than the exception. I have seldom met the case of the jealous actor who tries

THE IRISH SERVANT IN "MR. AND
MRS. DAVENTRY"

*It was rumoured at one time that this play was written by the late
Oscar Wilde*

to "kill" the other man's scene. I don't say I have never met it, but such cases in my experience have been rare. Gerald and Mrs. Campbell were sometimes so anxious to give me an opportunity that they failed to keep strictly to the author's lines. It is dangerous to "fool" on the Royalty stage, because the theatre is so small and intimate that the audience can see every blink of an eyelid. I remember the late King Edward (then Prince of Wales) being vastly amused at something one night and stretching so far out of the box as he applauded that we felt he was coming clean over on to the stage.

"Mr. and Mrs. Daventry" was not a great success, so Mrs. Campbell decided to revive "The Notorious Mrs. Ebbsmith." As I have said, the original production of this play was made by John Hare, who played the Duke of St. Olpherts, the part I afterwards played on tour. Of course I was very anxious to play the part in this revival. Pinero had never seen me in it (I don't think Pinero ever goes to see his own plays) and Mrs. Campbell had seen me only in the parts I had played with her. But she believed in me and was anxious that I should have the chance.

(Advice to young actors:

 If you are with a good manager who believes in you, stick to him. You cannot expect the public to believe in you until you get good parts, and the manager is the only person who can give them to you. Having gained the confidence of your manager, think twice before you throw him over.)

Pinero probably felt that an actor of riper experience should have the part; possibly he thought that Sir John Hare might be persuaded to take it up again. At any rate Mrs. Campbell arranged for me to meet Pinero, although she didn't hold out much hope of his accepting me. If Mrs. Campbell wanted anything badly enough she generally got her own way. But I rather suspect that Sir Arthur Pinero always got his. So I didn't feel very sanguine about it.

As a matter of fact I expect Pinero had already made up his mind that he would take a chance on me, for although he is notoriously good at selecting a cast, he could hardly estimate at one interview the ability of an actor to play such a character as this. However, I played the part.

After this Mrs. Campbell revived "The Second Mrs. Tanqueray" in which I played Cayley Drummle. It was at this time that I began to give up the use of grease paint whenever it was possible to do so. And it was due to a remark of Sir Arthur Pinero at the dress rehearsal.

He called out from the stalls, "Arliss, what have you got all that stuff on your face for?"

"All what stuff?"

"All those lines."

"Why, to make myself look old enough for the part."

"Well, you don't need them. You look quite old enough without."

This startled me rather, because I was barely thirty. I had gained my experience amongst actors who were

192

sometimes thrifty with their aitches, but who never spared their grease paint. They would as soon have thought of going on the stage without their nether garments as to appear devoid of a generous covering of paint. But Pinero's remark set me thinking. I began to realize that electricity had so changed lighting conditions in the theatre that paint was very apt to look like paint and nothing else. I have no doubt many of my fellow actors had thought this all out before, but it happened that nobody had mentioned it to me. Since that time I have always tried to eliminate paint wherever possible. Frequently, in order to create some facial illusion, such as great fatness or excessive thinness, it is necessary to use a good deal of artificial coloring. I can see no way out of that, but I am afraid that with our present-day lighting the illusion in these instances is only suggested and not really created. Thank heaven for the imagination of the audience! It helps the actor out of many tight places.

It was during the revival of "The Second Mrs. Tanqueray" that Mrs. Campbell was approached by George C. Tyler, representing Liebler and Company of New York, with a view to making an American tour. I believe that George Tyler did not himself come to London; he sent Al Canby, a very able man who afterwards conducted the tour. As far as I remember, the negotiations between Mrs. Campbell and Liebler and Company were not settled with that promptness which we associate with American theatrical business transactions. They were continually on the point of being satisfactorily closed and then again on the point of being definitely broken off. At last the contract was signed with the "Star" and it only remained to choose the company. There seemed to be a strong probability that I should not go. I believe the Lieblers insisted on some well-known leading man. Herbert Waring was popular in London, and as he was available at this time they selected him. George Titheradge was already a member of Mrs. Campbell's company and was most valuable to her in "Pelleas and Melisande" and "Beyond Human Power" — both of which plays were to be in her repertoire. These two actors were to be "featured" and were both expensive engagements. It became necessary then to "cut down" on the other people. I was by this time getting a decent salary and as I was by no means anxious to go, I did not make any effort to lower my price. I was married and had my home in London; my prospects were on the whole very good, and I saw no reason why I should leave the country. The management decided that they could not pay what I asked, so I considered the matter off. Mrs. Campbell expressed considerable regret but apparently she had to keep within certain limits. She must have exercised more than her customary persistence however, for I was engaged at the last moment, although I was obviously regarded by the Liebler Company as of no real importance. The whole company was engaged for four months — to leave in December and return the following April. Having settled to go, my wife and I looked upon it as a thrilling adventure; we did not dream that it would be more than twenty years before I played another season in London. We sailed on the *Campania*, known then as the "Ocean Greyhound."

My most vivid recollection as the boat left the harbor is the figure of Gerald Du Maurier, waving us farewell. It was a great disappointment to me that he did not come with us. He had been a member of the company during my whole time and I had a strong affection for him. He declined to leave England and remained behind to become the most popular actor in London.

Of course I was very ill on the journey. I'm always very ill on the journey unless the weather is exceptionally fine. But this was my first trip and it was December, and I knew nothing about Atlantic liners and their ways. I believed the steward when he told me that it was a fine morning and everybody was up; I believed the "old sailor" when he told me that if I felt ill the great thing was to get up and go on deck. And I would struggle up and fall into a deck chair, and Flo, who is an exasperatingly good sailor, would tuck me up and when she thought I was asleep would slip off to the library to look at the papers for a few minutes. How can the good sailors know anything about the sufferings of their poor seasick brethren! They think they know, but they don't. If only they would realize that they can never know! If only they would not be sympathetic.

(Advice to young actors crossing the Atlantic for the first time:

Don't believe the steward when you're feeling very ill and he tells you that everybody else is up and feeling well. Don't believe anybody who tells you anything. Don't get up and sit in a deck chair. If you do, when you are at your worst a terrible thing will happen to you: you will develop a *sixth* sense. As you sit, pale, green and inert, with your eyes closed, you will sense certain things not given to other people to know; you may hear a footstep that is strange to you, and although it is in the far distance, far away the other end of the deck, you will know that the man to whom that footstep belongs is going to walk towards you, is going to stop in front of you, is going to place his hand on your shoulder and say, "Aren't you feeling well?" And, oh God, you know that when he does it you'll be sick. But there is no escape for you. It is pre-ordained, you know it is bound to happen. And it happens. You fall down again in your chair; you are on deck and you know you are too weak ever to go back again to your cabin. You close your addled eyes and presently your ear detects through the lashing of the waves and the cries of the children who are tearing round you and asking their parents or guardians or nurses if they may have an ice-cream, or another cup of soup — terrible children — your ear detects a strong determined footstep in the distance and your sixth sense murmurs, "He is coming to you. This is the man with a remedy. Brace yourself." And he comes; it is inevitable; he stops in front of you. He is evidently examining you closely. Your eyes are already closed so that prayer is easy, and you pray that he may not speak to you. But he does. He says, "You'll soon be all right." What an idiotic thing to say! How does he think you can soon be all right — feeling as you are and the boat pitching and tossing as it is. He knows you won't soon be all right, but he wants to be sympathetic. You don't answer and you don't open your eyes, and he doesn't go away. You wonder what he is waiting for; you begin to feel that you are something in a museum and that he is looking in the catalogue to see what you are. Presently he says, "Ever try a glass of champagne and a dash of absinthe?" You mentally shake your head, having expended all your physical energy by the act of arresting your stomach on its way up. After a long pause he goes away. How is it that you know he is coming back again, remedy in hand? It is your sixth sense! Why should you suppose that a perfect stranger should go to the expense of ordering a small bottle of champagne and a dash of absinthe just because he is sorry for you? But he does and — see where he comes again! — the glass is in his hand; he says, "Now, drink this, and you'll be all right in no time." He raises your head and puts the glass to your lips and you drink it. You know exactly what is going to happen immediately after, but you drink it. And it happens. Take my advice. Stay in your cabin till the weather moderates. Do not venture on deck until you have some power of resistance.)

197

We got to New York in the evening and left for Chicago the next morning. I remember a feeling of disappointment when Flo and I on our arrival in New York went out to see Fifth Avenue, which we had heard so much about. It was not until we came back again to New York that I realized we had been looking at Sixth Avenue by mistake. Our first introduction to Chicago, too, was not very auspicious. We had been recommended to a boarding house. I believe boarding houses in those days were better than they are now; I am not sure because I have never stayed in one since that first tour. This would, I am sure, have been a most comfortable place under normal conditions, but the landlady was ill and I think there was a man in possession — a broker's man. Anyhow, we could get no attention. We had not yet been initiated into the mysteries of steam heat; we didn't know how to turn it on or off and there was nobody to tell us; we were nearly suffocated with the heat, and during the night the radiator proved to be one of those aggressive instruments that make a noise like artillery. In addition to this I was seized with the worst toothache that has ever attacked me; so on the whole I was desperately unhappy.

The next morning I decided I would have my tooth out, but it was Sunday and no one could direct me to a dentist. So I got hold of Al Canby who was always helpful, and he took me round to a large building. English dentists usually have their offices in private houses, so I was surprised to find a huge building filled with nothing but dentists — at least that was its condition on a week day, but on Sunday they were all off duty. We went from one office to another on the off chance of finding one occupied; for about fifteen minutes we were going up and down in the elevator from top to bottom, under the guidance of a friendly elevator man who took compassion on us. At last we struck a man who was just coming out and locking his office door behind him. He was a huge man about six feet six inches high, and broad in proportion, and wearing a large cowboy hat. I have never seen a dentist like him either before or since. He heard our story and said he would see what could be done. We all went into the office and my new-found cowboy friend placed me in a chair, made a deft movement with his toe from behind and in an instant my two feet were filling the space occupied a moment before by my head. It was one of those nerve-destroying chairs. Our friend removed his hat in order that he might get his head farther into my mouth and asked me if I wanted gas. I said, "No"; but Al Canby said I had stood as much pain as was good for me, and as he felt responsible for my performance to-morrow he insisted on my having gas. Our friend said he wasn't sure whether he had enough gas to make a real job of it; he took his hat off the gas tank and put it back on his head, and after a slight examination he said, "Well, I guess it'll do — let's pump it into you, anyway." He put the gag in my mouth. I had never had gas before, and I asked him if it were necessary for me to have that thing in my mouth. He said, "Sure, friend. If you didn't have that gag,

by the time I'd pumped this into you you'd be clench-
ing your teeth so tight I could never get your mouth
open." So I took the gas, and under its influence I
remained conscious that I was in the hands of the
dentist, but I thought I was condemned to hell because I was having a tooth out on a Sunday. I felt
myself going down, down, millions of miles in an
elevator; I knew that there was only one thing that
could save me from eternal damnation, and that was
to keep my mouth open. When I came to, the dentist
was saying to Al Canby, "Say, that's the strangest
thing. I've never known that to happen before in all
my experience. He opened his mouth so wide that the
gag fell out." I thanked him and apologized for
having detained him. He was a tremendous fellow
of a type that was new to me. I had been in America
barely sixty hours, and I thought as I looked at him
that he probably slew buffalo on a Sunday as a
recreation, so I was much surprised when he wished
me good-by and said, "Well, I guess I'll just slip back
to the wife and kiddies."

As I look back on those first months in the United
States I find that my outstanding early impression of
the American people was their kindliness and their
helpfulness. I was continually surprised at the amount
of time and pains that busy men would expend in
order to give me pleasure or information. I have
since got used to this characteristic and take it almost
as a matter of course, but I trust I shall never fail to
appreciate it. Another attribute that struck me at
that time was the eagerness with which men in busi-

ness would listen to and consider the views of other men. It astonished me to see how gray-headed men, holding important positions in business, would listen with respectful attention to the views of an underling hardly out of his teens. I don't remember being surprised at the dimensions of things in America — heights of buildings, or width of roads and rivers; one soon adjusts one's mind to these conditions. We seem to be living in an age when Things no longer surprise us. It is the People who make the Things that interest me.

Mrs. Campbell's tour, from a business point of view, was, I believe, a triumphal one. We played to large and enthusiastic audiences. Personally I consider that her reputation in America was permanently injured by the efforts of a too-zealous press department. Publicity at any price seemed to be their slogan. Some reports that were widely circulated would lead one to suppose that she sat up all night playing poker and drinking cocktails. While in reality she was a most moderate drinker — if, indeed she drank at all — and she did not know one card from another. Her pet dog "Pinky Panky Poo" was exploited *ad nauseum*. As though she were the only woman in the world who behaved foolishly about her animals! It was the kind of publicity that might have been resorted to in an effort to foist upon the public an inferior musical-comedy star. Mrs. Campbell was apt to make a ridiculous fuss about Pinky, but no more so than most dog lovers. I remember, some years after, we happened to call at Mrs. Campbell's house in London. She had

had a serious illness and was still confined to her bed.

My wife, not knowing that the dog had died, said, "Where's Pinky?"

Mrs. Campbell put her hand across her eyes and said, "Oh, my dear, don't ask. Pinky's in heaven — sitting on God's knee." Her sense of humor never deserts her.

Mrs. Campbell's repertoire consisted of "Magda", "The Second Mrs. Tanqueray", "The Notorious Mrs. Ebbsmith", "Pelleas and Melisande", "Beyond Human Power" — I think that was all. Our New York opening was with "The Second Mrs. Tanqueray", in which I played Cayley Drummle. Flo and I were living in Twenty-fifth Street just off Broadway at a house kept by a very charming and cultured old lady, a Mrs. Liliendhal. It was a place frequented almost exclusively by actors. When I came in to breakfast on the morning following our opening, I found myself being shaken warmly by the hand by several men I had never seen before and congratulated on my press-notices. I was a good deal surprised because I do not remember that I had received any very special mention in the newspapers previous to this. But it seemed that the New York critics generally had spoken rather more than kindly about me. And from that day until the present, although the press has shown no hesitation in expressing an adverse opinion regarding my play or my performance if they felt it was deserved, I have always received from the critics a most earnest consideration, and in spite of the fact that most of them are unknown to me personally, I feel that they have for me a very solid friendship of which I am very proud.

With the appearance of these notices my fate was sealed. I was unaware of this because I did not know the ways of American managers. I knew that English theatrical managers were generally entirely ignorant of what was going on in any other theatre. If a new actor suddenly got his head above water, they either didn't see it, or regarded it as no concern of theirs. I was therefore quite unprepared for an offer which came almost immediately from Charles Frohman. It came by letter: I did not see Mr. Frohman for many years after this — and then only once. I will mention that later on. Nothing came of this offer, because we were unable to agree upon terms.

In the meantime Mrs. Campbell had put on "The Notorious Mrs. Ebbsmith" which established me very firmly with the critics. I may here remark without undue modesty that there was no great credit due to me for my success in the Pinero plays. Any actor with ability just slightly above the average would be sure to make a success in such parts. Everybody (almost) who has ever played Cayley Drummle has made a hit. I don't know any author who can equal Pinero in writing cast-iron parts for actors. I recall with much pleasure the attitude towards me of Herbert Waring and George Titheradge at this time. As I have said, they were "featured" players, and the publicity which I received was often undeniably at their expense, but they were amongst the first to offer me very hearty congratulations and there never arose the slightest antagonism or friction.

Soon after my offer from Charles Frohman a mysterious messenger came to the stage door of Wallack's Theatre during a matinée. He asked for me and told me in a mysterious way that Mr. Belasco would like to see me. I afterwards discovered that this aura of mystery was something that surrounded everybody who emanated from Mr. Belasco's office. There was no real reason for mystery. There was no reason why I should have been conducted with an air of secrecy to Mr. Belasco's sanctum and the door closed silently and darkly upon me. Why are all Mr. Belasco's assistants so inscrutable? I found nothing mysterious about Mr. Belasco — except his waistcoat. And after all, if he, as a theatrical manager, likes to wear a waistcoat suggestive of higher things, that is his affair. I can only suppose that these assistants live in the atmosphere of the theatre and carry with them, intentionally, an air of suspense which they know to be the very essence of drama. Mr. Belasco was very pleasant and quite human.

Mrs. Leslie Carter was at the very pinnacle of her career, playing "Madame Du Barry." The theatre was then the Republic. It was afterwards called the Belasco, but it went back to its old name, the Republic, when Mr. Belasco built his own handsome theatre in Forty-fourth Street, which now bears his name. I went to see the last performance of "Du Barry." I suppose Mrs. Campbell must have been playing "Magda" that night or I should not have been free. I did not play on "Magda" nights. The Republic Theatre was crowded to suffocation and I was much impressed both by the excellence of the production and the real emotional power of Mrs. Leslie Carter. Well, it was in Mr. Belasco's office in this theatre that my interview took place. Mr. Belasco said that he was producing a play called "The Darling of the Gods" — a Japanese play — in which he was starring Miss Blanche Bates, and he wished me to play the part of the Minister of War. I said that of course I must read the part first. He answered, I think, that I could not do this as the play was not yet finished. I demurred at this. As a matter of fact I was not anxious to stay. I liked America, but I had worked for several long years to get to London and as I had now reached my goal I did not wish to sacrifice it. I mentioned my salary, thinking it might frighten him as it had Mr. Frohman. But he agreed immediately. So I said I would think it over and let him know the next day. He spoke most kindly, told me to take all the time I wanted; told me of his association with Dave Warfield, and with Mrs. Carter; confided in me his plans and his hopes for Blanche Bates, and passed me over to one of his men of mystery who escorted me back into the great world. I talked it over with Flo and we decided that if he would make certain concessions we would stay in New York for another season and then go back to London for good.

The next day I returned to the Republic Theatre and intimated that I wished again to see Mr. Belasco.

One of the brotherhood gave me a wan but kindly smile, beckoned me with his index finger and led the way along the dimly lighted corridors; he stopped a moment in silence, gave me a reassuring look as much as to say, "Be brave, you will never regret entering our secret order," then opened the door of Mr. Belasco's chapel and closed it silently behind me.

Although some twenty-four hours had elapsed since my former visit it was obvious that Mr. Belasco had never moved since I left him. He had waited patiently and silently, perhaps without food or water, for my return, and lo! I was here. That, at any rate, was the impression I received. He at once became animated and very cordial; I could not have been received with more courtesy if I had been the President of the United States. I observed one peculiarity, and that was that he seldom stood still; he was either seated or walking to and fro. When for a moment he did stand still he seemed to have to steady himself by raising his hand to his forehead and hanging on to a handful of his luxuriant hair — much as ordinary people seek support from the strap in the subway. He was now seated.

I opened up with my conditions and after he had listened to me for a moment, he waved a kindly hand towards me, lifted himself by the hair into a standing position, picked two sheets of paper from a shelf above him and said, "Mr. Arliss, here are two contract forms, if you will take them home, and fill in anything you wish, sign them both and send them back to me, I will sign your copy and return it to you at once."

This I afterwards found to be Mr. Belasco's system — to create a bond of friendship and to inspire confidence in those with whom he was to work. I consider his great success as a producer to be largely due to following this broad and generous method.

Of course, it took the wind out of my sails. I carried the contract home as he suggested, and I have no doubt I asked for a great deal less than if I had had to fight point after point. My association with Mr. Belasco was always pleasant and Miss Bates behaved towards me with that same generosity which I have nearly always experienced at the hands of actors and actresses of great ability. Although she was the star, and I had a dangerously good part, she never once withheld her whole-hearted coöperation in anything that was likely to enhance the value of my character. The rehearsals of "The Darling of the Gods" were long and arduous. Almost from the beginning we rehearsed in Japanese shoes and kimonos in order to become thoroughly familiar with the costume. I would often watch Belasco with keen interest as he worked out a scene; sometimes when he met difficulty he would suddenly stop the rehearsal and walk up and down the stage for as long as half an hour in absolute silence; but when he found the solution it was worth waiting for. He had really no idea of time. Members of the brotherhood would bring him occasional meals of cake and milk, and sometimes he would go on till two or three in the morning. Personally I consider long rehearsals a mistake, but each producer must work in his own way. I remember feeling very tired and worn-out late one afternoon; we had been going on without a break since morning. Albert Bruning, who played a character "bit" magnificently, whispered to me, "Would you like a glass of buttermilk?" I said, "I should." I was not a drinking man and I did not believe in taking alcohol at rehearsals, but on this occasion I felt in need of a stimulant, and I did not for a moment doubt that Bruning's invitation was couched in words brimming over with American humor. I knew that, of course, he meant a whisky and soda.

"We have time," he said, and we slipped out. He led the way along Forty-second Street. We passed several saloons.

I said, "We had better not go too far. Won't this — "

He interrupted me to tell me that he knew where to get the best in New York. After we had walked five or six minutes longer and passed half a dozen more saloons, he took me down some stone steps and to my consternation I found myself in a small but unequivocal dairy — and to my horror he called for two large glasses of buttermilk! I didn't know the stuff existed outside of storybooks and old ballads. I couldn't even drink milk without feeling ill, but buttermilk — horrible! This was the first American company I had ever met and I thought to myself, "This is evidently the custom in America. I am the only Englishman in the company. I cannot let them think that we drink whisky and soda at rehearsals while they drink buttermilk."

I didn't know Bruning well enough to make a clean breast of it: in fact I think this was the first time we had spoken. He brought the two glasses — such large glasses — one in each hand, and gave me mine with pleasurable anticipation of my enjoyment. He took a long draught from his own glass and said, "That's the stuff!" I had never seen it before, but I took his word for it. It looked even more awful than I had pictured it. But his eye was upon me, there was no possible escape. I murmured inwardly, "For England", and drank it down. I wasn't in the danger zone during the Great War, so this was the nearest I have ever come to dying for my country.

The part of Sakkuri, for which I was cast, was, I believe, originally intended to be played with its humorous side dominating (I think Sir Herbert Tree afterwards played it in London from this angle) but as the rehearsals matured I am of opinion that Mr. Belasco was secretly pleased to find that I was developing rather the subtle villainy of the part and allowing the comedy to slide. He took tremendous care and interest in the "Torture Chamber" scene and introduced various bits of business that enriched it. But one day I got worried by the presence of some spies shooting about during a certain speech of mine and I asked Mr. Belasco if he felt it was necessary to have that action at this particular moment.

He said, "Do you find it distracting?"

I said, "I do rather."

"Then of course it sha'n't be done," he said. He looked at his watch and then beckoned every one on the stage to come round him. "Come here, folks. Mr. Thompson" (to his assistant stage manager), "bring your script here. Now, folks, I want you to understand this is Mr. Arliss' scene. Whatever he says goes. Mr. Thompson, I'm going out for half an hour, and Mr. Arliss will take this scene and whatever he wants done, you put it down in the script and it stays. It's Mr. Arliss' scene and he knows just what he wants. Now, folks, pay attention to Mr. Arliss," and he went out of the stage door. I suspect that he went no farther than the front of the house and that he watched every detail of what happened. But he was following out his system — to give me confidence. He came back apparently much refreshed by his half-hour's rest, and although I had done nothing of the slightest importance, he expressed himself much gratified at the vast improvement.

I am reminded here of an anecdote that Brander Matthews told me of Belasco's earlier days.

When Bronson Howard was producing "Young Mrs. Winthrop" he called on Brander at an hour that seemed obviously stolen from rehearsal.

"How is it you have come away from your rehearsal?" asked Brander.

"Well," Bronson Howard said, "there's a young fellow there who is assisting me; he seems to have ideas, so I've left it in his hands; he may discover something that I never knew was there." The young fellow was David Belasco.

We played "The Darling of the Gods" for an entire season in New York. It was a very beautiful produc-

AS SAKKURI IN "THE DARLING OF THE GODS"

tion and an exceedingly good company. Blanche Bates gave one of the most charming performances of her career. Ada Lewis had a very small part on the stage, but made up for it by being the life and soul of the company off. Robert T. Haines played the lead and smaller parts were filled by such unusually good actors as Albert Bruning, Mr. and Mrs. Charles Walcott, and Benrimo. Although business was big, I should think it unlikely that it was possible to make a profit in the Belasco Theatre with so expensive a production.

At the end of the season Mr. Belasco asked me to play the part on the road for another year. This was contrary to my ideas as I had intended to go back to London. But I talked it over with Flo and we decided that as the play had attracted considerable attention, it might be advisable to continue with it in the big cities. We therefore determined to stay in America for one more year and then go back to London for good.

On this tour we made many personal friends and we became more and more attached to America and Americans. We felt that we should leave the country with much regret when the time came for us to go. The play went on for another season, but this time I declined to continue with it. I found that I was in danger of being regarded as a specialist in Oriental parts. Already I was receiving innumerable plays written round Japanese noblemen, Chinese ministers and Indian potentates. I felt I was in peril of getting into a rut. Moreover, I had a desire to play a part which gave me more freedom of expression in both voice and action. The perpetual restraint of gesture and emotion which is part of the Japanese character began to get tiresome. So we booked our passage home. But it happened that just at this time Mrs. Fiske had decided to open her next season with a revival of "Becky Sharp" and she wished me to play Lord Steyne. It was a great temptation. I wanted very much to play with Mrs. Fiske, but I had definitely decided to go home. I talked it over with Flo and we concluded that it would be so splendid to be with Mrs. Fiske, that we would come back for just one year more and then go home to London for good. So I went to England and had pleuro-pneumonia. After that several English actors who had been unsuccessful in America told me that to go back to a winter in the United States meant certain death. But as no one could give me any actual assurance that I should not die if I remained in England, and as I knew from actual observation that there were a great many people still alive in America, I decided to take the risk. Moreover we knew that we were only going to be away for one more season, anyway. So I came back to Mrs. Fiske and remained in the bosom of her company for three years.

XI

MRS. FISKE AS A PRODUCER

MRS. FISKE's dominant characteristic was kindliness. Throughout the entire three years of my engagement there traveled with her always two of her relatives — "Aunt Mary" and Emily Stevens. Aunt Mary was a strange and aged trooper of surprising vigor and Emily Stevens was a most attractive girl still in her teens. I believe Emily Stevens' first part was that of an old servant in "Hedda Gabler" who goes on and makes up the fire. I know she used to regard herself as "a scream" in the part. She used to stifle her outbursts of laughter just long enough to go on and do her bit and then explode with merriment as she came off. I'm afraid that even "Cousin Minnie" never took this part of the entertainment in the proper Ibsen spirit. My engagement with Mrs. Fiske began at the old Manhattan. This theatre stood, I think, at the corner of Thirty-third Street on Broadway. I haven't the faculty of remembering the exact spot on which a building stood when once it is pulled down, but I remember that the stage door was just opposite a side entrance of a big store. I used to see the employees coming out at lunch time when I would be walking up and down outside the stage door, going over my part — a habit which I had formed in my earlier days at the Elephant and at Margate in "Repetition Alley."

I recall that one day I was standing by the stage door, deeply engaged in trying to work out some bit of business that had occurred to me, when I became conscious of two girls crossing the road, one of whom was apparently experiencing great difficulty in keeping her legs, and was only prevented from falling by the valiant efforts of her friend; as I looked up she had a violent collapse and with numerous hysterical screams she begged her friend to "help her off the ice." As there was no vestige of ice to be seen — it being early summer — and as the friend was staring at me in convulsions of laughter, I was forced to the conclusion that I had quite unwittingly been going through certain antics, which had attracted the attention of the girls and produced the seizure I have described. Thereafter I was careful not to lose consciousness of my surroundings when I was perusing my studies in the street — but I henceforth adopted the phrase, "Help me off the ice," to express a definite degree of surprise under given circumstances.

During my association with Mrs. Fiske, I played in a considerable number of pieces; amongst them were: "Becky Sharp" (revival), "Tess of the d'Urbervilles" (revival), "Hedda Gabler", "Rosmersholm", "The Eyes of the Heart", "The New York Idea" and "Leah Kleschna."

At the end of each season Flo and I definitely determined to return to London for good, but always eventually decided to come back again.

Mrs. Fiske's ability as an actress is universally acknowledged but her capacity as a producer is not so well known. During the early rehearsals of "Leah Kleschna", Mr. Fiske, who always directed her productions, was taken seriously ill and the entire work fell on the shoulders of Mrs. Fiske. The ease with which she piloted the play to success and the brilliancy of her suggestions surprised us all. Personally I have never ceased to regret the absence of Mrs. Fiske's advice when I am studying a new part. She had an uncanny capacity for suggesting the tricks of old age, or extreme youth, passion or suffering, in directing others; her character acting was superb and her constant warning to the actors was "keep it true — keep it true." Our great difficulty at this time was to prevent her effacing herself. She was so interested in getting the best out of everybody else that she always seemed to regard herself as a negligible quantity in the play.

I remember saying to her, "Are you going to speak all that with your back to the audience?"

"Yes," she said, "I want them to see your face."

"But," I remonstrated, "it's a very long speech for you to deliver in that position."

"Yes, I know," she sighed. "It's such a long speech, I want to get through with it as quickly as I can."

She never liked long speeches, and is never at her best in them in my opinion. Her great moments come in flashes — in silences, in exclamation, or in brief utterances.

"Leah Kleschna" had a very unusual cast. I can hardly hope to play again with three men so perfectly fitted to their parts as were John Mason, William B.

Mack and Charles Cartwright. John Mason would, in my opinion, have been the greatest actor in America if his private character had been as well balanced as his public performances. He had personality, great ability and a magnificent voice. But he had no control over the frailties of his nature. He had an extraordinary charm of manner. I remember some one saying, "John Mason always strikes me as a man who could really find great pleasure in his home; as a charming companion for some nice woman. I picture him as a man coming home at night to the fireside with his easy chair drawn up and his slippers on the hearth," and the reply of somebody who knew him well, was, "That's just the sort of man he is. But his slippers are always on the wrong hearth." Poor John! He was a very sweet nature, but he had no shame in him. He gloried in his indiscretions. I came across him one day folding up some nice clean new ten-dollar bills and putting them in envelopes with loving care. He confided to me that this was alimony that he was sending to his ex-wives. He said they liked to have it in cash and he never could bear to send them soiled money.

He knew every saloon and every saloon keeper from 25th Street to 42d Street. There was a saloon in 42d Street that ran through from Seventh Avenue to Broadway. Saloon keepers always listened sympathetically to the troubles of their regular customers. One of the frequenters of this place was a man who used to have occasional serious quarrels with his wife and when these domestic disturbances happened, he

216

would go into the saloon, have a drink, confide in the bartender and dash out again. This performance he would repeat at intervals of about ten minutes throughout the entire morning and afternoon. It happened that on one of these tempestuous afternoons John Mason went in, had a drink and walked over to the cigar stand to get a light for his cigar. He told me the story with great gusto. "George, for once in my life I was scared. I had just gone over to the cigar stand; I heard some one come into the saloon. I was stretching for a match when I became conscious of a man striding towards me from behind; he stopped close at my heels. I knew something was going to happen; I could feel his hot breath on the back of my neck. I didn't dare to look round. Suddenly he said, 'Do you know my wife, sir?' George, I was scared stiff: I guessed I did know her, but as I couldn't see the man I didn't know which one it was. I seemed to feel the muzzle of his pistol behind my ear. But I didn't let on. I struck the match and put it to my cigar when he hissed again between his teeth, 'Do you know my wife, sir?' 'No, sir,' I said; 'I do not.' 'Then, by God! you don't want to,' said the man and strode out into Seventh Avenue."

Charles Cartwright was an Englishman; he could play a certain type of villain better than any actor I have ever seen. His reputation was established in these parts in the old days of melodrama at the Adelphi Theatre, London. He had a somewhat monotonous method of delivery that implied great strength. His suggestion of malicious determination could be appalling. In private life he was a man with a perpetual grouch. When he was in America he was continually grumbling about the country and the people, and holding up England as a model of all the virtues. When he was at home in England he hadn't a good word to say for his native heath, and was perpetually protesting that America was the only country for any civilized person to live in. An unaccountable friendship sprang up between Mason and Cartwright. The two were always together and on tour Mason would "mother" Cartwright and always defend his grumbling and growling. But I once heard him administer a subtle rebuke. We were sitting at lunch in a restaurant in San Francisco. Charley Cartwright was being particularly fractious. He complained of everything, "Beastly draughty hole this is. Thank God, I shall soon be back in London and civilization," and he shivered and hiked up his shoulders. Presently he looked round and saw behind him an electric fan which was whirling round and blowing in front of it a brave little silken flag which flaunted the stars and stripes.

"God," said Cartwright, when he caught sight of this, "that's what it is. It's that damned American flag," and he shivered and stamped his feet.

"Feet cold, Charley?" said John quietly. "Well, don't look at it. You are not the first Englishman, you know, that it has affected that way."

At this time Mrs. Fiske was fighting the "Trust" as it was called. This was before the Shuberts came into power, and when Klaw and Erlanger were in absolute control. The consequence was we used to go into all sorts of little towns that we would never have visited in the ordinary way; we played in halls, in circuses and obscure theatres — anywhere we could get in. Sometimes, in towns that had theatres from which we were barred and where it was impossible for us to get a place to play in, Mrs. Fiske would engage a hall and read a speech to the populace telling them why it was she could not visit their city. Our journeys were often long and tedious and on railways to which it seemed time was no object. I remember on one journey in the wilds of Texas when our carriage had been standing still even longer than usual, we got out to see the cause and found that we were all alone on the line. Ours had been the last carriage on the train; it had been insecurely coupled and had parted company with the remainder of the train without any one knowing it. I think we were there for three or four hours; there was no habitation visible except a small shack in the distance. One of our wits asked Mrs. Fiske if she wouldn't like to go over and explain why we were not playing there this season. Eventually an engine came panting up and took us off in state. It seems to me that during my association with Mrs. Fiske, I visited every corner of the United States. Her quarrel with the Trust certainly placed her at a disadvantage. But in towns where she was very strong, it had a possible commercial value. The fact that we were playing in some building apart from the regular theatres gave an added interest to our visit and often resulted in huge audiences.

Towards the end of my third season with Mrs. Fiske, a somewhat momentous conversation took place between Flo and me. I had been talking of our return to England and suddenly Flo said, "Don't you think we had better face matters?"

I looked pained. I am always pained when Flo asks me to face matters, because I know it means that I have to make some uncomfortable decision. Of course I said, "What do you mean?" although I knew perfectly well that she was going to point out that we had been here too long to go back.

She said, "Do you realize that you've entirely dropped out of any position you had in London and that you are building up some reputation here? We must remain in America and you must become a star." That's so like Flo; she will go to extremes. I am continually having to rebuke her for that.

I said, "Do not let us confuse the main issue. Let us discuss whether we go or stay."

"No," she said, "the two things go together. If you stay it's quite time you starred."

I said, "No."

She said, "Why?"

I said, "I will tell you." I have always found it difficult to make Flo listen patiently to my perfect logic when our opinions do not coincide, but in this instance she held herself in absolute but unrespectful silence while I expounded my reasons. I told her that I was very comfortable under the management of Mrs. Fiske; that she was a distinguished actress and that I had become associated with her in the public mind;

that as a supporting actor I was comparatively free from responsibility because it really didn't make any vital difference to anybody else whether I succeeded or failed; that starring anyway was a vulgar and ostentatious boasting of one's supposed ability — a shouting from the hoardings that "I alone am worth the money": that I shrank from such unseemly conduct and that I couldn't bear the strain. — At this Flo cross-countered and said, "Nonsense." — I said again, "What do you mean?"

She said, "I will tell you." (With acerbity.) She proceeded with her rebuttal. I listened in absolute and respectful silence. She said there was no more vulgarity or boasting about an actor having his name in large letters than was displayed by a candidate for the presidency of the United States; that as a matter of fact it showed far greater sportsmanship, for when once a president is handed to the public they have to keep him whether they like him or not, whereas it is within their power to leave the star severely alone. "And as for strain, that's simply absurd," she said; "as a supporting actor you have strain if you like, because you have to bite and scratch for every bit of acknowledgment you get. But for the star it's perfectly easy: you just stand in the center of the stage in the limelight and everybody dances round you."

I was at a disadvantage in this argument, because I knew in my heart that to a great extent she was right. While an actor is struggling to rise, every step upward is mainly due to his actual ability and to his comparatively unaided effort. As soon as he becomes a star everybody rushes to his assistance — the author, the producer, the limelight man, all conspire to force him into prominence and to cover up his deficiencies. It is my opinion that an actor probably does his best work before he becomes a star. His most spectacular successes are generally made after that period; but there can be little doubt that as soon as the way to success is made easy, the art is liable to deteriorate. I might have continued the argument of my case against my wife on the score of the nerve-destroying responsibility, but I knew she loved responsibility and courted it, and I was aware that my desire to evade this inevitable condition of stardom was mere cowardice, so I was too proud to fight her on this issue.

But as a star the sense of my obligations to the management, the author, the company and the audience has ever remained a terror to me. The knowledge that every one is relying largely upon me frightens me. There is always the possibility that after a company has been engaged and large sums of money spent on the production, I may prove to be utterly unsuited to the part, and the play may have to be withdrawn. Or that having got a success I may lose my voice, or get some trumpery illness that would necessitate the closing of the theatre and the throwing out of work of innumerable people. These spectres are forever hanging over me. But as I knew that this was no valid argument against Flo's case, I had to take refuge in satire.

So I said, "Of course, we need not take into consideration the fact that I have to find a manager. As soon as it is known that I have any desire to star, there will be a wild dash from every manager in New York."

To which Flo replied, "Tcha!"

So I decided, being of a vindictive nature, that I would make an attempt to do as she desired. I went to my old champion Fred Latham, who was then representing Charles Dillingham. He said that Mr. Dillingham was thinking of running a male star in the legitimate and he thought I was "just the man for him." I remembered this expression and I knew at once that his principal would raise some objection. I was right. Mr. Dillingham considered my terms were too high. I knew it was no use approaching Mr. Belasco, for he had previously thought of starring me and had abandoned the idea. Mr. Fiske would have done it but he had no play. Luther Long offered to write a play for me and then decided that I was not strong enough to carry one on my shoulders. I had for a long time formed an opinion that there was a great opportunity for a stock company in New York, that might eventually develop into a National Theatre. It was not to be run on the ordinary stock-season lines, but more on the method of the Theatre Française. The main idea was the keeping together of a number of first-class actors in one theatre who should work together for a sufficiently long period to establish themselves as a unit. It was somewhat complicated but I had it all worked out in detail. To give the scheme a fair chance against initial failure required a considerable amount of money or great influence, so I went to Charles Frohman. I had never met him before. He listened with patience to my proposal and decided against it. He said, however, that he would very much like to have me under his management, but that he would not star me. So we parted and never met again. Then chance took a hand and decided the whole thing in my favor.

Mr. Alexander Konta, an American citizen but a Hungarian by birth, had secured the rights of a piece called "The Devil" by a young Hungarian author named Franz Molnar. It was playing in Budha Pesth with great success. He approached me, I believe, because of his recollection of my performance of Sakkuri in "The Darling of the Gods." The play reached me act by act as it left the translator's hands in Budha Pesth. I read the first act and was very favorably impressed. The second act maintained the promise of the first and when finally I got the whole play I knew that I should have no difficulty in finding a producer. I was still with Mrs. Fiske so it was agreed with Mr. Konta that we should take the play to Harrison Grey Fiske; he decided without hesitation to put it on. I thereupon turned over the entire control to Mr. Fiske, merely making the stipulation that I should play the part. This was at the end of the season 1907–1908 and it was arranged that I should open in the fall of 1908.

I then returned to England as was my custom at the end of each season and during my absence it transpired that although Mr. Konta had actually bought the rights from an accredited agent, the play, owing to the fact that there was no copyright arrangement

"THE DEVIL"

One of Franz Molnar's earliest successes

between Hungary and the United States, was in fact
public property and could be presented by anybody in
America who could obtain a script. It was, therefore,
decided that I should return early and make a production in August instead of September, in order to be
first in the field. Soon after this it became known that
Colonel Savage had a version of the play, which I
think came to him through a German source, and
that he was preparing it for production. I could never
understand why, at this point, the two managers did
not come together and arrive at some amicable commercial arrangement, and I have always regretted that
that course was not taken, but as I then knew nothing
about the business end of theatre management (I
know very little about it even now) I did not interfere.

The upshot was that on the night of August 18,
1908, there were produced two versions of the same
play bearing the same title "The Devil", at two
separate New York theatres. As the theatrical season
had not really started, and theatregoers were craving
some diversion, this unusual duplicate production
created quite a furious sensation, and on the first night
speculators were getting as much as ten dollars a seat
— an unheard-of price in those days.

Before our advertising matter was put out, Mr.
Fiske asked me whether I wished to be starred or
featured. Remembering that my original success in
America was a great deal due to the fact that I had
"come in on rubbers" and wishing to postpone the
evil day of stardom as long as possible, I elected to be
featured. As it turned out, I had, however, the per-

haps unique distinction of becoming a full-blown star in one night. This was by no means due to any sensational success on my part, but merely a strategic movement on the part of my management. As Colonel Savage was advertising heavily all over New York "The Devil", and as there were two of that name in the city, it was considered advisable that we should have a trademark, so whereas on the eighteenth the electric sign outside the Belasco read, " 'THE DEVIL' with George Arliss", on the nineteenth one of those mysterious mechanics who manipulate electric signs with such amazing ease, caused it to read "GEORGE ARLISS in 'The Devil.'" At one bound I became a star and an obedient husband (an unusual combination) and since that night I have never made any effort to escape from that position in which Flo had decided to place me some three months before.

My chief regret was that I was never again to appear with Mrs. Fiske. As far as I remember she was now playing "Salvation Nell" written by that amazing young author, Edward Sheldon, then, I believe, about twenty-two years of age. As a matter of fact we did play together once more in the second act of "Hedda Gabler" in Milwaukee. She was appearing in some near-by city and I was in another close at hand and we met to give a flying benefit for the Milwaukee Humane Society.

"The Devil" was, in my opinion, an exceedingly clever and entirely artificial play. It was "machine made" to the last degree, but the lines were so good and the central character so entertaining that one

ceased to be critical of its construction. If it were
played to-day I think it would appear old-fashioned,
but I cannot be sure of that. The character of the
Devil was an interesting one to play. To the characters on the stage he had to seem to be a very open and
sincere man of the world, and yet the audience must
be aware that this was merely an assumption of
honesty. If, in order to deceive the people on the
stage, he struck a note of real truth and sincerity, he
was in danger of also deceiving the people in the
front. In order to prevent this confusion I found it
necessary to overact all my emotions in a slight degree
so that the audience might feel that although they
could tell I was lying, the unsuspecting people in the
play would never realize it. This gave the audience a
pleasant appreciation of its own intelligence, a condition of mind that it is often beneficial to create.
Whether my overacting was as subtle as I wished it
to be I cannot say: it is more than likely that it was
not. I am always anxious that an audience should not
be perplexed and so I might have overdone it. My
opinion is that an audience should never be confused.
If the play is what is known to-day as a "detective
play", then to puzzle is probably a necessary condition of the contract. But to puzzle is not necessarily
to confuse. If it is what is known as a "problem
play", then the author may perhaps leave the problem
unsolved; in this case he should make it clear at the
end of the play that he intends to say to the audience,
"I don't know the answer to this. Do you?" But to
suggest that he does know, but won't tell, is, I con-

sider, absurd. To send the people away saying, "What did he mean" by this or that, is in my opinion bad art. He should show clearly what he means and then leave them to discuss as to whether they think him right.

The writer of a book may be allowed to be so subtle or abstruse that the reader in his library or in his hall bedroom may find it necessary to turn back and read a passage a second or third time, but for the theatre, until the day comes when any member of the audience may be allowed to stand up and say to the actors, "Excuse me, would you mind saying that again", I say until this privilege is allowed, I contend that it is the duty of the writer of a play to make his meaning so clear that it may be gathered by any person of average intelligence at one sitting. People who, having paid for their seats, fail to understand what an author is driving at, don't pay again to find out. The man who goes a second time to a play is one who has thoroughly understood it and enjoyed it. I am not suggesting that an author should write "down" to his public: that is a fatal thing to do. But he should not consciously write above their heads. That is an ignorant thing to do, and is usually a sign that he has less intelligence than the majority of people for whom he is writing.

(Advice to young authors:

There is a large number of unintelligent people in every city, and I am happy so say that many of them go to the play. But if I may be allowed to offer a word of warning, I would say that I have discovered by long experience, that once these unintelligent individuals are in the theatre and become part of that unit which we call "the audience", they take on a dangerous and uncanny instinct which is perilously like intelligence. Do not monkey with them.)

My starring career, then, had a very propitious beginning. We ran some six months in New York and finished out the season on the road. As far as I remember we made a good deal of money, and I suppose we should have made more if there had not been other Devils in the field. Mr. Fiske now began to look for a new play for me for the next season. It is never easy to find a star-play for a character actor: it is particularly difficult to discover one for me. I can neither be dashing nor beautiful. I have never tried to assume either of these valuable attributes since I wore pink tights in Hammersmith. I might be very good as sweet old gentlemen, but they generally annoy an audience. So it becomes necessary to look for some unusual character. As no play was forthcoming we examined some of the "best sellers" of the period.

W. J. Locke had just made a great success with his book "Septimus." Mr. Fiske thought this might be a suitable character for me. So he had the story dramatized and we determined to try our luck with it. I ran it for a short time in New York and then finished the season with it on the road. Its career was reminiscent of that consoling medical term, "the operation was successful but the patient died." It was an excellent dramatization, skilfully contrived.

The principal female character was played by Emily Stevens — her first big part — and there was a very good supporting company. Every one who saw it professed to like it, but apparently nobody recommended it to a friend. It is generally conceded that newspaper notices and advertising are but of small value to a play unless the audience talks about it with enthusiasm after leaving the theatre. It is the "mouth to mouth" advertising that tells. Our business kept on a dead level of mediocrity. We seldom played to disgracefully bad business but the receipts never went high enough to check the steady shrinkage that was taking place in the size of my head.

Whenever one of my plays is a great success, or a persistent failure, I always try to find a reason. It is possible that I never discover the right one, but it is an interesting game to play. I commence by ruling out the possibility that it is my fault. Not entirely from reasons of vanity, but because I consider it logical to start with the hypothesis that any one actor is seldom bad enough to ruin a good play and never good enough to carry a bad one to any considerable degree of success. My conclusion about "Septimus" was that it was a charming story which should never have been dramatized. It was almost impossible to discover this until it was too late. The character in the book was that of a delightful person whose mind was entirely absorbed by the study of inventions. He continually failed to realize the importance of the things that really mattered in his life. He forgot appointments, he forgot people, he forgot his meals,

AS "SEPTIMUS"

The absent-minded inventor, drawn from W. J. Locke's novel

his costume, even himself. He was called upon during the play to make a great sacrifice. While the story was in book form the author could cleverly impose upon his readers the agonized emotions experienced by this strange being at a time when he made frantic efforts to save the good name of the girl he loved. That was fairly easy for Mr. Locke to do. But when this same character became an actual flesh-and-blood person, walking about on two legs, plain for everybody to see, the audience failed to be moved to a similar extent by these emotions expressed by the actor; not necessarily because the actor was not giving an adequate portrayal of those emotions, but because the onlookers had grown to know the character so well that they were apt to conclude that what would have been a heart-breaking surrender for another man was in reality little or no sacrifice for Septimus. They had learnt that he had the capacity for forgetting so strongly developed that in a few hours he would probably overlook the fact that he had done this thing at all. These are the dangerous pitfalls that it is practically impossible for a producer or an actor to see until he is too far on the road to turn back. But these things are sent to try us. If Septimus had been more prosperous George Tyler would never have said to me, "It's about time you got a success", and if he hadn't said that I should probably never have played "Disraeli."

XII

"DISRAELI"

THE breakfast hour is a time when one doesn't expect anything to happen except eggs and the morning paper. But on this particular morning George Tyler happened too. It was at the old St. Nicholas Hotel, Cincinnati — now no more, I believe. I had seldom seen Tyler since the Mrs. Patrick Campbell season. Had it been dinner time we should probably have said, "Why, my dear old chap, I am glad to see you. What a surprise. How well you're looking." But being breakfast we said, "Hullo, what are you doing here?" I think we said it together. Tyler, it seemed, was passing through, on his way to administer aid to one of his companies. He said, "Sit down and let's have breakfast together."

To invite companionship at breakfast requires courage. But it is just this initiative and self-sacrifice that has made Tyler what he is. I sat down. If we did not talk of Shakespeare and the musical glasses, we discussed almost every other kind of entertainment; we also talked of actors of various degrees of ability and success, including myself. It was then that Tyler made his memorable remark: "It's about time you got a good play." I knew he meant that I was in imminent danger of fading into obscurity.

I said, "That's all very well" (breakfast time was

232

beginning to tell) — "but how is one to get a good play?"

He shrugged his shoulders and said, "If you've got any ideas we might get one written for you."

Now it happens that morning is my best time for ideas: it is astonishing what a flood of ideas you can get whilst peeling an egg. No man seeking ideas should have his eggs "opened" in the morning. So I started off with my most brilliant idea, I forget what it was, but I know I considered it a good one.

George Tyler, in his Napoleonic way, took it, examined it, wrestled with it, laid it out pale and lifeless and then proceeded to spread it on the tablecloth with the flat of his knife. And that finished it. One by one, I watched my cherished ideas go under the knife and listened to him as he said, "Frankly speaking, I don't think much of it. In other words, I should call it absolutely useless."

I became discouraged. I had used my second egg and was about at the end of my brilliant conceptions. There was a pause while Tyler continued to spread my last suggestion very thin on the tablecloth. I felt I should say something, so I murmured, "Of course, I once had an impression that a play written round Disraeli should be interesting, but — " and I looked wearily round for the waiter, feeling that my career as an actor must come to an end as soon after breakfast as possible.

Suddenly I became aware that the operation with the knife had ceased and that Tyler was putting both his hands into his trousers' pockets. I thought he was about to pay the bill; but he didn't take them out again. I became conscious that he was glaring at me with surprised eyes.

I thought, "Somebody has picked his pocket. He has lost all his money." I expected to hear him shout, "Gone, every cent." Instead of which, he merely said, "That's an idea." I was disappointed at this remark because I had been giving him ideas for the past thirty-five minutes; the tablecloth was covered with them. I was about to venture some observation of this kind when he continued in a terrible crescendo, "That's a damned good idea." I was greatly surprised at this. Of course I knew it was an idea; I believed it to be a good idea, but I never thought it was a damned good idea.

He was staring at my face so hard that he evidently couldn't see the rest of me, for although I was still sitting where I sat he said, "Sit down a minute; let's talk about that." I made a movement suggestive of attaching myself still more firmly to my seat as he said, "Damned if you're not like him too." I accepted the compliment modestly. I saw that I had made a hit. I could see that he wanted to talk as soon as he had got his breath. I knew that in that case it was no use my trying, even if I wished to. So I remained quiet and listened to him growing more and more enthusiastic. The waiter kept on coming up to see what he was asking for, and going away again unnoticed.

When Tyler receives an impression it is either useless or there's a million in it. I had made a million dollars for him in one minute. Everything was suddenly changed. My "career", so far from being at an end, was only just beginning. He pointed out the possibilities from every angle, told me how long it would run in New York and finished up with, "There's a fortune in it. It can't fail."

The waiter brought some ice water. Then we got down to real business. He said, "There's only one man in the world to write the play and that's Louis Parker. I am sailing for Europe in ten days and I am going to see him. If he agrees to write the play will you do it under my management?"

I believe a scenario writer, if he were preparing this for the movies, would "fade out" on that episode and would immediately introduce us to "The Parker Home in London", disclosing a magnificent library, with the opulent-looking Mr. Parker, wearing a worried look, sitting opposite the opulent-looking Mr. Tyler, talking volubly, with the sub-title "There's millions in it"; cut back to me walking impatiently up and down my magnificent suite in the one-night-stands; cut back to Parker and Tyler shaking hands, with the sub-title, "I'll do it." Then, after showing a flash of Tyler handing in a cable, followed by a dull scene of the inner workings of a British telegraph office, followed again possibly by pictures of the bottom of the ocean with fish swimming nonchalantly round the Atlantic cable, followed immediately by an exciting scene of the interior of an American telegraph office, contrasting it with the British office by showing the rapid movements of the operators and a complete absence of cups of tea and golf-sticks; open out to picture of me breaking the seal of a cable and reading, "Parker agrees to have Disraeli play finished by October."

At any rate, it was a cable to that effect that I received. I went to London in June and met Tyler immediately at the Victoria Hotel, Northumberland Avenue. We entered into an agreement drawn on half a sheet of notepaper and unsigned by either of us, which was the only contract that ever existed between us. My belief is that a supporting actor should have a "cast-iron" contract, but "a gentlemen's agreement" is the only one that is any use between a star and his manager.

Tyler then went back to New York. I took an early opportunity of calling upon Louis N. Parker; his name had of course been familiar to me for many years — ever since the days of his first great success "Rosemary." He had always been a most prolific writer and could generally be depended upon to turn out anything he took in hand at short notice. I had never met him before and he had never seen me. I was rather appalled at our first meeting. His library was large and handsome, and opened into a garden. There seemed to be every book that any one would ever be likely to want and more than any one could ever read, but there was a pleasant relief of bright brasses, and pottery, and statuettes, and many souvenirs of his long theatrical association. He sat with his back to a wall of books, at a huge semicircular desk which rendered him impregnable to physical attack by managers or actors; in fact, it occurred to me at the time that with about three good machine guns he could have kept a whole army at bay. I wondered how he got out, but I found as he rose quickly to greet me that there was just room enough for his body to pass through without disturbing the back wall. He was rather short and rather stout and rather fierce. In reality, I afterwards found out, he was brimming over with kindness and good nature, but he had a brusque way with him and a keen eye that was a trifle terrifying at first. I told him I had called to show him what I was like and he told me he was very glad. I told him that I hoped he realized that I was really waiting for the play and he said he did. But he begged me to leave him entirely uninterrupted in the matter; I should have it by the date agreed upon. I said I trusted him entirely. He said I might. We shook hands; we were polite — exceedingly polite. I mention this fact particularly because it was almost the last time we were exceedingly polite to one another. We afterwards became very rude and very friendly.

I think I did not hear again from Parker until September.

During the intervening period, I had produced a one-act farce at the "Palace", London, called "Widows' Weeds." It was the original version of "There and Back" that I had written years before.

In September I had a message from Parker saying he would need more time than he had anticipated. I said I would wait. I think it was the first of October that Parker asked me if I would call upon him. I was shown into the library and found him entrenched behind his battlement. To the best of my recollection the conversation went like this:

PARKER. I don't think I can write this Disraeli play.

ARLISS. Oh.

PARKER. I've tried hard enough, God knows, but it's no go.

ARLISS. Oh. Why?

PARKER. Well, it just won't come, that's all.

ARLISS. Oh. Well. How's that?

PARKER. Well — his life: it isn't dramatic — theatrically. He was in love with his own wife, and nobody else, damn him! He did lots of great things, of course — but no good for the stage.

ARLISS. Well — er — then you haven't done anything?

PARKER. I haven't done any good, if that's what you mean.

ARLISS. You see, I've been depending entirely on this play for my next season.

PARKER. My dear Arliss, I know that, and I'm horribly sorry — But I can't do impossibilities. I don't want you to think I haven't tried. I've written an entire first act. And I'll read it to you if you'd like to hear it."

So he read it. And as he went on I became more and more surprised. And when he had finished I saw that he had practically suggested the whole play. I cannot understand to this day why he failed to realize

238

this. Perhaps his mind was running too much on "Pomander Walk" which Tyler was shortly to produce in New York; or perhaps he was tired and needed a mental stimulant. The fact remains that when I said, "What are you worrying about? The story is there," he sat up like one who had just been awakened from sleep, and within about two hours he had made a rough draft of the entire four-act play. After this and throughout the writing of the play I was a constant visitor to his library. Together we spent many interesting hours and before the play was finished we had many friendly fights.

Parker is a most enthusiastic worker; his characters become real living people to him and when he reads his plays aloud he does so with conviction and with great feeling. As each important scene was written I would go to his library and he would read from his manuscript. If I made any objection or criticism he became at once depressed and irritated and then we would walk up and down and "slang" each other until the point was settled, when he at once became happy and enthusiastic again. I remember one scene I objected to as being too long and talky. I said, "Have we got to have that scene; is it necessary?"

He looked fiercely at me and said, "Of course it's necessary; the thing has to be explained."

"Well," I said, "couldn't it be done without words?"

"What do you mean?" he said techily. "Don't stand looking at me with that Sphinx-like face of yours. Tell me what you mean."

I said, "Couldn't it be done with a look?"

"What look! Which look!" he said in a state of irritation bordering on insanity. So I showed him what I meant. He stared at me for a moment and then took his blue pencil and ran it through the scene and said, "Of course it can. But how the hell was I to know that you could do that?"

That was one of the few delicate compliments that passed between us at this time. But in reality my association with Parker throughout this entire Disraeli period was most delightful and it founded a strong friendship that is not likely to be broken.

"Pomander Walk" was produced in New York on December 20, 1910, and proved a great success. On the same day I was handed the completed manuscript of "Disraeli" and we began rehearsals by the end of the month. Louis Parker produced the play himself. The costumes had all been designed and the make-ups suggested by Percy Anderson, who was at that time considered the greatest authority in London for that kind of work. Of course my own make-up was left to me. I took infinite care in my preparations. I visited every gallery in London where there was likely to be an authentic picture or bust of Disraeli and I made sketches that carefully recorded every line of his face. When I am going to play a new part I devote considerable time at home to the study of my make-up. Unless I can present to myself in person the man I have visualized whilst studying the part I cannot portray him with conviction. When I take my last look in the mirror before going on the stage for a

"DISRAELI"

The character study which is likely to be remembered by American audiences as George Arliss's greatest success

first performance I must be able to say to myself, "There he is; you look like him; now go and behave like him." With Disraeli I felt I had a fairly easy task. My wig had been built in exact imitation, following the lines of drawings I had made from busts in the London galleries. I sat down in my room with my grease paints round me and my sketches before me — and the door barred against intrusion, as usual. I worked with care and precision, registering every line and shadow as my notes directed. It was a long process, but at last it was done, and behold, I didn't look anything like Disraeli!

Flo is always my first and most important critic on my make-up. She has an artist's eye and can generally be relied upon to see at once what is wrong. She knows that after my first experiment is completed I shall unlock my door and come to her and say, "How's that?" So she generally contrives to be sitting in a distant corner of her room that she may get a first impression of me in some perspective. She will say at once, "Your color is too high" (or too pale), or "Your brows are too heavy" (or too close), or some useful criticism of that kind.

On this occasion I went to her in a state of despair. I said, "What's wrong with this make-up? I've done everything I can, and I don't look a bit like him."

Flo took one glance at me and said, "I don't like those trousers."

Of course that was an irritating thing for her to say, when I was so worried about my face. I said, "These are my street trousers; I'm not going to wear these for the part; it's my head I'm thinking about, not my legs."

She knew that; the fact is she was so disappointed with my make-up that she wanted to gain time; she knew about the trousers. She said, "Just stand there a moment — just there. Now keep still a moment — don't shuffle and hop about." (Flo gets like that when she's worried.) "Now stand over there." (She's terribly autocratic on these occasions.) She looked at me for a full minute and then said, "You're sure you're not going to wear those trousers?" I only groaned. I knew she was puzzled. "Well, there's something wrong," she said. "Now stand perfectly still and let me look at you." I stood — feeling like a tired horse. Flo screwed up her eyes and at last she said deliberately, "I know what it is. You've been working with all those drawings you made, and you've put all the lines on your face that were on his face."

I said, "Of course I have."

"Well, you see, darling, by a merciful dispensation of Providence, you haven't got his face. His was broader and larger and heavier; so to use all the lines that you found on his face is merely to distort your own. What you have to do is to take out about half of those lines and make use of your own features, using only such lines as will suggest his." Of course she was right. It's strange how those women sometimes get intelligent ideas!

We gave the first performance at Montreal on January 23, 1911, and after two or three preliminary weeks we went to Chicago for a "run." We had a really beautiful production. Tyler had done everything possible to give it a fair chance. In the light of its subsequent popularity it might be supposed that the play was an instantaneous success. But it was nothing of the kind. I cannot remember now what the press said about it, but certainly the public took no interest in it at all.

A number of actors who were also playing in Chicago saw the play and liked it. David Warfield was playing "Peter Grimm" and giving a remarkable performance. Forbes-Robertson was playing, I think, "Hamlet." I remember he said to me, apropos of my poor houses, "Have you ever made any money at this business — I mean real money, enough to save? — I haven't." I believe within the next few years he had made a considerable fortune; and in the last years of his career he played always to tremendous business.

Douglas Fairbanks was making what I believe was his first starring appearance in a farce in which he leapt over everything on the stage and hung onto the gas pipes — the name has escaped me. He gave a professional matinée and when I met him afterwards I said, "I saw you in a stock company at Baltimore when I first came to America in 1901 and I knew that you were going to make a name for yourself." He shrugged his shoulders and said, "I hope you're a good prophet, but I doubt it. There are plenty of Douglas Fairbanks in the world, but there's only one George Arliss." At the present moment I am afraid there are a great many people who are unaware of the fact that there is even one George Arliss in the world, but there are very few who are old enough to have their eyes open who don't know that there is one and only one Douglas Fairbanks.

For several weeks in Chicago we played to abominable business — I think between three and four thousand dollars a week. Any other manager would have thrown up the sponge, but Tyler fought on. If conditions then had been as they are to-day it would have been impossible for us to continue; we should have been put out by the theatre management and "Disraeli" would never have been heard of again. But if Tyler believes in anything he is as tenacious as a bulldog. In fact, this courage of his convictions has cost him several fortunes if I'm not much mistaken. He sent from New York numerous play doctors and producers, with directions that they were to find out what was the matter with the play. Without wishing to hurt the feelings of any of these gentlemen I feel bound to record my opinion that none of their suggestions had any influence on its future. There was only one change of any importance and that was the end of Act III. The curtain on that act failed to draw any great applause, and it is an accepted rule (and a good one) that the third-act curtain in a four-act play should "come down with a bang." Various suggestions were tried; Mr. Parker even went so far as to write in a new character which had no other business in the play except to make a curtain. This was done in desperation, for such a course in a play of this kind was almost surely doomed to failure.

At last a device was found: it was just an old trick revamped; perhaps rather unworthy of so good a play. But it served the purpose and brought the curtain down on delighted applause. As more than one of the advisers that Mr. Tyler employed have said in bold print that they invented this curtain, it is only fair to Mr. Parker that I should declare that they are mistaken. I happen to have the original manuscript of the suggested change as it was handed to Mr. Parker, who at once adopted it and improved upon it. But I doubt if even that had any material influence on the success of "Disraeli." The play was there as it came from Parker's hands, and the changes were so slight as to be negligible. It has also been said in print that from the time this new curtain was devised for Act III the business commenced to pick up. This is more or less true, but in my opinion our growing popularity was not due to this single development in the construction of the play. The fact was that it was just beginning to be known that the play with the funny name — Disraeli — was worth seeing.

Apart from the Jewish population, I think very few of the theatregoers of Chicago knew anything about Disraeli. One of the newspaper men assured me that most of the people he knew thought it was a tooth powder. Even in Philadelphia there was a young lady (I have this on the authority of Owen Wister) who said she "didn't know whether he was in the New Testament or the Old." A few people were beginning to talk about us. Influential Chicagoans began to come and all expressed surprise at the poor houses;

they commenced to regard us as a civic responsibility and telephoned to their friends that we were worth seeing. H. H. Kohlsaat (who afterwards became my close and valued friend) called on me and said, "Look here, you've got a fine play here. We must let people know about it; I'm going to take you round and show you off." He was most indignant that Chicago was so indifferent. He insisted on taking me to all the clubs and introducing me to men who "might be useful." Kohlsaat was a remarkable man; he was at the time a very busy man, but he always found time to make friends, and to help them when they needed help.

Then the Drama League took a hand. This was in its early days; in fact I believe its entire membership was under five hundred. The League, under the leadership of Mrs. A. Starr Best, began to take a very great interest in the welfare of "Disraeli"; I was made the first actor member of the Drama League, and Mrs. Best and her associates worked with a will for our success. That Louis Parker was not unmindful of this will be gathered from his reference to the Drama League in these verses which he wrote some time later. The play was published and dedicated to me, and on the flyleaf of the copy *de luxe* which he sent me, he wrote:

Dear Arliss, in the April days
　　We met and talked and laughed and swore
　Until the play grew more and more
　　The kind of play that Arliss plays
　　And then the snows of Montreal
　　　　Crowned all.

246

"DISRAELI"

Upon the shores of Michigan
  When the poor play showed some fatigue
The endorsement of the Drama League
  Made Dizzy quite a different man
    We saw the booking, after trouble
      Double.

And now New York upon your brow
  Has placed a crown of bay and myrtle
You can indulge in genuine turtle
  The taxi's your conveyance now
    And as for me I share with wonder
      The plunder.

So while your clever head I bless
  And lay this tribute at your feet
Think of me till again we meet
  As one who's proud of your success
    And prays we two may soon repeat it
      Or beat it.

LOUIS N. PARKER

New York,
NOVEMBER 21St, 1911

Owing to the interest of the Drama League, to the individual efforts of my personal friends, and mainly of course to the qualities of the play itself, our business began to grow, but improvement was very slow. Then Tyler wrote to me and said that if I would consent to play on Sunday nights he could arrange to hold the theatre, but not otherwise. I had always strenuously opposed Sunday work and to depart from my principles in this direction was a great sacrifice for me. But I felt that so much depended on the next few weeks that to refuse would be unfair to those associated with me in the production. So I consented. But although our business now began to go up by leaps and bounds, our Sundays were always poor. After a few weeks we discontinued this Seventh-day performance, and since then I have never played on Sunday — and never shall. If I had my way I would close all theatres and all movie houses on Sunday. I would make it a day apart. I would withhold all the ordinary amusements that are to be found on week days except outdoor sports, and so force people to seek some other kind of entertainment. There is no reason why it should be a dull day for anybody. There are always good books which we never have time to read on week days. There are hobbies to be pursued. If the worst comes to the worst, why not sit at home and converse for an hour or so? It is surprising how intelligent other people can be when you really get to know them. For those who must have external amusement I would have all the Art Galleries and Museums wide open and made as attractive as possible. I would have classical music and high-class concerts.

The people who were driven to these resorts because there was nowhere else to go, would very probably grow to look forward with pleasure to this change from a "steady diet" of pictures and theatres. I do not suggest that this class of entertainment is necessarily better, but it is different and is likely to open up in one's mind fresh ideas and a new train of thought, which at any rate may be stimulating. An unbroken routine in our amusements may be as bad for us as the steady grind in our labors. My friends of the concert stage and the musicians will perhaps say, "What about us? Why are we to work on Sunday?" Well, my friends, with you it isn't compulsory, as it would be with the actor. You can refrain from appearing without breaking the run of a play. You can take your choice.

The season in Chicago was for me a unique experience. I have never before or since played before a succession of audiences with whom I felt in such close personal sympathy. This sensation has come to me on occasions in various cities, particularly in Boston, but in Chicago during this Disraeli season it was repeated night after night. I think the reason for it is to be found in the fact that our audiences were so small that everybody who came in felt they had made a discovery; our earlier audiences were mainly composed of women, and I think they regarded us rather as a foundling that they had come upon, starving by the wayside. They seemed to nurse us and fondle us (most improper but quite true) and to regard us as their own particular property. The same people would come time after time, and by degrees they brought their friends to show them what they had found; and then the friends took a personal interest in us. Although our business grew to be quite big by the end of the season, I don't believe we ever drew the general theatre-going public of Chicago. We remained to the end a select Mutual Admiration Society.

I shall never again experience the emotion that overtook me at the final matinée when I came forward to speak a word of farewell. My agitation was not caused by the prolonged applause, but by the great silence that followed; there came across to me then a wave of friendship so strong that it enveloped me and left me almost overcome. Nearly every member of the audience had been to the play five or six times — some ten — some twenty, and they were swelling with pride that their child had now grown strong and healthy and was going out into the world to make a name for himself. I am bound to believe that such concentrated thought in an audience sets up a physical action which is registered through the ether on the mental organism of the person to whom it is directed. We speak of the magnetism of an actor, but comparatively few people realize the magnetism of the audience. When a crowd gives noisy evidence of its approval it may be possible to gage the degree of its interest by the quality or volume of its applause. But what of its silences? An actor knows that an audience may be silent and yet convey to him the impression that it is literally vibrating with sympathetic interest and understanding: and another audience may be equally silent and yet be unsympathetic and vacant.

During my long association with this play I had many delightful farewell experiences, but none so memorable as this. I played Disraeli for five successive seasons! In some respects this is a painful reflection, for there are so many other parts I want to portray and I know that I shall not have the time to devote to them.

An historical character is always interesting to perform because one never exhausts its possibilities. This may of course be said of any well-written part, but the imaginary character is not offered the same opportunity of stimulation. Side lights on Disraeli's character were continually being admitted from unexpected angles. An old number of *Punch* would tell me that "Mr. Disraeli said to the House — 'so-and-so.'" I would pick up a book from "All in this row 10c." that would give me some illuminating allusion to the Prime Minister. Souvenirs, letters, photographs, were sent me from all parts of the world. Elderly men and women who had known him personally would call upon me and tell anecdotes that would thrill me to the core. One of the most charming compliments I ever had came to me from Lady Gregory whose name is so well known in connection with the Irish Players. She has been a widow for many years, but during her husband's lifetime they had been intimate friends of Disraeli. She came to see the play and told me afterwards that the reality of the character had so carried her away into earlier years that she turned instinctively to speak to her husband. All actors who play good parts have compliments showered upon them, so I make no apology for repeating any little pleasantry of this kind. President Taft was delighted with the play and did me the honor to send for me to his box between the acts. He recently told me that ever since that time whenever he goes to a play he asks himself "Do I like it as well as Disraeli?"

"Everybody" came to see "Disraeli" and during

my five seasons with the play I had the good fortune to meet a great number of distinguished citizens and visitors. In spite of its great success I feel that to say "everybody" came is a considerable over-statement. I believe that we only drew a more or less restricted section of the public; that there were certain strata that we never touched at all. It is an extraordinary thing in my estimation, that of all the hundreds — and I suppose thousands — of people that I have met who came to see Disraeli, I cannot recall one who had not seen the play more than once. Four or five times seems to be a low average. A man came round to my dressing room one night and told me that he felt he ought to meet me because that was his twenty-fifth visit. There was some excuse for him, for it transpired that he was a member of a firm of European bankers that had helped to raise the money for the purchase of the Suez Canal. But there was no excuse for a certain elderly gentleman with a flowing white moustache who came to every Wednesday matinée in New York and always occupied the same seat. I became curious to know who he could be and set my manager on to do some detective work. He found out that his name was Weston and that in his day he was a well-known professional walker. If the play had drawn all classes of theatregoers and had had the same appeal as it appears to have had to those who composed our audiences, it would be running still to crowded houses.

Amongst the autograph letters of Disraeli now in my possession there is one that so exactly suggests

the character in the play, at the moment when he
bluffs the Manager of the Bank of England, that I
think it may be interesting to repeat it here — particularly as Parker could never have seen it before he wrote
the play. It bears no date.

Dear Baily: Your bill is due 17th. Yesterday after
long years of negotiation, suddenly and unexpectedly
I settled with Hume. He accepted an offer wh. he
refused two years ago. A sum down, wh. is ready,
tho large, and the balance in equal instalments in
five years from 1847. Never was anything better arranged, without any lawyers, and at Grosvenor Gate,
principally by Mrs. D.: no judgement, wh. he fought
hard for, and no security but my personal covenant.
This is the greatest coup I have yet made and makes
me free. I think I shall be able also to bring the
settlement of the floating claims, projected last year,
also to bear, and thus will be terminated my long
distracted affairs. My principal object in writing
this is to say that if it be indispensable *I will by return
send* you the £500 for the bill due 17th but it will
draw me to the backbone, leaving me in fact no balance. If therefore you could arrange it *for a month* it
wd. be very agreeable. Pray let me know and believe
me, Ever Yrs ffly, D. Carlton, June 12th. [Then,
writing on the flyleaf, he says:] You are aware of the
present critical state of my affairs and can imagine
that I was in fact prepared to agree to any terms
wh. Hume might have dictated, whereas he himself
surrendered.

The final observation on the flyleaf suggests that a
great deal of gentlemanly bluffing had gone on at
Grosvenor House before Hume surrendered and before

Disraeli brought off "the greatest coup I have yet made." His readiness to give the credit of the victory to "Mrs. D." is also interesting and sounds the note in his character which Parker played upon so charmingly in the drama and which was in my estimation the keynote of the success of the play.

After the first night at Wallack's Theatre, New York (September 18, 1911), the stage-door man planted some corn in a diminutive garden outside the stage entrance, and told me it would be in prime condition long before I moved out. We played till the following May and reopened there in September, 1912, for a further short season. The corn looked remarkably healthy; as there was only one ear I refrained from eating it and hung it in my dressing room as a mascot.

I think I was very fortunate in my associates in the play; during the five years I had comparatively few changes. The charming Elsie Leslie (the original Little Lord Fauntleroy) was my first leading lady. After two years, however, she decided, much to our regret, to retire into private life. Violet Heming, very young and very beautiful, followed her as "Clarissa." The part of the adventuress has always been played by the alluring Margaret Dale, who never missed a performance during the whole five years, and who played again with me in the revival and also in the screen version of the play. Miss Marguerite St. John was the Lady B. in the original production and was followed by my wife who gave a most touching performance and who continued in the part until the end of the run. Dudley Digges was my stage manager for about seven years. He should owe me a grudge for having been the means of hiding him from the public for so long a period. During that time he seldom acted unless he was obliged to, but he could go on for any part at any moment, and when such an occasion arose through illness or some other cause he generally gave a better performance than the original. He and I first met in Mrs. Fiske's company and we always believed in each other. I think there has seldom been a company of actors or actresses who were so united and worked so pleasantly together for so long a period. Our Christmas dinners and such festivities became like family parties with the sting taken out.

Amongst my most cherished possessions are the many tokens of affection that I received from the company and also from the working staff during those five years. Always on Primrose Day some unknown admirer would send me a pot of growing English primroses — this being the bloom that Queen Victoria had designated as Disraeli's favorite flower. It is impossible for me to set down even a small percentage of the many pleasant things of this kind that happened to me in the Disraeli days.

During our run at Wallack's Theatre a juvenile performance of Disraeli was given at a matinée. Three of the principal parts were played by the Tobin children — the two girls who have since developed into such charming actresses and their elder brother, George. George Tobin played my part; I had a most difficult task in making him up; he was so small that he didn't seem to have any face to work upon: I succeeded at last however in making him look uncommonly like a miniature of myself. Then I went in front to see the performance, anticipating a great deal of fun and enjoyment. I watched it for a time with great interest, but as the play went on a queer sensation began to overtake me; I was afraid. I have said that when I go on the stage to play a part I have to forget myself and visualize the man I am impersonating. I suppose this is common to all earnest actors. Little George Tobin was so ridiculously like me — every movement, every look, every inflection of the voice, that I became terrified that I should never be able to see the part again except as a tiny little man toddling about the stage and imitating me. I had to leave the theatre and walk for miles to try to rid my memory of the picture. But when I played that night, and for weeks afterwards, I was nothing but a little creature trying to behave like a big one; and all the company around me looked to me like giants. In time of course the memory began to fade, but it was an eerie experience and one which I hope I shall never have again.

Our success in New York was repeated in Boston where we played for about six months. My wife and I took a small furnished house in Brookline and settled down as good citizens.

There is some difference of opinion between the inhabitants of Boston and those of other cities as to whether or not Boston is the Hub of the Universe. I take no side in this controversy, my knowledge of the universe being limited largely to streets considered sufficiently important in which to build a theatre, and spots which are regarded as sufficiently near the noise and clatter of railways and street cars to make them desirable sites for the building of an hotel. But I will go so far as to say that Boston is a very pleasant place to live in. And, if I may again give advice to my fellow man, I would suggest that when you are there should you be seeking companionship — female companionship — don't go to the dance halls amongst the flappers, but pick out some lady, — almost any lady, over seventy, and if she takes to you you will have the time of your life. But don't be put off with some immature substitute in the fifties or sixties; be sure that she has reached the allotted span of life.

At seventy the Boston lady says to herself, "I have done my duty as a wife and mother; I have earned the love and respect of my grandchildren and my great grandchildren; now I am going to have a good time." But before you attach yourself to the lady, you must be sure that you are in good physical condition; you will need all your strength. She will call for you in the morning at ten; if it is winter put on your woolen underclothing and get out your heavy coat, because it is probable she will have an open car waiting for you; she has had experience and she knows that fresh air is good for you. You will get into the car first and she will leap in after you. She will then proceed to take you everywhere; she will be splendid company, chock-full of charm and information and high spirits. You will go to lunch in some historic spot

where your body and your mind will be simultaneously fed. After that when you are thinking that she
really ought to go home and lie down, she will help
you into the car again and take you everywhere else.
When eventually she lands you exhausted but happy
at your hotel, she will bid you a hasty and affectionate
good-by, advise you to rest a while, and tell you that
she has just time to get to her bridge party. When you
wake up, after a few hours' rest, you will realize what
a wonderful time you have had. It is quite possible
you will fall in love with her. I generally do.

During our Boston engagement, I hurt my hand
with the result that for more than ten weeks I played
with my right arm in a sling. This puzzled the audience and gave occasion for a good deal of discussion
between the acts. I got frequent reports of people saying, "Why I never knew Disraeli only used one arm,"
and almost invariably a well-informed friend would
say, "Didn't you! Oh, yes, he always carried his
right arm in a sling." I discovered that many were
disappointed when they afterwards saw me play the
part with the normal number of hands. Possibly the
evidence of the misfortune from which I had been
suffering had invested the character with a certain
amount of additional sympathy. I had, myself, grown
so used to manipulating all my business with one hand
that the first night I was allowed by the surgeon to
use my right arm my performance seemed to me
strange and unnatural.

I cannot sufficiently express my gratitude to my
Boston friends. They did not take us up as a passing

fad, but they gave us a friendship which has been maintained with increasing warmth at each succeeding visit. I hesitate to mention people that I have met but casually; perhaps however I may be allowed to speak of so outstanding a figure as the late John Sargent. I had the good fortune to meet him several times somewhat intimately, and to be the solitary visitor admitted to his temporary studio at the Library whilst he was working on his frescoes. But I could never "get near to him." I admired him tremendously and should have rejoiced if he had shown the slightest interest in me. I made desperate efforts to draw him into conversation but never succeeded. I don't think he ever spoke to me of the play; I am not even sure that he knew I was connected with a theatre. I tried him on art; I mentioned my brother Fred who is an artist and the interesting work that he was engaged upon for the Indian Government, but I got no response beyond a monosyllable. He made me feel that he had mentally taken my measure and decided that I wasn't worth while. He seemed to be cold and stern. And yet his friends have told me that he could be warm and responsive; that his passion was music, and that if you sat him down at a piano he would become gay and boyish. I have no feeling of resentment for his attitude towards me. A man as big as he should be allowed to be contemptuous of some other people. I set down my impression merely as a matter of record. Such acquaintanceship as I had with him was through Mrs. "Jack" Gardner who was one of his most intimate friends.

Mrs. Gardner had a striking and fascinating personality.

With characteristic initiative she called on us at our little house in Brookline without any kind of warning or introduction, and from that time she remained our devoted friend. She insisted on introducing us to all her closest acquaintances. If she were going any distances such as to Manchester or Gloucester she would beg leave to borrow our car. She said, "I can't afford to keep a car of my own, because I am having to keep all the policemen and postmen in the United States." This was an allusion to the tremendous duties she had to pay the Customs on works of art which she bought in Europe to add to her marvellous collection in her palace at Brookline. At that time I believe the duty on imported antiques had not been removed. She knew and loved every one of her precious possessions, and I believe she never acquired anything that did not appeal to her personally for either its beauty or its artistic merit.

I had the good fortune too to meet Mrs. Fields, who entertained me with many stories of her intimate friendship with Dickens and Thackeray. Mrs. Thomas Bailey Aldrich was then a striking figure in Boston and was one of our dearest friends. She would pay me the compliment at that time of seeking my criticism on certain chapters of the book she afterwards published with such gratifying results under the title of "Crowding Memories." One of the most delightful of the group of women was Mrs. Bell who was then eighty-four. I met her at many gatherings. No dinner party in which she was included was ever dull. She generally kept every one in peals of laughter and I never heard her repeat herself. She lived in a small house with a small back garden. For a time she kept a pig in the yard and when asked why on earth she kept it, she said, "Well, we must have something to put things in." I must curb myself in setting down my recollections of this Boston visit or I shall be led on to tell tales of the Merrits and the Montagues, and Cecilia Beaux (who did a picture of me), John Hays Hammond, Jr. (who is always working on some revolutionizing invention), the inimitable Beatrice Herford, Major Higginson, the Howes, the Peabodys, the Hoopers, the Lorings, Robert Shaw (with his wonderful collection of theatrical records now housed in the Widener Library, but at that time a private collection), the amazing Mrs. Osgood and her daughter the beautiful Mrs. Fiske Warren, and so many others whose friendship and kindness to us both have been unswerving.

When we were leaving it was apparent that our time would not permit us to pay a leisurely farewell visit to all our friends, so the Montagues arranged a Sunday dinner to be partaken of in five or six separate and distinct establishments. We were not aware of this conspiracy and accepted the invitation to dinner in good faith. We were therefore much surprised when, after soup, our hostess got up and the whole party of eight wished us good-by. We were bundled into a waiting limousine and driven to house number two, where we arrived just in time for the second course.

Fish having been consumed, the party rose and saw us safely into the patient motor-car and we were whizzed off to house number three, which we reached in time to find the third course about to be served. This was repeated until the end. It had been so carefully arranged in the matter of time that none of the dinner parties was seriously dislocated. The final course of this peripatetic meal was partaken of in the sixth house, where all the parties from all the other houses finally assembled for coffee. Whether this was an original idea for a farewell dinner I cannot say: I have, however, never met it since. But I really must stop writing about the pleasant Boston people or I shall become emotional and consequently more tedious than ever. I find it very difficult to gage how far the recollections that interest me are going to be entertaining to others.

(Advice to Intending Readers of Recollections:

Approach the volume with patience and a Christian spirit. If for instance, I, as the writer, should be led away to tell you at great length all about my Aunt Emma and the time when she was so kind to me, don't say "Heavenly powers! What is all this about Aunt Emma? What do we care about his Aunt Emma!" don't thereupon treat the volume in a way that is liable to endanger its binding; be calm and try to remember my position. The memory of Aunt Emma is vivid in my brain; her character is enriched by the thousand and one good qualities which you can never know about. In writing about her I have perhaps lost my sense

of proportion. But have I? How am I to know?
You might perchance be very interested in her.
And suppose I didn't mention her at all, and then
something came out about her afterwards, you
would be the first to say, "Why didn't he mention his Aunt Emma? Rather snobbish of him!"
So approach "Recollections" with fortitude and
forbearance.)

To pursue "Disraeli" through all its travels would
be to write a guide book to the United States. It
seems to me that in the five consecutive seasons during
which I played it, I appeared in every corner of the
country. I am always grateful to George Tyler that
he never made any attempt to cheapen my company
throughout the long period. The performance in the
most obscure one-night stand was on the same plane
as that given during the New York season.

XIII

FIRST NIGHT AGONIES

It might very naturally be supposed that having had five years in which to collect plays suitable for my use that I should have no difficulty in finding a successor to "Disraeli." As a matter of fact I hadn't anything. I had read hundreds of plays. Statesmen by the dozen had been dug up by diligent authors — Gladstone by the bagful; Pitt, Chesterfield, Palmerston and a host of others. If an actor makes a success as a Prime Minister, authors insist that he shall be a Prime Minister to the end of his career, or at least a member of the Cabinet. After I had played the Japanese Minister in "The Darling of the Gods" I was inundated with Japanese and Chinese characters. After "The Green Goddess" it was taken for granted that all star parts written for me must be gentlemen of color. If only authors would not write plays expressly for me, I should be so much obliged. I want them (or some of them) to keep on writing plays but to write them for somebody else, and then send them to me. By that means I might get something that will suit me. The only success I have had that was designed for me was "Disraeli" and that was written by a man who had never seen me act. I except "Hamilton" because in that I was a collaborator.

So at the end of the season 1914–1915 when I closed with "Disraeli" I found myself without a play. I was not unconscious of the tragedy of my position. I had been looking for something for the past four years and there seemed to be no adequate reason why the succeeding four years should not see me devoted to silent meditation in the library. When trouble of this kind overtakes me — or indeed any other kind of trouble — and I find myself in New York, I always go to Brander Matthews and he generally gives me good advice and consolation. This has been a habit with me ever since I met him first in 1901. I recall that first meeting very vividly. Flo and I had just arrived in New York from England.

Flo said, "We must call on my aunt and uncle, Mr. and Mrs. Brander Matthews."

Of course no sane man wishes to call on his wife's aunt and uncle, so I murmured, "Must we?"

"Certainly we must," she said; "Aunt's a darling and I know you'll like him." Flo always insisted on my liking the people she likes.

"What is he?" I asked.

"He's a professor," she said shortly. I think my reply to that was, "Oh, my hat!" "Don't be ridiculous," said Flo. "He's Professor of Dramatic Literature at Columbia University and a very distinguished man."

I said, "All right, I'll go. But I don't like professors; they always make me feel unnecessarily insignificant. Don't let's stay more than five minutes."

So we went. At the end of two hours Flo had to drag me away. And ever since that day, if ever I need advice or if ever I have an hour or two to spare, I ring

up Brander and his response is, "Come right in with
your boots on, as the alligator said to the piccaninny,"
or words to that effect. We have written a play
together (one of those good plays that have never
been produced). Not that I particularly wanted to
write a play, but because it brought us continually
together; at each meeting I would lead him on to
talk for an hour and by that means I learned more
about the drama of the world than I ever dreamed I
should know. My association with Brander endowed
me with a free education in the drama and the
"British rights" to all his most amusing anecdotes.
I don't think I ever have quite as good a time as when
we are alone for the express purpose of "swapping"
stories and opinions.

But occasionally in those earlier days he would give
a special luncheon for me, inviting people that he
thought I ought to know. It was in this way that I
first met Augustus Thomas, Clyde Fitch, W. D.
Howells, Mark Twain, Francis Wilson, Bronson
Howard, Joseph Jefferson and many other interesting
men. I shall never forget the thrill I got when I
found myself seated next to Mark Twain at luncheon.
I believe I have mentioned that my earliest reading
was Mark Twain and the Bible. I think I read Mark
Twain first. At this luncheon I was more fortunate
than the others who were present. They were mostly
men who had something to say and wanted to say it.
Mark arrived in great form; he took the stand and
kept it nearly the whole afternoon. I was in luck; I
had nothing to say, and more than anything in the

world at that moment I wanted to hear Mark Twain talk. He had, as every one knows, a most picturesque head, lit up by those keen and humorous eyes, and decorated with his shaggy hair and brows. But what interested me most was his manner of telling his yarns. Everything he said seemed to be spontaneous, spoken with a slow and fascinating hesitancy. But as the afternoon went on, my experience as an actor told me that there was method in the telling of all his stories; they had been carefully "constructed" so that each point should come in its right place and should lead up to a climax.

I met Joseph Jefferson only once. He was the guest of honor at some large gathering of men; I was much impressed by his vivid personality and his youthful vivacity. I remember he used a device for escaping the ordeal of making a set address, which I have since borrowed on occasions. He said that he did not propose to make a speech, but as it was possible he had special knowledge of certain things connected with the stage in which his friends present might be interested, he would be very glad to answer any questions that were put to him. This led to a most entertaining hour in which he disclosed his opinion on many points. I met him with Brander after the meeting and asked him if he thought that the great expense of production — meaning the considerable attention paid to scenery and effects — had tended to improve the art of the actor. He thought for a moment and then said, "I should say No! In the old days when scenery was much simpler the actor had to exert all his powers to excite in the imagination of the audience all that was lacking in the 'production.'"

This seems sound common sense, although I think it is open to argument. Personally I believe I can be a more convincing king sitting on a well-built throne than balancing on an inverted soap box. I have tried both. But to return to 1915.

Brander made some good suggestions; one was that I should revive "The Professor's Love Story", but I think the play was not available at that time. Finally I went to England to look over the ground. There I read innumerable manuscripts. With Louis Parker I talked over the possibility of a play written round "Cagliostro" but after a great deal of thought and labor on his part the idea was abandoned. Chinese Gordon was suggested and passed over. I visited Justin Huntly McCarthy. I knew he was a great lover of Pepys and I thought he might be able to offer me a Pepys play. But he couldn't undertake it at such short notice. We also discussed the Old Marquis of Queensberry known to posterity as "Old Q.", but he failed to establish himself as a central figure for a play. Israel Zangwill whizzed me off to his charming country home, took me into a lovely garden which delighted and exhilarated me and read me a Jewish problem play which depressed me exceedingly. Then I called on Knoblock at his chambers in The Albany and we dug up Edgar Allan Poe and buried him again. Then Knoblock said, "Have a look through my books and notes over there and see if you can get an inspiration." While I was seeking for inspiration, he was discussing with an art dealer the possible acquisition of a piece of priceless red lacquer such as only dramatists who live in The Albany would ever dream of considering. I came across some notes on Paganini that arrested my attention. I didn't know anything about him beyond the fact that he was probably the greatest violinist that ever lived; but ever since I could remember there had been in a shop window in Wardour Street a full-length plaster statue of Paganini which always interested me. It looked like a trunk of an old gnarled oak rather than the figure of a man.

I suppose a character actor is always likely to be interested in a "make-up" and I at once saw myself as this skinny and attenuated black figure. I called out "What about Paganini." It happened that Knoblock knew all about him and was immensely attracted by him as a stage figure. Within five minutes the play was decided upon. And so my next character was "Paganini." After the first night my friends crowded round me, shook me warmly by the hand and congratulated me. But we all knew there was something wrong. I felt it when the curtain fell. And when my friends beamed at me and said, "Most interesting!" I knew I hadn't struck a success. "Interesting!" Fatal word. Nobody ever told me "The Green Goddess" was interesting, "How thrilling" was the expression used there. That meant success! But "interesting!!" So, I've no doubt, is an operation for appendicitis. Again I found out, too late, what was the matter. I hadn't learnt my lesson from "Septimus" it seemed. It was plainly exactly the same trouble. Just as "Septimus" was so far engrossed in his inventions that what would have been a sacrifice to another man was but an incident to him, so Paganini's passion for his music burned every other emotion into ashes. It was in vain that Margery Maude — looking and sounding exactly like her fascinating mother Winifred Emery, as I first remember her — in vain that she poured words of love into my ear: the audience knew that she was not in love with me, that she had no deep and enduring passion for the man; it was his music, his violin, that had carried her away. In vain that I tried to manifest passion, to suggest that my whole heart went out to her. Those amazing critics — the people who had paid for their seats — knew it wasn't true. They knew I had only one love, only one mistress, and that was my violin. I have no doubt that this impression which the audience got so unmistakably was exactly what Knoblock intended — it was true to life. But it was the kind of truth that is interesting and not thrilling; which is just the difference between success and the other thing. "Paganini" was by no means a failure; it carried me through the season and we opened again with it the following year in New York for a short run, but it was on the whole a disappointment.

This was followed by a revival of "The Professor's Love Story." A delightful play; old-fashioned, but I suppose any piece that has been plagiarized a hundred times is likely to seem old-fashioned. It is surprising what a number of professor's love stories in different disguises have passed through my hands during the past twenty years. But this early effort of Barrie's

"PAGANINI"

In the play written for George Arliss by Edward Knoblock

has all the elusive charm of dialogue that has delighted us in his later plays. Sir James confessed to me, the only time I ever met him, that the construction was rather shocking to him now. He expressed some amusement at the comfortable way he had moved his characters on and off the stage to suit his own convenience, with a sublime unconsciousness of the struggles and troubles that beset the more mature dramatist in the effort to make these entrances and exits appear spontaneous. During this season Miss Margery Maude left the company and her place was taken by the amazingly clever Jeanne Eagels. Miss Eagels continued in the part of the Secretary until the end of the run. She then played Clarissa with me in a short revival of "Disraeli", and afterwards Mrs. Reynolds in "Hamilton." Three distinct parts, each played with unerring judgment and artistry!

"Hamilton" remains to me a most pleasant recollection. It is one of the few plays of any value that has ever come to me "out of the blue." It was sent by an unknown author without introduction. When I read it, I was at once attracted by the character and the story. I considered that it needed to be reconstructed in parts and largely rewritten. So I interviewed the author, Mrs. G. W. Hamlin, of Canandaigua, and suggested a collaboration to which she agreed. Mrs. Hamlin is probably the only woman alive who is a good wife, a good mother, a good housekeeper, a good friend and a good playwright all in one. She is also, I believe, the only author extant who, having agreed to collaborate with a star, has

271

not afterwards said or implied, "Of course it was really all mine." She would have a good case, too, for she has since written two exceedingly good plays without any interference at all. She was entirely unlike other untried dramatists that I had met. She never once wept over her own pathetic lines, nor did she ever refer to the play as her baby or even as her little papoose. I was very grateful to her for that. During our association in the writing of "Hamilton" her unselfish and generous attitude towards me surprised me always and left me ever her devoted friend. I have often heard that collaborators are dangerous and that it would be well if some scientific means could be devised by which they could be segregated; but to any one requiring a model collaborator, I have much pleasure in highly recommending Mrs. G. W. Hamlin or Professor Brander Matthews. When Brander suggested that he and I should write a play together he said, "You know, George, you are quite safe in writing with me, because if the play fails the critics will say, 'Ah, too much Brander Matthews,' and if it succeeds the credit will surely go to you."

While I was busy preparing "Hamilton" I came to the conclusion that the best place to write is in a top room of a large hotel. I have tried my own comfortable study but have found it too comfortable for intensive labor. I have tried the seclusion of a country cottage in the summer time, with no sound but the birds and the rustling of the trees. The birds and the trees are for me bad company. They behave in precisely the same manner as those wicked actresses that young men are warned against when they first go out into the world. They beckon me and chirrup at the outside of the window; they say, "Come on, leave all that stuffy old work; come with us; we will give you a good time." And I am too weak to resist.

The production of "Hamilton" brought me more personal correspondence than any play with which I have been connected, including even "Disraeli." Fortunately we had been reasonably careful to stick to facts in the construction of the play; we had spent a great deal of time in digging up old records. The Historical Society of Philadelphia gave us a mass of information and Mr. McAdoo, who was at that time Secretary of the Treasury, offered us every assistance in his power. Strange to say, there is hardly any record of Alexander Hamilton in the present Treasury Building. There is a rather poor but very large painting of him in the Secretary's office, but that is about all. I say it was fortunate that we were secure in our facts because descendants of almost every character in the play descended upon us in most unexpected places. Each of these living representatives had the engraving of his particular ancestor hung up in the best room at home and burned incense under it. If their idol failed to come forth as a hero in our play, they asked the reason why, and defied us to prove that he was not only a hero, but a saint. It was lucky for us that the duel is out of fashion or we should many times have been challenged to mortal combat. Just what the method of procedure would have been in the case of a duel with collaborators I cannot say. Perhaps our opponent would have been allowed to use a shot-gun. Sometimes we were met in a more Christian spirit. Many of the great-great-grandchildren greeted us warmly and gave us most interesting and intimate information of their ancestors. The present representatives of the Hamilton family were particularly pleasant and agreeable, although they had the broadest field for fault-finding. Numerous treasures were presented to me, including a lock of Hamilton's hair contained in a locket worn by him at the moment of the duel; books bearing his signature; shoe buckles; engravings; letters and many other souvenirs. Strange to say, the majority of these gifts came from Wall Street men; this surprised me because I had always been given to understand that the exceedingly light musical plays are designed mainly to meet the demands of the manipulators of the market.

"Hamilton" was not a spectacular triumph, but it was a gratifying success. On the first night in New York I was anxious, nervous and decidedly depressed. Having a double responsibility of authorship and of presentation, I found that the optimism of the author was overshadowed by the pessimism of the actor. The morning following the first night I met my friends Frank Gillmore and Francis Wilson at an Actors' Equity meeting and told them my varying sensations of the previous evening; they dared me to write the experience for the *Equity Magazine*. I sent them this sketch, which having been written at the moment will probably convey my feelings more vividly than I should express them now.

" ALEXANDER HAMILTON "

The play which Mr. Arliss wrote in collaboration with
Mrs. G. W. Hamlin

A FIRST NIGHT

SCENE I

*New York—Star's dressing-room on the street-level. It is
the first night of a new play. Star arrives looking pale
and haggard and knowing it; he has always looked like
that on every first night. It is a religion with him. He
would as soon think of dancing at a funeral as of
smiling on a first night. Jenner, his dresser, receives
him with forced brightness.*

JENNER. Evening, sir.

STAR (*with the air of a man who has travelled many thousands of miles and eventually finds himself on a desert
island*). Well, here we are.

JENNER. Yes, sir.

STAR (*letting his coat fall from his dry, shrunken body into
the hands of Jenner*). Got to go through with it, I
suppose.

JENNER. Yes, sir.

(*The Star disrobes with the air of a martyr, and in a
silence that throbs.*)

STAR. Isn't it colder to-night?

(*Jenner murmurs something that does for yes or no.
Star slides into his dressing gown, and remembers that
he put it on just that way when he was about to undergo
an operation in a private hospital at Boston.*)

JENNER (*hanging up clothes*). Going out to supper
to-night, sir — after the theatre?

STAR (*mastering a convulsive shudder, and speaking with
the air of a man who knows he is to be hanged by the
neck before eleven, but must cunningly conceal the fact*).
No — not to-night.

(Sits before his make-up box and remembers that day when he was a happy, careless boy; decides that life is not worth living. He begins to make up. During the next twenty minutes, no one really speaks. But out of the mouth of the Star come unexpected sounds — "Rotten" — "Oh, help" — "What's the matter with the damn stuff" *— and several long, groaning sighs. Nothing more except for one awful moment when a small boy in the street, who has found a crack in the blind through which he can see in, shouts,* "Oh, my Gawd, what a face," *which is the cue for the quick exit of Jenner, and noise without. In course of some space of time that is interminable and yet too soon determined, the Star is dressed, and stands before the mirror with dull, weary eyes. There is a knock at the door, giving him a shock which he is sure will shorten his life, and the stage manager says,* "I'm going to ring in — you look fine," *and is gone. The band strikes up, and the Star endeavors to determine rapidly whether if he invested everything he had in the world at five per cent., he could leave the stage and have enough to live on in some unpretentious way up-town — when, enter his wife.)*

HIS WIFE *(brightly)*. Well, old man, how are you feeling?

(The Star gives her an agonized, resentful, appealing look.)

HIS WIFE *(very brightly)*. You're not going on the stage like that, are you?

STAR *(almost swooning)*. Why, what's the matter? Like what?

276

HIS WIFE. Well, you look ninety. You're supposed to be thirty-five, you know.

STAR (*alarmed*). Do I?

(*Stands in front of mirror, and suddenly assumes excessive youth.*)

HIS WIFE (*looking critically at his reflection*). Yes, I don't mean that you want to go on looking like one of Ziegfeld's Follies. You want to look like a man, but not an old fossil.

(*Star looks at her, wondering why he ever married.*)

HIS WIFE. Now, buck up. It's going to be a great success, and you're going to be splendid.

STAR. Thank you, dear.

HIS WIFE. Now, don't be nervous. Good luck. Pity that waistcoat isn't a shade or two darker.

(*Goes brightly out.*)

STAGE MANAGER. Just going to ring up.

STAR (*with unexpected bravery*). All right, let 'er go.

(*When the overture is finished, there is a horrible moment of quiet. Then the Star hears the murmur of applause, and he knows the curtain is up.*)

STAR. Shut the door, Jenner, and let me know when Mr. Blank comes off. I don't want to hear anything until then.

(*Jenner goes out, and the Star is alone. He poses before the mirror until he hates the sight of himself. Jenner comes back apologetically with another pile of telegrams.*)

STAR. Time for me?

JENNER. Not yet, sir.

STAR. How are they taking it?

JENNER. Not like it went at Atlantic City, sir.

(*Exit.*)

(*Star is alone again. He suddenly says, "Oh, my God." This is when he remembers that he will have to make a speech. He soliloquizes.* "What was that I thought out — 'Ladies and Gentlemen, allow me to thank you for your kind reception of our new play.' ")

(*Stage hands assemble outside window in street, and voice of super-master, who is waiting to go on in the last act* — "Success, of course it won't be a success. These costume plays never are. I've been in dozens of 'em. They're all failures. Besides, this one is twenty years behind the times.")

(*Star rushes out of the room.*)

(END OF SCENE I)

SCENE II

THE SAME, *after the play* — *A crowd of friends of the Star bubbles round from the front, bringing with it the air of the idle rich; a jumble of words, alluring perfumes and flashing shirt fronts. The Star waits anxiously for their verdict.*

FIRST LADY FRIEND (*seizing him wildly by the hand*). Well, aren't you pleased? You certainly ought to be. You went through it as though you had been playing it for years. What a long part it is, too. I can't think how you remember it all. I want you to meet Mrs. Williams, one of your greatest admirers. She has seen you in everything.

278

MRS. WILLIAMS. We had a perfectly lovely evening. So interesting.

STAR (*daring to hope*). Did you like it?

MRS. WILLIAMS. Like it! Why, I don't know when I have seen anything so — why it's so — (*opens her mouth very wide with the hope that some useful word may settle upon a somewhat large, expansive red tongue which she exposes. The word not being within reach, however, she falls back upon "interesting" with great emphasis*).

ACTOR FRIEND (*darting forward and shaking Star by the elbow*). Excuse me — I won't interrupt you, old chap, but — Great!

(*Darts away before the Star can question him.*)

THE AUTHOR. I want you to meet some friends of mine. All people from my city. Mrs. ——— Mr. ——— Mrs. ——— Miss ———. (*Introduces nine people.*) (*They all say, "Wonderful", and "So interesting", and "Couldn't have believed", a number of times, during which the author of another play which is running on Broadway gives a friendly wave from the back of the crowd and stage whispers, "Perfectly bully" — "Can't stay" — "Got some people waiting."*)

STAR (*calling after him*). How's your play going?

AUTHOR OF OTHER PLAY (*coming back rapidly and shaking hands*). A sell-out almost every night — well, I'll tell you — the first week was a trifle seesaw, but now — well, Saturday on the two performances we played to — (*Whispers*). Good night, dear boy. Perfectly bully. (*Quick retreat.*)

OLD FRIEND (*in Star's ear*). It's all right, old man, except for your main theme. There's no drama in adultery any more, you know, — not in New York; it's just a comic episode. So your big scene will always go for nothing — otherwise with a little pruning —

ELDERLY LADY. May I shake hands with Mr. ———. I almost called you Hamilton. We had a perfectly wonderful time. I want to introduce my niece's daughter, Ramona. Yes, quite an unusual name for a child — isn't it? — She is crazy to go on the stage. What parts do you think she ought to take up? Of course, you can't tell without hearing her recite, but (*in confidence*) her talent is perfectly wonderful, and her diction — she has such diction, you know — I should have taken her to Mr. Booth or Mr. Jefferson, if they had been alive, because those are the parts that I think she ought to play, but then I'm no judge.

SOCIETY LADY FRIEND (*introducing a long white arm with a hand at the end of it*). I only want to say one word, "Wonderful", and how young you looked too, and so did your wife — I could never have believed — please give her my love and tell her so. Good night. Quite wonderful!

FRIEND FROM LONG ISLAND. Good night, dear boy. So good of you to send us the seats. Saw and heard splendidly. My wife's crazy about it, aren't you, dear.

WIFE (*taken by surprise*). Crazy! (*With emotion.*)

280

CROWD LEAVING. Can't tell you how much we enjoyed it. — So artistic! You always give us something worth while. — You must come and dine with us one evening, but, of course, you can't very well — How long will you be in New York? — Oh, yes? All winter, I am sure — A little over their heads, I think, but we loved it. (*Exeunt all but Star's wife, Jenner and Star.*)

STAR (*to his wife*). Well, what do you think?

HIS WIFE (*evasively*). Well, you heard what they said, didn't you? Everybody seemed delighted.

STAR. Do you think they did?

HIS WIFE. Now get dressed, and come along. (*Kisses him — a suspiciously protective and maternal kiss, and exits to her own room.*) Jenner and Star alone.

STAR (*after slight pause, beginning to undress*). Well, it's over, thank God.

JENNER. Yes sir. (*Undressing proceeds in silence.*)

STAR (*invitingly*). My clothes look all right?

JENNER. Yes, sir, they looked very good. (*Dressing proceeds. Further pause.*)

JENNER. Shall I bring the pictures down from the 'ouse, sir, — the ones you always 'ave 'ung up in the dressing room and 'ang them up 'ere, sir.

STAR (*techily*). Why — I don't know — I suppose so — don't worry me about that to-night — do as you like.

JENNER. Very well, sir. (*Long pause.*) I should think this play ought to do very good at Boston, sir.

Star is still alive the next day, much to his own
surprise.

Jenner having dressed me and undressed me for
more than twenty years has not only an intimate
knowledge of my wardrobe, but knows what I'm
thinking about, what I've forgotten and what I am
likely to be thinking about the day after to-morrow.
When he is in my dressing room my dressing room is
full, except for a small space for me to creep through
to my bench. Not that he is fat; he is merely large
everywhere and appropriately impressive. He has
two claims to distinction beyond other men: one is
that he is happy and contented with his job and the
other that in a slight altercation some years ago he
knocked out Young Corbett. He is, therefore, most
valuable in intervening between me and insurance
agents, to say nothing of the vendors of *Editions de
luxe*.

My wife and I continued to play Hamilton all that
season and we reopened with it the following year,
but at that time everything conspired against theatrical prosperity; there was the general unrest of the
interminable war — the closing of theatres on Mon-
days (and sometimes Tuesdays too) as a coal-saving
measure; then came the influenza scare of 1918 during
which a theatre was liable to be shut up at any
moment by the Health Commissioners. Every theatre
on my route was closed, one after the other, so that
at last, after waiting nearly a month for the skies to
clear, we were compelled to abandon our tour and go
back to New York.

It was during the spring of 1918 that a number of us did a three weeks' tour of flying visits with "Out There" for the benefit of the Red Cross. The idea was conceived by George Tyler, who undertook the tremendous task of arranging the tour.

Surprisingly small parts were played by amazingly big stars, who were anxious to do their bit for the cause. From memory I recall the names of Mrs. Fiske, Laurette Taylor, Helen Ware, George M. Cohan, H. B. Warner, Chauncey Olcott, James K. Hackett, O. P. Heggie, James T. Powers, George MacFarlane, and there were others whose names have escaped me. We visited, I think, seventeen cities in three weeks, opening in Washington and closing in Pittsburgh. It was no uncommon thing for us to play to forty thousand dollars in one night, and at Pittsburgh a signed programme realized twenty thousand five hundred dollars. Laurette Taylor has written and published an amusing and detailed account of this tour. After "Hamilton" there followed in succession "The Mollusc" (with which I played Barrie's charming one-act play "A Well-Remembered Voice"), "Jacques Duval" (from the German) and Booth Tarkington's Bolshevist comedy-drama "Poldikin." It was during the run of Poldikin that I made my first moving picture.

XIV

BEFORE THE CAMERA

For several years tentative proposals had been made
to me to enter this new field of the actor's art but
something had always intervened. It was now proposed that I should make a picture of Molnar's
"Devil" — the play which had been my first starring
vehicle on the speaking stage. It happened that I
had two other pressing offers to do pictures at this
time, so the people who wished to do the "Devil"
signed a contract with me before making any photographic "test." This is a dangerous thing to do,
because many men who can act do not screen well.
It was therefore an anxious time for me and for them
when I went down to the studio to have my first test
made. The director was James Young, who had been
an actor of reputation before he elected to devote his
time to directing pictures. He had an enormous
respect for acting as an art, and a considerable belief
in me as one of its exponents. He knew that an actor
is a sensitive creature that must not be worried or
badgered if he is to appear at his best. I was curiously
ignorant of studio conditions and everything seemed
strange and discouraging around me, as I walked into
this large and queerly lighted workshop. James Young
realized my sensations and glided softly to my side.
James Young is lithe and supple; he can glide or leap,
or hang on to the arc light by his teeth or turn a

284

somersault without touching the ground and is willing to execute any one of these capers in order to encourage an actor. This was the moment for the glide. He spoke softly to me with a charming bedside manner. This in itself was no mean accomplishment as there was a great deal of knocking and shouting in progress in all parts of the studio. He told me not to be anxious or nervous. He was terribly kind and considerate. I felt that this was probably the way the dentist spoke to King George the Fifth before he took his teeth out. He led me to a spot where there was a table and a chair and some gentlemen in their shirt sleeves with green faces who appeared to be waiting for me. James Young smiled upon me and said, "Well, what shall we do?" I looked at him wildly. He now leapt a little bit to encourage me. He leapt six feet to the left of me, clapped his hands, and leapt back again to my side.

"Now," he said, "let us invent a little story for the test. Suppose we try this. You are seated at the table; you open a letter and find that it is an offer for you to make a motion picture; you think, 'Shall I do it.' You decide 'Yes. But what play shall I select?' You reach for your book of programmes of the plays you have already performed — Septimus — You shake your head. Paganini — 'No. Ah. What is this? "The Devil." The very thing. Yes, I will do "The Devil."' You write a note accepting the offer, seal it, decide you will mail it yourself — and go off. How's that?"

James here gave an imitation of Professor Blondin

285

jumping lightly off the slack wire after having walked safely across Niagara Falls — and smiled at me encouragingly.

I said, "All right."

James said "Ah", clapped his hands, turned to the group of hired assassins who awaited his signal, said, "Boys, this is Mr. George Arliss," and then told them what I was about to do. "Now we won't shoot for a minute; you just rehearse it by yourself and say when you're ready." And he went into a corner and tried over some difficult steps just to keep himself in condition.

I went through the business two or three times. My whole thought was, "How am I to get the meaning of this thing over without speaking a word." I wished some one would come and give me some hints; but I was left severely alone. At last I said I was ready.

James at once glided to my bedside, asked soothingly after my pen and ink, stationery, book, chair; finding all was well, he ordered the camera man to begin the operation and from then he never took his eyes off me until the end.

When I heard the grinding of the camera and realized that for the first time its deadly work was directed at me, I became cold with fear, but my long training as an actor led me to go through without squealing; the camera with its relentless grind was my audience and I was brought up in the school of actors who would die before they would confess fear or suffering to the audience. I went ahead. Opened my letter — expressed surprise — thought "Shall I do it", decided "Yes"; reached for my programmes — discarded Septimus; decided against Paganini; came to "The Devil" — started — The very thing! Wrote my letter of acceptance; decided to mail it myself and went off. When the camera stopped I felt as though I was let out of a cage, but I said, "May I do it again? I am sure I can do it better." So I did it again, this time with a little more assurance and with determination that my facial expression should leave no doubt as to my meaning. As I finished I looked round for James, and found that he was sideways in a large armchair apparently giving an imitation of a shrimp during the process of boiling — with his eye fixed on me.

I said, "How was that?"

He said, "Great."

I said, "Really?"

He said, "Fine — perhaps just a leetle — but we will see it to-morrow!" Here he leapt into space and came down amongst his hired assassins to whom he now introduced me individually. I found to my relief that they were not really green, and that they were in fact not assassins at all, but kindly, smiling men who were deeply interested in my future — the camera man, his assistant and the property master. The tests were "rushed" and I was sent for the next day to go and see them.

Waiting to see yourself come on the screen for the first time is another uncomfortable sensation. You wonder what kind of a person is going to appear and when you see him you are shocked and disappointed but you thank Heaven it is no worse. I am thankful I was left to myself in the making of this test, for I

287

learnt a lesson and learnt it very thoroughly. When the thing was thrown on the screen there I was; I saw myself, but it seemed to me somebody else; I watched this person narrowly and critically from my seat in the dark room; the camera man was there and so was his assistant. James was there too; I couldn't see him, but I knew he must be chained to his seat, for nobody moved. This is what we saw. A gentleman seated at a table trying not to look nervous. He picks up an envelope with exaggerated nonchalance — opens it with a flourish, takes out the letter as though he were producing rabbits from a hat, reads the letter with a series of varying facial expressions such as no man has ever accomplished before; looks out into space and thinks for so long that he appears to be listening to the angels singing; reaches for book of programmes; turns over the leaves with much shrugging of shoulders and shaking of head. Stops suddenly; starts as though he had read that the British Isles had been swallowed up and every soul lost, thinks "Shall I commit suicide" — reaches for note paper — writes a farewell letter, — seals it — thinks "Shall I stab myself now with a steel pen, or shall I go out and drown myself in the Hudson?" Decides on latter course and goes off. During the presentation of this tragedy somebody must have unchained some part of James, for before the lights went up I found his head resting lightly on my shoulder and it was murmuring, "Don't you think perhaps just a leetle?"

The lights went up and found me a figure of shame.

But as I said, I learnt my lesson. I had always believed that for the movies, acting must be exaggerated, but I saw in this one flash that *restraint* was the chief thing that the actor had to learn in transferring his art from the stage to the screen. A broader method is required for the stage; this is perhaps partly due to the fact that there are certain distractions on the stage that do not attach to the movies; the spoken word for one; expression and gesture are more clearly defined on the screen; there is the telltale close-up, with which the speaking actor can never be threatened. It is fortunate that I proved to be an apt pupil, for we began the picture in real earnest within the next few days. My experience in the movies taught me many things that have been useful to me in the theatre; first and foremost it brought fully home to me the value of sincerity; I found that every flicker of an eyelash, every shade of thought, was registered on the screen, and so I reason that what is seen by the camera may be felt by an audience. The art of restraint and suggestion on the screen may any time be studied by watching the acting of the inimitable Charlie Chaplin. Apart from the all-important cultivation of restraint, I found practically no difference between the method of acting required for the screen and that which I had always applied to the stage. How far it is necessary for an actor to change his method must I suppose depend upon his manner of acting on the speaking stage. I suppose that a more restless actor or one whose effects are gained by rapid motion would experience greater difficulty.

It is true it took me many weeks to get used to the habits of the studio. During the years in which I have more or less directed my own affairs I have always opposed the frittering away of time at rehearsals. I can find no excuse for the systematically unpunctual star. No man has a right to waste the time of others, however great his position may be by comparison. Let a star or a director work his company as long as he likes within reasonable limits in order to insure a good and smooth performance; but to waste their time is presuming on his authority; and it is moreover commercially unsound. The dissipation of valuable time seemed to me the besetting sin of the studio. Possibly I am unfair in this criticism; perhaps all the interruptions and delays are unavoidable, but I found it very difficult to accustom myself to them.

My contract called for me to be ready for work at 10 A.M. and finish not later than 3:30 P.M. This restriction of time was necessary for me, because I was acting at night and was compelled to take some rest before the performance. I realized, therefore, that with the heavy overhead expenses of the studio every moment was of value. It was not at all unusual however to have a working day like this; I would arrive on the scene at ten o'clock. The camera man and James would be there. James was always on time; the camera man never seemed to leave the studio. James would say to me, "You look great this morning. We must wait a few minutes. Mr. Thomas is on time but he had a make-up that I thought was a trifle too dark — he's just changing it. Those rushes that came

in this morning were grand — just saw them run off.
I believe we've got time to dash down and let you see
them. Harry (to camera man), you had better come
too." We go down and see rushes, in all of which I
feel I could do better if I could do them again. In
three quarters of an hour we return and Mr. Thomas
is there, all ready. James says, "That's better, Mr.
Thomas; fine. Now off we go. Wait a minute.
Where's Miss Lucy? She puts her head in at this door,
you know. Tell Miss Lucy we're waiting for her."
The assistant goes down for Miss Lucy; returns with
the news that she has not arrived. Her home is rung
up and Miss Lucy says she was told she wouldn't be
wanted to-day, but she will come at once. There is a
council of war as to whether something can be done
until she arrives. This is found to be unpractical.
After the lapse of an hour the lovely Miss Lucy
appears on the scene dressed and ready. There is some
discussion as to when she was told that she wouldn't
be wanted and who told her and what right had he to
do so and the matter is then dismissed.

James says, "Now, then, we've got to push along.
All ready, Harry. Shoot." Harry, who is always
patient, begins to grind and we all commence to act.
After the first few feet of film Harry suddenly stops
and says, "Wait a minute. That tie Mr. Arliss is
wearing comes out all white; it'll look terrible."
There is a further pause of ten minutes while I dig out
another tie. James now cries "*Shoot.*" We act beautifully until we are nearly through the scene, when
James says, "Wait a minute! What are those flowers

doing on the table. Didn't I tell you no flowers in this scene. Those are the flowers he gives her later on. Kill that, Harry. Take off those flowers. Now once more. Shoot."

Harry begins to grind. I attempt to revive my waning vitality and spontaneity, when a voice from heaven rumbles forth. "Wait a minute."

Everything stops.

James says, "What's the matter."

The voice replies, "This lens has broke; I'll have to change it." James says soothingly to me, "He's got to change his lens." I am amazed to observe that no one around me shows the slightest irritation at these interruptions. James, who is the soul of good humor until he is vexed, asks me if I have ever walked on my hands. I tell him that I used to do it at one time, but gave it up when I decided to learn the violin. In order to while away the time, he throws himself on to his hands and walks round the set. Some other sports are indulged in and then, after what seems to me an interminable interval, the new lens is ready. It is then disclosed that Mr. Thomas' stomach has been troubling him this morning and he has just slipped to his room to take something for it. Some diversion is here created by the arrival of three musicians attached to three instruments — a harp, a violin and a diminutive piano. It transpires that one of our ladies has declared that she cannot act without music. James asks the trio if, in the absence of Mr. Thomas, they will oblige with something dreamy. They do so. Several ladies have arrived by this time and everybody agrees that the music is perfectly wonderful, and that the violinist is perfectly wonderful, and we all wonder why he is not snapped up by the Metropolitan Opera House. Everybody asks them to play something else and we are just settling down to a pleasant musicale when Mr. Thomas is seen pulling himself together and approachng the set.

There is now nothing to wait for; we all brace ourselves for a great effort as James says, "Shoot." But Harry has a hawklike eye; he says, "Wait a minute," and everybody stands at ease. Harry has discovered that the music has so affected Miss Lucy that her make-up is all spotty round the eyes. She retires to her room. I observe James approaching me with measured tread and a strange unfathomable look in his eye; he stops before me and says, "I want to see you do Richard III on the screen. Wouldn't it be great! You remember when he says" — his body begins to shrink and he proceeds to give a remarkable performance of Richard III. He then turns lightly to Hamlet and we have just settled down to an afternoon with the Classics when the lovely Miss Lucy arrives, looking lovelier than ever. Her beauty so affects the violinist, who is already affected by the fact that his music has affected her, that he starts something into which he puts his whole soul. It is so beautiful that no one dare interrupt and we listen in rapt attention to the end.

We are just about to return to work when a noise starts in the set behind ours such as it seems impossible could be brought about by human agency. This makes

James angry, and in a tremendous voice — bigger than Richard III — he commands that there shall be silence. The noise ceases, but a number of men come towards him and there is a considerable amount of conversation. Then another director approaches James affectionately and tells him that this scene behind ours must be scrapped, because they need the space to build a scene that he is almost waiting for. James, who is now roused, says he doesn't care how many scenes they want to build, they can't do it now; he is not going to have his actors handicapped in this way. Then the other director weeps (directors can do everything) and James, who never can resist a director's tears, consents to listen. The director points out that it is now within fifteen minutes of lunch time and if James will dismiss for lunch now he will have the scene scrapped by two o'clock. This is agreed upon and as I do not lunch when I am working, I stand and wait till the scrapping is accomplished, learning another lesson in patience and resignation. Out of regard to my friend James, I am bound to point out that this waste of time does not necessarily imply bad direction; things are always happening in the movies that nobody could have foreseen; it is nevertheless somewhat trying for the actor who is fresh from the legitimate stage.

I never cease to be surprised at the lavish expenditure on movie productions, at the art of the scene designers and at the extraordinary ingenuity and ability of those who carry out these designs. Nothing is too difficult for them and every one in a studio seems willing to make any sacrifice in order to get an effect on the screen. I have the greatest respect for the screen and its people. It is unfortunate that the newspapers seem to find so much profit in the reporting of the peccadillos of those who are guilty of spectacular misbehavior in the quest for happiness or for publicity. The public in time believes that the conduct of these few is a fair example of the manners of the movie world. They do not take into account the thousands of steady hard workers who are the real backbone of the industry. My acquaintance with the wickedness of the movie actors and actresses has been gained entirely through the press. I have never met any of these dreadful people or if I have I've been unaware of their wicked ways.

Work in the studio is arduous; it is by no means all beer and skittles. To me it is always interesting, but rather exhausting. I got a great deal of pleasure and relaxation out of location work — in the country on charming sunny days. I was never better in my life than when we were on location with "The Ruling Passion." That was a picture in which I worked in a garage, and when I had on my overalls and was puttering about outside my workshop, I began to realize the pleasures of being a "working man." We had a garage built in a country road, with a pump fitted for the supply of gasoline, and everything complete. I was supposed to be at war with the garage opposite and marked down my gas as low as fourteen cents to compete with my neighbor. Our building was so real that drivers of cars would pull up, attracted by the price, demand gasoline, then the thing would be explained, they would notice our painted faces and good-humoredly drive off. Of course we had no gasoline, simply the pump.

One day during the lunch recess, I was sitting in the little office of the garage and one of the property men was standing by the pump. I saw a car draw up and as none of the actors were about, there was nothing to intimate that it was not a veritable garage. I heard the owner ask for five gallons of gas and to my surprise I saw the "props" attach the pipe and begin pumping; he didn't know I was in the office; I saw the man bring out a roll of bills and for the moment I feared our property man was going to take the money, so I was much relieved when I heard him say in an offhand way, "No charge to-day."

"What?" said the man, "How's that?"

"Mr. Rockefeller's birthday. Drive on," said the props, and off went the delighted owner. This is about the only movie wickedness that I have encountered. I was party to the crime, for it amused me so much that I could not resist allowing him to go through the same performance with another unfortunate driver before I intervened.

I have always been grateful for my movie experience; it has taught me a great deal. I will not enter the discussion as to whether acting is an art — although I have my opinion — but given certain physical attributes I consider an actor requires less ability to achieve popular success upon the screen than upon the legitimate stage. The director of the movies is of far more

"POLDIKIN"
The hero of Booth Tarkington's play on Bolshevism

ultimate value than the producer on the stage. An actor of limited experience can be trained to give effective moments; enthusiasm and fire may be injected into him by a talented director long enough for the pictures to be taken by the camera. But every theatrical producer knows that after he has worked like a slave with a bad or mediocre actor, the effect of his labor may remain for two or three performances, the spark may glow for a short time, but it will surely die out, and the performance will become dull and lifeless.

As I have said, I was still playing "Poldikin" at the time I made my first picture. "Poldikin" contained some of the choicest comedy that I have ever read. Booth Tarkington had taken tremendous pains in the writing of the play and had drawn some exceedingly good characters. A curiously modest man, Tarkington, considering his great ability and his acknowledged position in the literary world; he is in close sympathy with the actor and is always anxious to see his point of view and to conform to suggestions when possible. There are authors who are contemptuous of the actor and his opinions. This I consider is an unwise attitude for a dramatist to maintain, for an actor often has an intuition as to how a point may be best conveyed to an audience; this subtle apprehension is not always given to dramatists — particularly to those who are primarily novelists. Booth Tarkington was a perpetual delight to me. It was worth sitting up to the small hours to watch his keen eyes blazing with enthusiasm, and to catch the infection of his amazing chuckle. The trouble with "Poldikin" was that an American audience could not take seriously the warning that there was danger to them in Bolshevist propaganda and perhaps they were right, as audiences generally are. The consequence was that the deep and earnest intention of the author failed to impress them and the play was accepted merely for its comedy value.

I had now been with George Tyler for ten years — ever since "Disraeli." I had watched him go gray in his efforts to find plays that would please both me and the American public at one and the same time. His digestion was not what it was when he first took over the responsibility of my career, and just now his rest at night was disturbed. "Poldikin's" days were numbered and I was screaming for another play. George Tyler was beginning to weigh himself every morning, when lo! Winthrop Ames appeared and offered to nurse me for a little while whilst Tyler got some sleep. But when it actually came to this point George Tyler and I found that we had become a habit with one another which we were loath to give up. Tyler is one of the best friends any actor can have. He may think he's a hard-headed business man, but he is as full of sentiment as an egg is of meat. I knew that he would have stood by me, and found plays for me until I was aged and toothless and even then would have put me in an all-star revival. But Winthrop Ames had "The Green Goddess" for immediate production, and the Rajah was so obviously a part for me that we accepted the inevitable. The sting of parting was to some extent relieved by my being taken over as a sort of loan without any definite time being fixed for my return.

"The Green Goddess" was one of those unusual productions in which everything that was expected really happened. We felt reasonably confident of success and we got it. In striking contrast to "Disraeli" it was an assured hit from the first rise of the curtain. For the benefit of the struggling young actor I record a forcible example of the advantage of gaining experience before attempting to leap to the top rung of the ladder.

Within the first week of the production of "The Green Goddess," my Stage Manager was suddenly taken ill and was removed to a hospital. This left the entire responsibility on the shoulders of the Assistant. Assistant Stage Managers have not the same standing as Assistant Managers in business. I find as a rule that if I wish to make any inquiries or lodge any complaints in a business house, or in an hotel, I am referred to the Assistant Manager. The Manager appears to be a very exclusive individual, occupying an office remote from the vulgar world. When I am crossing the ocean, I am referred to the Second Steward; there may be a First Steward, but I have never seen one. But the Assistant Stage Manager is, as a rule, little more than a glorified errand-boy. He may have capabilities, but he is seldom given the opportunity of testing them.

Both Winthrop Ames and I were, therefore, much surprised when our Assistant at once took the reins with a masterly hand and ran the stage without a hitch. It seemed all the more remarkable as this particular Assistant happened to be a girl — Maude Howell. When we sought an explanation of this phenomenon, we discovered that Miss Howell had had the good sense to thoroughly learn her business in a stock company before she attempted to ally herself with an important New York production. The illness of the unfortunate Stage Manager was prolonged, and Maude Howell assumed the position and has remained my Stage Manager for the past seven years.

I am grateful for "The Green Goddess" because it brought me considerable financial return; but I think perhaps I am chiefly grateful because it brought me in intimate relationship with William Archer and Winthrop Ames. I need not dwell upon my admiration of Ames as a producer; his work is so widely appreciated as to make that unnecessary. But it might be well to point out how great was his share in achieving success for "The Green Goddess." I think the play was more or less "cast-iron." I believe it would have done well if it had been put on by even the most ordinary director. But I do not believe it would have stood the slightest chance of the lasting success which it attained if it had not been for the imaginative faculty of Winthrop Ames. Archer was the first person to admit this on all occasions when the success of the play was under discussion. Indeed his admiration for Ames was so great that it was a long time before I could get him to talk about me at all.

Archer was a tall well-built man of the raw-boned

"THE GREEN GODDESS"

*William Archer's first and only play. He wrote it as the result of
a dream*

Scotch type. His face might have been considered stern and even hard if it had not been for his kindly and humorous eyes which completely denied the austerity of his features. I never saw him dressed in anything but black and I never saw him with his coat unbuttoned. In all weather, rain or shine, he always carried an umbrella. He was by temperament retiring and reticent. For a long time after the production of "The Green Goddess" I was firmly under the impression that he considered my interpretation of the Rajah had from an artistic standpoint ruined his play. The first night came and went. I received many congratulations from my friends, but not a word of commendation from Archer. He would meet me smilingly and pleasantly and say how delighted he was with the business; he would tell me how much the success of the play was due to Ames, but not a word about me! And it was not until some months later at a luncheon given to him that in a public speech he was able to pour forth upon me, much to my amazement, all the kindly thoughts and appreciation that his honest, taciturn Scotch nature had never permitted him to say in private. And then gradually I began to find out that he never lost an opportunity of expressing to other people his regard and affection for me and of giving me far more credit than was my due. And little by little those barriers of silence and reserve broke down between us and a warm and affectionate friendship was established. I was very proud of his friendship and deeply grieved when his sudden and comparatively early death robbed me of the privilege of the long association to which I had looked forward. He was so transparently honest, with such a keen brain and clear eye, that I cannot imagine anybody having sufficient presence of mind to tell him a lie. I remember Sir Arthur Pinero saying, "I regard Archer as one of the most honest, upright, kindly men that I have ever known." That was at lunch one day when Archer was still well and strong, during the time that I was playing "The Green Goddess" in London in 1924. I was sitting between Pinero and my old friend, Sir Gerald Du Maurier. In reply to Pinero, Du Maurier said, "Yes, I feel that too. Although, you may remember, Pinero, that when he was the dramatic critic of the *World* and I appeared in the first production of your play 'Trelawney of the Wells' he said in his criticism 'Not even the acting of Mr. Gerald Du Maurier could entirely ruin this brilliant play.' That was not very kindly, was it, Pinero?"

"No, Gerald," said Pinero, "it wasn't. And not true either."

My respect for the memory of William Archer is such that I feel very strongly that those who are interested in the drama should be brought to realize the value of Archer's influence on the theatre during his active life, and the great loss the stage has sustained by his death. A large majority of the present generation know him merely as the author of "The Green Goddess." This in fact is one of the least of his achievements. It was he who first introduced Ibsen to the English-speaking world, and for that alone we owe him more than we can ever estimate. I suppose there is no serious playwright to-day who has not directly or indirectly come under the influence of Ibsen. Personally, I consider many of Ibsen's plays, as plays, are overrated, but his technique in most instances is unsurpassed, his influence will remain when his plays are forgotten. William Archer was for twenty years dramatic critic of the *World*, an important English weekly. During that time he became acknowledged as the leading critic of the English stage. The arts have always been stimulated by serious, well-considered criticism and equally I believe that when an art is treated by the majority of its acknowledged critics in a flippant manner as the art of the theatre often is, it is likely to lose its true value and importance in the minds of the public. When Archer sat down to write a criticism of the drama, he devoted himself entirely to an earnest consideration of his subject; he gave no thought to the impression he might make on his fellow critics and he never strove to produce a blaze of literary pyrotechnics. He wrote to the best of his ability, and in the best English at his command. And this earnestness and sincerity was reflected not only upon the public but upon the rising dramatic authors of the time. It is significant that about this period — from 1880 onward — the old-fashioned claptrap of the stage began gradually to disappear. The United States at this time was still looking to England for the drama. This was before America had gained confidence in her native dramatists — in fact, there were then few American playwrights of any note. The good influence, therefore, that Archer brought to bear on the English stage was automatically reflected in America. In my opinion Archer's straightforward, earnest criticism and his hatred of humbug were in a great measure responsible for the general improvement in dramatic literature. It is my conviction that it was his strong critical faculty that shook his confidence in himself as a playwright and kept him for many years from attempting to write a play. He knew that it required something more than a knowledge of the stage and a facility for writing to make a playwright. He told me that the complete story of "The Green Goddess" came to him in a dream. He was greatly impressed by its dramatic possibilities; but he was so sure that he had not the special ability to write a play that he approached first Pinero and then Bernard Shaw with the suggestion that one of them should collaborate with him. I believe that Shaw's remark after listening to the story of the play was that "he didn't write for the movies." Archer then set to work and did it himself and in my opinion wrote one of the best-constructed plays of recent years.

I played "The Green Goddess" in America for three consecutive seasons and in 1924 I opened with it at the St. James' Theatre, London, under the management of Gilbert Miller. I persuaded Winthrop Ames to maintain his interest in the London season, and largely out of friendship for me he went over to England and superintended all rehearsals. I had not played in London for more than twenty years, so I need not say that my anxiety was intense. These moments of

nervous strain in an actor's life are very severe and
whatever victory may ensue, it is by no means cheaply
bought. From the opening night there was no doubt
of the play's success. We ran an entire year, from
September 6, 1923, to September 6, 1924. Archer was
held in such esteem that I am sure there was not a
critic in London who did not rejoice at his good
fortune. I am frequently asked to describe the difference between an American and an English audience.
It is, I think, somewhat interesting to record that
having played "The Green Goddess" for three seasons
in the United States, I found no more difference in a
London audience than if I had been taking the play
from New York to Boston, or from Boston to Philadelphia. Every situation, every point, line for line,
brought precisely the same response as we had habit-
ually received in American cities.

My own personal experiences were crowded with
interest for me. Every theatrical institution went to
the utmost limits of kindness and hospitality. American clubs and associations opened their arms to me
and welcomed me as one of the family. Gordon Sel-
fridge, the American whose spectacular success as a
merchant in London is known I believe wherever the
English language is spoken, and who is acknowledged
by all London shopkeepers to be the man who "put
Oxford Street on the map" as a shopping center, had
an entire Green Goddess window in our honor. Shades
from the past appeared to me in my dressing room at
the St. James' Theatre night after night; people I had
not seen since my early touring days drifted in and out

in an eerie procession. Charming leading women of long ago reappeared as charming gray-haired old ladies. Child actresses brought me their children to kiss and dashing soubrettes now long past their prime came and kissed me. Leading men relegated these many years to the rear ranks came timidly in and made me feel sad and guilty. As I have never yet succeeded in feeling more than twenty-five at the most, it was hard for me to realize that I had known all these people in their youth; it all seemed strange and unreal to me.

William Archer in his quiet and restrained way enjoyed the popularity that came to him with the success of his play, for though he had for many years received the appreciation of a limited circle of people, he had never before been made a fuss of by the larger public. We were often asked together to luncheons and receptions and I think it pleased him rather when now and then I would tell a story at his expense. There was one experience during the rehearsals of "The Green Goddess" that I sometimes told and which he always listened to good-humoredly. The last act of the play in its original form was admittedly weak until Winthrop Ames took it in hand and invested it with a weird, uncanny suggestion of impending catastrophe that resulted in maintaining the interest to the fall of the curtain. We had had much discussion about this act, and Archer knew its weakness. Ames is a past master in the art of stage lighting and when we came to the final rehearsals he decided that this whole scene must be relighted. Archer was not present but I sat next to Ames in the orchestra. He called the electricians and at ten o'clock the next morning he started rearranging all the lighting effects. It happened that about noon Archer called up the office and asked to speak to Mr. Ames. The secretary answered, "Mr. Ames is not here. He and Mr. Arliss are both over at the theatre relighting the last act." There was a sudden click of the telephone at the other end, and within a few minutes Archer appeared at the theatre in a state so nearly bordering on anger that he surprised us all. The fact was that he had misunderstood the secretary. He thought she had said "rewriting."

When I was playing "The Green Goddess" in New York the company gave me a surprise by presenting me with a bronze bust of myself modeled by Ivan Simpson. This event was rather extensively commented upon in the newspapers, so a year or more later when we played in Chicago, the press agent decided that there was no harm in doing a good thing twice; he sent a notice to the Chicago papers that the company had that evening given me a surprise by presenting me with a bust of myself by Ivan Simpson. And he got his publicity. At a luncheon during the London run of the play, I had just told the relighting story and Archer was called upon to speak. As he rose, I saw he had a twinkle in his eye and I knew he was preparing something for me.

He said, "I understand Mr. Arliss is creating quite a reputation in America by making curtain speeches which consist of stories mainly about me. I have great satisfaction in getting one on him. I am going to read you a little clipping which I have culled from a New York paper." He then produced from his pocketbook a small cutting from, I think, the *New York Sun*, and read it. It ran:

"Out in Chicago where George Arliss is acting 'The Green Goddess' the company got together and presented Mr. Arliss with a bust of himself modeled by Ivan Simpson. There was a similar ceremony during the New York run, when the company presented Mr. Arliss with the same bust. There have been, however, no accounts of the intervening festivities in the course of which Mr. Arliss seems to have given the bust back to the company."

The final fall of the curtain which marks the end of the run of a play is always a sad moment for an actor; if the run has been short there is the mournful reflection that the play has failed; if it has been long, it becomes a touching and melancholy farewell to an old friend. As I put off my costumes of the Rajah for the last time I had the depressing feeling that everything was at an end for me. It seemed that I should never find another play in which I should be so warmly received and so pleasantly remembered. My position was precisely that in which I had found myself at the end of "Disraeli." I had no play. Once more I was threatened with retirement and extinction.

I had made many friends amongst the English managers and there seemed to be a general opinion that I ought to stay in London. But nobody had a play to offer me. Gilbert Miller was ready to put on anything I might suggest, but I had nothing to offer. Frederick

Harrison gave me a pressing invitation to go to the Haymarket Theatre if I should for any reason forsake the St. James. Harrison was one of the oldest London managers, having been lessee and manager of the Haymarket Theatre for a quarter of a century or more. During my year in London a strong friendship sprang up between us. We usually met at strangely "untheatrical" places — the Bath Club or even at the exclusive Marlborough and we would talk shop by the hour. I never met him in his office — in fact, I seldom met any London manager in his office. On reflection I think I have seldom met any American manager outside of his office. During my season of "The Green Goddess" in London I did not become acquainted with the business habits of managers sufficiently to be able to speak of them with authority, but my own experience was that when I rang up a manager at ten thirty I was told that he was expected between eleven and twelve. By one o'clock I had missed him because he had just gone to lunch; and at three o'clock he was expected back any moment. It may surprise many American managers to know that in spite of this apparently malignant and lingering disease, the midday lunch, the London manager contrives to accomplish a great deal of work. But he does it in a leisurely fashion that must be very exasperating to the hustler.

Gilbert Miller suggested that I should revive "The Darling of the Gods" but I am desperately afraid of a play that is twenty-five years old, no matter how good it may seem to me in perspective. The treatment of plays during the past fifteen or twenty years has so changed that anything written before that period is likely to seem old-fashioned. I don't say that the up-to-date play is better, but it is superficially different.

I determined that I would not accept any play that I could not control for both America and England, and that any arrangement must be made in conjunction with Winthrop Ames. My intention was to include London in all my future tours; making the first production of the play either in London or in New York. Frederick Harrison was much concerned on hearing that I had absolutely nothing to produce and nothing in sight. He said he would make a great effort to find a play for me and if he succeeded he would let me have it even if I was not able to produce it at his theatre.

I had for years been promising to take Flo to China and I was just about to get a map to find out where it is, when a cable was handed to me; it ran: "Read new play by Galsworthy Old English and cable me your opinion as part for you." I secured a manuscript from Ames' agent in London. I approached it with moderate interest and without much hope. I had read so many plays that had been recommended to me that I had become pessimistic. But any play of Galsworthy's must be worth reading. Gilbert Miller had gone to New York and had presented me with the use of his large and comfortable office at the St. James' during his absence. I carried the manuscript there and locked the door. The first page was not very reassuring; I found that the part was that of a tremendously stout

"OLD ENGLISH"
Which proved a phenomenal success throughout the United States

old gentleman literally rolling in fat. I thought of my own one hundred and forty pounds all told, but I read on. And as I read, from page to page and scene to scene, I felt a pleasant warmth creeping over me, and gradually I found that I was putting on flesh; and by the end of the first act I was so stout and heavy that I could hardly move. I started to get up with difficulty in order to open the window and was quite shocked when I rediscovered my own miserable frame. I didn't get up — I feared to further break the illusion — I read on to the end and then took a taxi to the telegraph office and cabled, "Will do it if you are willing to take the chance." The fact was that I knew I couldn't reproduce the part as Galsworthy intended it. I could not simulate rolls of fat. But here at last was the part of a real man — not a mere stage figure, but a human character. I felt I had known him for years or that perhaps I had been such a man in some previous incarnation. In due course came a reply, "See Galsworthy he will probably die in coils at the idea of your attempting the part it is up to you. Winthrop Ames."

I lunched with Galsworthy and broke the news to him during the fish. Being my host he deemed it impolite to die before the meal was over, by which time he had partially recovered. How serious was the shock I shall never know: but he consented; placing his trust in Providence and Lyle Swete — and both served him loyally. Lyle Swete came to America to produce the play and much of my personal success is due to his suggestions and to those of Winthrop Ames.

My surprise and disappointment came when I made inquiries for the English rights. I found that Frederick Harrison not only owned the London rights of the play but he had already made all arrangements for its immediate production and had engaged his company. He had had the manuscript of "Old English" in his pocket during all those weeks that he had been trying to find a play for me and had never for a moment dreamt that I should consider the part suitable for my own use. And so I was unable to play it in London. It may as well be confessed that neither I nor Mr. Ames believed that the play would be a great success: we knew we should have a good deal of pleasure in doing it, but we thought it would run only one short season. We believed it would attract but one class of people, and when that class had been drawn upon, business would go to pieces. Everybody in London shook their heads when they heard I was going to bring it to America. Even at our final dress rehearsal there was a considerable amount of head shaking. "Old English" has, in fact, proved the greatest financial success I have ever had.

I have an advantage over many other writers of reminiscences and that is, I have been in personal contact with a large number of my readers — at least, I like to think so. May I allow my imagination to go so far as to conjure up a friendly pressure of the hand as I bring these recollections to a close — with a future yet to be accounted for.

END

INDEX

INDEX

INDEX

Cave, Joseph A., proprietor and manager of the Elephant and Castle Theatre, 54–60; a Benefit of, 68–69.
Chicago, production of "Disraeli" in, 243–250.
Children's party, 9, 11–16.
Clearness, a feature of acting, 227–229.
Clemens, S. L., Arliss's early acquaintance with writings of, 35–36; as a story-teller, 266–267.
Clown, the, 63.
Cobbe, manager, 126–127.
Cohan, George M., on Red Cross tour of "Out There" company, 283.
Collaborators, 272.
Conquest, George, theatre manager, 52.
Craig, Gordon, pupil at Miss Thorne's School of Acting, 137.
Creamer, Auguste, his company, 74, 76–80; his humor, 88.
Curzon, Frank, produces play of Arliss's, 169.

"Daggs", 8.
Dale, Margaret, in "Disraeli", 254.
Daly, Charles, stage manager of Theatre Royal Margate, 132, 140.
"Darling of the Gods, The", 205–211, 309.
Dentists, 198–200.
Denton, St. John, theatrical agent, 89.
"Derby Winner, The", 172.
"Detective plays", 227.
"Devil, The", double production of, 224–226; Arliss stars in, 226–227, 229.
Digges, Dudley, stage manager for Arliss, 255.
Dillingham, Charles, 223.
Disraeli, autograph letter of, 252–254.
"Disraeli", suggestion of idea of, 232–235; the writing of, 236–240; Arliss's make-up for *Disraeli* in, 240–242; initial lack of success of, 242–244; change of third-act curtain of, 244–245; grows in favor, 245–248; close of the Chicago season of, 250; success of, 250–252; in New York, 254, 255–256; the company, 254–255; the Tobin performance of, 255–256; in Boston, 256, 258; through the United States, 263; revival of, 271.
"Doing daggs", 8–9.

Doncaster, 76.
Drama League, interests itself in "Disraeli", 246.
Dramatic schools, 43, 128.
Drury Lane Theatre, the dramas of, 31.
Du Maurier, Gerald, as *Strephonal* in "The Fantastics", 185; helpful to Arliss, 190, 191; his popularity, 195; and William Archer, 302.

Eagels, Jeanne, versatility of, 271.
Edwardes, George, of the Old Gaiety Theatre, 17, 151, 156–161, 163–164.
"Egotism", definition of, 170–171.
Elephant and Castle Theatre, 46–48; the audience of, 50–53; the company of, 53–54; the proprietor and manager of (Joseph A. Cave), 54–59; pantomime at, 63–65; Benefit Nights at, 67–69.
"Elixir of Youth, The", 20.
Elliston, Sydney, stage manager of the Old Gaiety Theatre, 159.
Elocution Classes, 16, 43.
Emery, Winifred, 270.
Evans, Charles E., in "Widows' Weeds", 170.

Fairbanks, Douglas, 243.
"Fantastics, The", 180–182, 185.
Farren, Nellie, actress, 17, 46, 156.
"Fatty", 12, 13, 26, 27, 34.
"Feeders", 104.
Fields, Mrs. James T., 260.
"First Night, A", 275–282.
Fiske, Harrison Grey, directs Mrs. Fiske's productions, 215; produces "The Devil", 224.
Fiske, Mrs., her dominant characteristic, 213; repertoire of, 214; as a producer, 214–215; her character acting, 215; fights the "Trust", 218–219; member of "Out There" company on Red Cross tour, 283.
Fitch, Clyde, 266.
Fit-up tours, 92–93, 95–96.
"Fly-posting", 152.
Forbes-Robertson, Sir Johnston, 52; his success, 243.
"Friar of Orders Grey, The", 10.
Friends, the value of, 94, 174.
Frohman, Charles, makes offer to Arliss, 203; refuses to star Arliss, 224.

INDEX

INDEX

Tobin, George, in "Disraeli" performance, 255–256.
Trafford, Bill, 23–24.
Tree, Beerbohm, anecdote of, 91–92.
"Trust", the, 218–219.
Tulloch, Augusta, leading lady at the Elephant and Castle, 68.
Tyler, George C., approaches Mrs. Campbell for American tour, 193; his connection with "Disraeli", 232–236, 244, 263; conceives idea of "Out There" tour, 283; as a friend, 298.
Types, the insistence on, 176–177.

Vanbrugh, Irene, of Miss Thorne's school, 137.
Vanbrugh, Violet, of Miss Thorne's school, 137.
Vaudeville Theatre, 177–178.
"Vicar of Wakefield, The", with limelight effects, 93–94.

Walcott, Mr. and Mrs. Charles, 211.
Walnut Man, the, 6–7.

Ware, Helen, on Red Cross tour of "Out There" company, 283.
Warfield, David, 243.
Waring, Herbert, in Mrs. Campbell's company, 194, 203.
Warner, H. B., on Red Cross tour of "Out There" company, 283.
Warren, Mrs. Fiske, 261.
"Well-Remembered Voice, A", 283.
"Wellington, The", public-house, 107.
Weston, Edward Payson, the walker, 252.
"Widows' Weeds", 169, 237.
Williams, Arthur, in "Widows' Weeds", 170.
Wilson, Francis, 266, 274.
Wogan, Mrs., 81, 82.
"Woman's Revenge, A", 154, 155.
Working-man's club, 36, 37.

Young, James, director of moving picture studio, 284–288, 290–294.

Zangwill, Israel, 268.